A Woman Called Murn

A Story of Love, Loss, and Perseverance

Deborah L. Burris

ISBN 978-0-578-29020-1
Library of Congress Control Number 2022906721

Printed in the United States of America

Published by Bel Canto Publishing, LLC
Carbondale, Illinois
belcantopublishingllc@gmail.com
belcantopublishingllc.com

Dedication

This true story is

For all the *children* who had someone who taught them by their actions the
meaning of *agape* love,
for all the *children* who never experienced such love.

For all the *adults* who gave their all to the children they raised,
for all the *adults* who didn't know how.

For all the *children* who needed someone to step up,
for all the *children* who had no one who came to their rescue.

For all the *adults* who were always there for their children,
for all the *adults* who couldn't because no one had ever
put their needs first.

For all the *children* who were successful because of the
adults who championed their aspirations,
for all the *children* who weren't because no one
encouraged or supported their dreams.

For all the *adults* who had opportunities and took them,
for all the *adults* who didn't have a chance in life.

For all the *children* who experienced faith and its power,
for all the *children* who were left to their own devices.

For all the *adults* who were part of a child's village and travels,
for all the *adults* who traveled their own path apart from their child.

For all the *children* who were loved regardless and could always come home,
for all the *children* who had nowhere to go.

For all the *adults* who were like a woman called Murn,
for all the *children* who were like my little sister and me.

Acknowledgments

It seems everyone has a story and I didn't believe my story was particularly unique. I spent two hours drinking coffee with my college trumpet professor and now author telling my stories about my mom and my life. I wasn't sure my stories were unique enough for a book. At the end of our conversation, Larry Franklin looked at me and said, "Do you still think you don't have a story to write?" Larry's encouragement that day set me on the course to write my story. I'll forever be grateful for those two hours we spent talking.

My university teaching career in teacher education introduced me to many amazing and wonderful public school teachers. One exceptional high school English teacher read much of my early writing, spending time conversing with me, encouraging me, and providing feedback that allowed this book to come to fruition. Sheri Hunter was instrumental in moving me along the path to writing this book. Her kind words and constructive guidance at the beginning motivated me to see it through to the completion.

I never imagined myself even close to being a non-fiction novel writer. Two dear friends spent hours and hours, painfully reviewing page after page, line after line, and word after word giving me feedback. I will forever be indebted to Marta and Harry Davis for their skill, suggestions, corrections, and never wavering support.

Good friends are often called on to help provide you with honest feedback, helpful ideas, and suggestions. I am blessed to have so many wonderful friends along with my sister Pam, who throughout the process read my manuscript, some more than once, and shared their honest opinions and critiques. Your friendships and opinions have always been appreciated throughout the years and none more than during this endeavor. In addition, there are so many I have asked to read the manuscript to obtain a variety of readers' reactions or sought help in various facets. I thank each of them for their willingness to commit their time on my behalf: Dixie, Nadine, Suzy, Bill, Margaret, Carissa, Jeanine, Brad, Jeff, Sharif, Shirley, and Arthur.

I am so grateful for the detailed and focused final editing of this book. Janet Travis Miller, your comments, corrections, and professional skills were crucial to the completion. As a friend from our years in junior high school, you have made this book more special by your skill, heartfelt memories of Murn, and our refound friendship after fifty-four years. I will always treasure your contributions in bringing this book to closure and honoring Murn.

I believe everyone needs a cheerleader and I certainly had one from the first word to the final sentence. Her encouragement never failed. She was always willing to listen to my reading of specific sections to her for her reaction, her reading of a chapter at a time, and discussing specifics of my stories helping to clarify them which often sent me back to the computer. There will never be enough words to thank her for her part in the telling of my story. But more than that, based on her reading, she ended up loving Murn although they had never met. Thank you Rolanda Quick. My buddy, my pal, the Thelma to my Louise, the Lavern to my Shirley, and well, my dear friend. Murn would have loved you and so do I. But for the life of me, I don't know why! Thank you from the bottom of my heart

I'm grateful most of all to EtEt, Daddy, Mother, and Grandma Troutman for giving me a memorable life, one which taught me love and understanding. But above all, I'm grateful to my mom, a woman called Murn, who gave me all she had to give: encouragement, courage, support, confidence, faith, and a wonderful life. But more than anything, she gave me LOVE.

A Woman Called Murn

A Story of Love, Loss, and Perseverance

CONTENTS

PROLOGUE

Death…the permanent, irreversible end of life. Too often Death is associated with the living being who died. While the threat of Death no longer matters to them, Death is a living, breathing entity for those who loved them and must continue life without them. From the moment a loved one passes, Death becomes a stalker, hovering over the shoulders for the rest of the days of the lives of those who are left. The younger you are when Death introduces itself to you the more you become aware of its heartless nature. Each year Death cruelly updates the calendars with death dates and birthdates of loved ones. Our birthdays and holidays are no longer celebrated with them. Death creeps into our thoughts and reminds us when we see families together that it will never be the same for us. It whispers that we will never have anyone who will love us unconditionally as they did and it enthusiastically surrounds us with a wall of sorrow making us more unapproachable with each loss. As time passes, Death screams the silence of never hearing their names spoken; their voices are heard only in our memory. Death laughs at our successes and achievements that can no longer be shared or celebrated with our loved ones. As time passes, Death smirks as friends tell us that death is a part of life, that you have others who love you. Death chuckles because Death knows they haven't met yet. And for each being that Death takes from us, it steals a little more of our joy each time. It rejoices in our loneliness even when we're in a crowd and especially when we're alone. When you begin to enjoy life and happiness begins to enter your world, Death heckles and jeers until you pull back. Death lives and breathes on the very existence it stole from those we love. We grow up learning to hide our relationship with Death in order to fit in. While on the outside we learn to appear normal to others, on the inside we know that Death always clings to our shoulders and is just waiting to snatch the life of another person we love. And when our friends finally meet Death personally, we know their lives will never be the same, that we are now in a circle of friends who share an uninvited guest until the day Death comes for our own breath.

But sometimes, on a rare occasion, a person comes along who dares to stare Death down, to persevere when others may give up or cease to live life. This person finds the strength to push Death behind her and move forward with purpose and determination. One who defies Death and refuses to give in to the fear of what it's to bring. She tells Death it will not decide for her, she will live until she and God decide her job is done, and only then will Death be welcome. This is a story of an exceptional woman who looked at Death and said "Not now" many times. This is a story of the armor of love she wore, the sword of courage she carried, and the perseverance through faith with which she won each battle with Death and the losses it took. This is the story of a woman called Murn.

CHAPTER 1

Leaves of the Branches

My Paternal Family

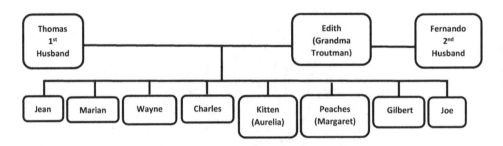

Thomas 1st Husband — Edith (Grandma Troutman) — Fernando 2nd Husband

Jean | Marian | Wayne | Charles | Kitten (Aurelia) | Peaches (Margaret) | Gilbert | Joe

My Maternal Family

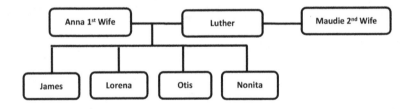

Anna 1st Wife — Luther — Maudie 2nd Wife

James | Lorena | Otis | Nonita

CHAPTER 1

The Fox and the Hound
Pre-1954 – Summer 1954

I came into the world on a hot, humid day in June 1954. The temperature was 94 degrees and the humidity as high as it could register for a town that sat between two rivers. As far as I know, I was wanted. But my parents brought me into their complicated world, which complicated mine. Children enter the world every day, sometimes with a mother and father who have anxiously awaited the birth of their child. Some children are born knowing two mothers, or two dads. Some children are born and never know their birth parents. Children come into the world because two adults often do not make wise choices when conceiving a child, or because the parents truly want a child. And sometimes the adults want each other more than they want a child. Regardless, a child enters the world not by the child's choice, but by the choices made by the two adults. To understand my story, it's important to understand the life of my parents before my arrival.

My mother was born on Valentine's Day, a day that is perceived to be filled with love, romance, and affection, but so often it is filled with disappointment, sadness, and frustration. That defined my mother's life, a dichotomy of emotions. As I grew up I realized that everyone, including me, was drawn to the vivaciousness and magnetic vacuum that Mother could draw you in with. Her laugh, the twinkle in her eye, the sense of humor, and the warmth of the names she would use when she talked to you – "honey, sweetheart, darling, sugar" – somehow made you feel special. It wasn't long before I realized that my mother was like Forrest Gump's box of chocolates; you never knew what you were going to get. The day of the month, something

13

someone said or did, didn't say or didn't do, loneliness or not enough alone time, full moon or new moon, happy or sad, angry or numb – to understand my mother one must understand her life long before me.

Mother grew up during the Depression on a little dirt farm located on Bird's Point in Mississippi County, Missouri, a small area along the Mississippi River just southwest and across from Cairo, Illinois. Bird's Point was one of the first settlements in Mississippi County. In the late 1800s, it was a community of about 400 with a ferry that transported cotton across the river along with a train that carried goods to Cairo. During the years following the 1929 stock market crash and the resulting Great Depression of the 1930s, the small town diminished to nothing more than dirt farming and sharecropping. Poverty struck hard and the residents that were left were considered the lowest of the low. Their homes consisted of shacks covering dirt floors and food consisted of what could be raised by the dirt farmers.

My maternal grandmother, Anna, married my grandfather, Luther, when she was 16 or perhaps 17 years old. Her mother had to provide a letter of consent for her to marry my grandfather. Anna had two younger sisters that lived with them and she had four children with my grandfather: my mother, and her two brothers, James and Otis, and a baby sister named Nonita. Mother's young life on Bird's Point is a mystery. She never spoke of it other than to tell very few people some of the horrible acts she experienced as a child.

Before the four little ones were school age, my grandmother took her two sisters and left my grandfather while he was out working in the fields. When she walked out, she left her four children: my mother who was six, James who was seven, Otis who was younger, and baby Nonita. When my grandfather came home late in the afternoon, he found the four little children sitting in a corner, hugging each other and crying. There were no food, no water, dirty diapers, and no supervision the entire day.

There were no pleasant stories of my mother growing up, no memories of holidays or birthdays, and no fond tales of friends or family during her childhood. My grandfather was an evil man and my mother as a young child became his replacement for his wife. He sexually abused my mother throughout her childhood and into her early teens. Mother's education was defined by the time, the place, and the circumstance. The school on Bird's Point was a little one-room schoolhouse where the teacher might have had an eighth-grade education and the curriculum was limited and only somewhat accurate.

Mother's education ended in the eighth grade and the skills she learned up to that point were equivalent to what now would be considered a third- or fourth-grade education. As a pre-teen, Mother learned that sex and men were going to be a continual thread throughout her life. A group of her male friends, along with one female friend, raped her. The female friend held her down as each of the boys took a turn. When she began to date, my grandfather told her to "make it pay." I can't imagine what my mother's life must have been like for her growing up as a young girl in a home without a mother and with a wicked father.

Her father eventually married another woman, Maudie, when my mother was about 11 years old. By then, a woman in the house would make no difference regarding the sexual abuse my mother had endured from her father and continued to endure. What Maudie did provide was lovingkindness that my mother had not experienced as a child.

The effects of my mother's abuse and poor self-image manifested themselves in her search for love from a man who would fill her emptiness. The view she believed society had of her motivated her to claw herself up in society by selecting men who she believed would help in her quest. She was not going to spend her life as that helpless little poverty-stricken, abused girl. She was going to do whatever it took to rise from her ashes and not be looked down on by anyone. Mother married her first husband, a man named Johnson, in the spring of 1939 at the age of 17. During this marriage, she had a child right away. Her husband took the infant out of her arms and she never saw it again. She divorced him 18 months after they had married. A year later she married Howard when she was 19 years old. With him she had a child who died at birth. On October 12, 1944, her second husband was killed in action during World War II.

Alone again, young, and determined to be accepted by the social classes beyond her upbringing, she had to support herself and look good doing it. Occupational options were minimal for women at that time. With my mother's limited education, opportunities were even more restricted. Her employment consisted of waitressing, retail work, counter work at dry cleaners, and once as a Bell Telephone operator. While she was often capable of getting a job using her femininity, she often lost the job once she had secured it due to her emotional thunderstorms which would develop without warning. Seldom was she fired, but often she walked off the job in a hailstorm of cold, icy comments followed by a confident exit out the door. Her jobs, married or not, provided her with the financial security she never had as a child and ensured her desire for material things and the ability to maintain her appearance.

As a young woman mother was beautiful. She had thin yet shapely legs like the "gams" many men were taken by, bottle-blonde hair in the latest popular style, long, beautifully manicured fingernails, and an air of sophistication and sexuality like that of movie stars who appeared on posters and in movie magazines. Stories of her walking down the streets of Cairo and how she turned the heads of those who passed by her were told by individuals who knew her or knew of her during those years. Although her name was Lorena, many called her "Blondie." It was easy to see how men were attracted to her and how women were protective of their husbands in her presence. Mother always entered a room like royalty: back straight, shoulders squared, chest raised, arms at her side, and head back. Once she entered, she would strike a pose and cock her head to one side as if to say, "Here I am; take me or leave me." Whether she was having a good day or a bad day, it was as if she was entering a masquerade ball – statuesque, with a disguise concealing who she was and from where she had come. Her expression, depending on her emotions at the time, was that of the Greek masks of tragedy and comedy. Her face always told her emotional state – happy, mad, or sad – but her posture was always royal.

Two years following her second husband's death, now 24, my mother married an Alexander County, Illinois, judge in December of 1946. With Bob, she gave birth successfully to a girl, Pam, in the spring of 1950 and a boy, Tom, in the fall of 1952. The judge's family was well off and included a woman who served as a maid and nanny. The judge's mother lived with them and was extremely controlling. His mother did not care for my mother and felt that her son had married beneath himself. He was the middle child and suffered from epilepsy, resulting in an overprotective mother. His family were staunch Catholics. Other than the belief that God existed, organized religion was foreign to my mother. As the years passed, the conflict between the two women gave Mother an excuse to seek another man's affection.

Mother loved to dance and with her brother James and his wife, Faye, they frequented a popular honky-tonk called the Turf in Cairo. The Turf was frequented by gangsters and mobsters who had money to spend and always entertained women.

Oddly enough, Mother never drank or smoked, strange for a woman who frequented such places. It wasn't liquor or cigarettes that she was seeking, it was the company of men. By this time in her life, it became a never-ending quest; Mother began finding her self-worth in the affection and adoration of men. When the interest waned or the affection didn't sedate her raging desire for acceptance and love, she searched for another man whose infatuation and desire made her feel she was valued. One place to find men was at the VFW. Mother began sitting on a barstool at the VFW courting my dad.

I can see why Mother was attracted to Daddy. He had a non-arrogant cockiness about him. He was handsome with a strong jawline, steely eyes, dark hair, and a slim frame on which he carried himself with an assured walk. He always had one hand in his pants pocket and the other holding a cigarette, or stood with his hands on his hips or in his pockets. His physical features were complemented by his confidence with people and a love of joke-telling, teasing, and kidding when interacting with anyone he met. Daddy was born almost 10 years after my grandmother had her sixth child, making him the seventh of eight children. As a child, he had older siblings who often cared for him. The sisters, Jean, Marian, and Kitten, assisted their mother in his care and nurturing. The brothers, Charles and Wayne, were busy working on the farm and helping their father. With the attention of so many older siblings, it's no surprise that Daddy was used to being the center of attention.

When he was in second grade he was infatuated with his teacher. One day one of his classmates brought the teacher a flower. Like most teachers would have, she thanked the little boy and exclaimed how beautiful the flower was. This did not sit well with Daddy. On the way to school each day, my dad passed by a house with beautiful flowers in the yard, so to win the affection and attention of his teacher, Daddy stopped by the house with the beautiful flowers on his way to school the next day. Instead of taking the teacher one flower, Daddy thought she would be more impressed with many flowers. Proud as a peacock, Daddy marched up to his teacher and presented her with an entire rosebush he dug up from the house with the beautiful flowers. I guess he impressed the teacher but not my grandfather. Together, Daddy and his father walked to the house with the beautiful flowers and paid the owners for the rosebush.

When Daddy reached fourth grade his teacher voiced a concern to his parents. She told them Daddy was a very bright little boy and he could learn anything. But she was concerned that he was very nervous and couldn't sit still. He exhibited discomfort when having to focus for extended periods and the discomfort kept him from focusing. His mother and father decided to remove him from school, leaving Daddy with only a fourth-grade education. He continued his education at home with his parents and siblings. I loved reading the cards he gave to me because his handwriting was elegant; it was beautiful and bold with sweeping lines that represented the confidence and pride he had regardless of his limited formal education.

My grandfather attended automotive school in Michigan and when he returned, he opened the first automobile garage in Vienna, Illinois. When Daddy was 11 years old, his father died from a heart attack at the age of 53, leaving my grandmother a young widow with two young boys – my dad and his younger brother, Joe.

Marian and Daddy were especially close. As a young teenager Daddy worked in the mom-and-pop grocery owned by Marian and her husband, Harry. He delivered groceries, stocked the shelves, and ran errands as they needed. He and Marian grew closer and closer as the years passed.

As many young men did when our country called at the start of World War II, Daddy lied about his age and enlisted in the Army. At 17, he had a boyish face with soft eyes and full lips, with barely a hint of facial hair.

Physically he had a thin frame standing less than five-foot-seven, with his conventional, brown hair side-parted, slicked-back sides, and roached up top contributing to his height. He entered basic training and followed in his father's civilian footsteps, focusing his training in the motor pool. Based on his performance, he earned the rank of a technical sergeant, earned four promotions in his first year, and served as an instructor for driving heavy trucks. He was stationed in the Philippines where the colonel chose him as his personal driver. Typically, the colonel would just send for a driver from the motor pool, but this colonel came to the pool and chose my dad specifically. Although chauffeuring the colonel sounds like a safe and comfortable assignment, Daddy spent his days driving to and from and along the front lines where the Japanese and our forces were engaged in combat. During the days and months he spent in the jungles of the Philippines, he carried with him a small New Testament Bible and a small English dictionary, the Bible for faith and the dictionary for knowledge. While he dodged the bullets and grenades, he didn't escape the life-threatening grasp of malaria. He was lucky he survived. For his bravery in driving through battles and the time spent at the front lines without cover, he was awarded two Bronze Stars. That same bravery and strength would be called on often throughout his life.

Like many of the soldiers who returned from World War II, alcohol consumption returned with Daddy. Perhaps it originated with the guys "throwing back" a few when on leave, but once many came home it was used to dull the pain and memories of what they had witnessed and participated in during their time in battle. Daddy had been weak as a child, but having malaria damaged his nervous system beyond repair. Between the horrors of war and the debilitating grasp of malaria he experienced, alcohol later became his lifelong crutch. When he returned from overseas, Daddy became a juvenile officer on the police force and was fortunate to find a lovely, good Catholic girl named Edna.

Daddy attended the family church and sang in the choir. He had a beautiful deep, bass voice. The years after I was born I never heard him sing that much but I remember one afternoon I was with him as he was tiling a floor in a local restaurant and we were listening to the jukebox playing Johnny Cash's recording of "Ring of Fire." Daddy sounded just like Johnny Cash, deep and rich. We played that song over and over with both of us singing.

He and Edna soon married. The family thought the world of her. While it was a happy marriage, Daddy was active in the VFW and would often go alone to have a beer and visit with guys who shared the same or similar experiences of war. Despite a wonderful wife and having escaped the life-threatening dangers of war, he could not resist the lure of my mother. She set her sights on him and he let down his guard. I guess the easiest way to describe it was the fact that they had interlocking pathologies.

As I understand, my mother chased my Dad. As everyone knows, a woman chasing doesn't insure the catching unless the man wants to be caught and vice versa. Either way, they caught each other. I have to assume my parents loved each other, but they complicated their lives and the lives of others by their actions. My mother divorced Bob, yet my dad remained married. Mother followed my dad to Michigan where he attended automotive school to be certified as a mechanic. Mother became pregnant with me.

Disappointed that my dad didn't immediately divorce Edna, Mother, pregnant with me, had no other option but to marry Bob for a second time. When I was born my mother's second marriage to Bob had been less than a year – poor timing on my mother's part. This complicated my birth because when a married woman had a child with another man, the child was presumed to be the child of her husband. However, according to family members on both my dad's and my mother's side, I was conceived in Michigan. When my dad did finally divorce Edna it devastated her. After I was born and Daddy's divorce was finalized, my mother divorced Bob for a second time, left her two children, Pam and Tom, with their dad and his mother, then she and my Dad married. There were casualties on both sides. I guess it was appropriate that since their marriage was complicated, bringing me into the world would be complicated as well.

CHAPTER 2

Leaves of the Branches

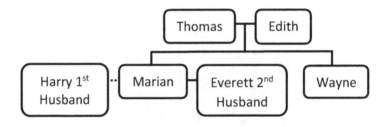

CHAPTER 2

Every Team Needs a Pinch Hitter or Two
Pre-1954 – Summer 1954

I would imagine that most people don't know or remember much about their early years unless their parents told them, or relatives told them, or they have seen pictures that partially tell their story. My earliest years were told to me by my paternal aunt, Aunt Marian.

Before I was born, Aunt Marian's first husband, Harry, had died. Marian and her second husband, my Uncle Everett, lived in Villa Ridge, an area north of Cairo. Aunt Marian was a housewife who was active in church and Uncle Everett worked on the GM&O railroad. Aunt Marian was a small but fiery little woman who barely stood five feet tall with a 17-inch waist. She had strong, muscular arms that extended from broad shoulders, both of which assisted her literally and what would be figuratively throughout her life. As a child, she contracted polio. This resulted in one leg and foot being shorter and underdeveloped compared to the other leg, creating a lifelong significant limp requiring the substituted use of her upper body to assist where most people depend on two strong legs. As if polio wasn't enough, she also had rheumatic fever.

When Aunt Marian was baptized it was by full immersion. Usually, a person's feet stay on the bottom of the baptismal pool as the minister supports you with one hand on your back and the other with a handkerchief holding your nose as you are "dunked" backward into the water and then raised. Aunt Marian, however, posed a problem; her lower body was so light due to the withered leg that she floated up and the minister couldn't get her legs down and her back up without basically lifting her to stand up. Quite a moment for them both! I guess it was a good thing the Lord was there to help!

When she was about seven years old my grandfather took her to the doctor to seek advice as to how to help her walk easier with the withered limb. The doctor strongly suggested that they measure her for a brace. Even as a seven-year-old, she had established strong will and determination. She informed the doctor and my grandfather that if they put a brace on her leg, she would tear it up. My grandfather looked at the doctor and said, "If Marian says she'll do it, she will." They left the doctor's office that day with my grandfather's bill minimal and my Aunt Marian satisfied with the large dose of submission she had administered to those two grown men. I guess it was her physical challenge that established her fearless confidence and determination.

I don't know if having polio gave Aunt Marian the confidence and feistiness she had all of her life or she was just born with it. She always laughed about a time when she was a young teenager and all of her siblings along with her mom and dad were sitting around the dinner table. Her brother Wayne was evidently sweet on a girl at school and Aunt Marian knew about it but Wayne hadn't told anyone. As a sister might, she decided to bring it up at the table one evening by announcing that Wayne had a girlfriend. Without looking at her, Wayne said, "Shut up, Marian."

Well, as most siblings might interpret such a comment, she continued with her encouragement. "C'mon, Wayne, tell us her name."

Again, Wayne prompted her to be quiet, "I said, shut up Marian!"

"Well, I think you should tell us all…" and before she could finish her sentence, Wayne threw his fork across the dining table and the tines hit Aunt Marian directly in the forehead just above her eyes, leaving three small divot scars that she carried all her life. That same fearlessness she carried like a badge of honor. She feared nothing and would always get to the bottom of any situation, regardless of the consequences.

A neighborhood grocery store often became a place where friendships developed. Aunt Marian and her first husband, Harry, owned and operated a mom-and-pop neighborhood grocery store. Harry had come to this country with his cousin as an Irish immigrant. There was a problem when they arrived at Ellis Island, as he and his cousin were both named Richard Richards. Two individuals could not enter the country at the same time with the same name, so Harry changed his name to Harry Jones.

Aunt Marian's second husband, Everett Lipe, was a bachelor who worked on the railroad and had an apartment near the store. Everett would get off work, clean up and walk to the store, where he would eat his supper and then get his lunch for the next day. He would ask for a couple of slices of bologna and cheese, maybe some ham, along with a sleeve of crackers. Aunt Marian or Harry would slice the lunch meat and this young bachelor would have a soda and eat his lunch meat as he visited with Marian and Harry. Then they would wrap up his lunch for him to take with him for the next day.

It wasn't long before Harry was diagnosed with tuberculosis and was confined to his bed in their apartment upstairs above the store. Aunt Marian ran the store alone for years without Harry's help. Their Jack Russell terrier, Snookie, became Harry's guardian and company. Snookie would run notes up and down the stairs between Harry and Aunt Marian throughout the day. When Harry died at home, Snookie wouldn't leave the bedside. Aunt Marian said she and Snookie grieved together as she continued to run the store now as a young widow, completely alone. Harry had been a well-known businessman. The flowers at his funeral cascaded across the front of the church, surrounded the casket, and flowed into the aisle, a symbol of the respect Harry and Aunt Marian had earned in the community.

In time, that young bachelor who worked on the railroad asked Marian to marry him. She said yes, sold the store, and became Mrs. Everett Lipe.

I've always heard that opposites attract.

Aunt Marian was young and Harry was much older. She had a temper and Harry responded appropriately, calming her down.

Aunt Marian was fiery and Uncle Everett was a quiet man. His stature was much larger than Aunt Marian. He had thin hair on top and full cheeks with deep jowl lines that made him resemble William Frawley, better known as Fred Mertz on the *I Love Lucy* show, though he was taller and less portly than Frawley and certainly more of a teddy bear than Fred Mertz. Uncle Everett grew up as a country boy who loved baseball so much that he went through his senior year in high school twice just so he could play ball. He was so good he was courted by the major leagues but had to decline the offer in order to help support his mother after his father died. He and Aunt Marian made a complementary couple; she decided and he agreed.

CHAPTER 3

Leaves of the Branches

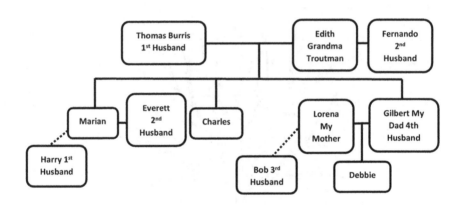

CHAPTER 3

Unto Them a Child Is Born
Summer 1954

I was born in the elevator, perhaps a prediction that life has its ups and downs. Mother and Daddy lived in Cairo, but Mother's doctor was across the river in a tiny town in Missouri. Daddy had taken Mother to her appointment for a checkup and her labor began as they arrived. My daddy had to get the ambulance from Cairo to come across the river to take Mother and me home. And that was the beginning of my life.

I'm not sure of the order of places, but I know there were seven or eight places my mother and daddy and I lived before I was six years old. Right after I was born, we lived on 25th and Walnut Street where we had a maid and nanny named Hattie. Aunt Marian told me she was at home one day when she received a phone call from Hattie telling her, "Miss Marian, you need to get over here right away. Miss Lorena has been sitting on the bed with that baby in front of her for the past three hours just staring at her."

Aunt Marian rushed to the house and gently picked me up and handed me to the maid. She told my mother, "Lorena, let's get you dressed and take a little ride." Mother complied and Aunt Marian took her to a doctor. Mother was suffering from postpartum depression. The doctor told my aunt that he would give Mother a series of three shots over several weeks and if she didn't respond, they might have to consider other alternatives. Within a few weeks, my mother responded to the second shot. After that, we moved in with Aunt Marian and Uncle Everett at Villa Ridge for most of my first year.

My first Christmas was when I learned to crawl. I was six months old and before Christmas I would only crawl backward until Daddy brought home a soft rubber Santa that stood about a foot high. When you squeezed it, it made a whistling noise – as soon as I heard that, they said I began crawling forward to get the toy. It seems as though I did several things differently. I sang before I spoke: "Ma, ma-ma-ma-ma. Da, da-da-da-da," all in a sing-song pattern. I guess I was meant to become a musician from a very early age.

During the period when my mother, daddy, and I lived with Aunt Marian and Uncle Everett in Villa Ridge, I remember Aunt Marian telling the story of my hair having grown out just long enough where she could curl it around her finger and put a bow in it. She went to town one day to run some errands and when she came back, Mother had me in the basement and had cut off all of the curls. Aunt Marian said she turned around, went back up the stairs to her bedroom, and cried. We celebrated my first birthday with Aunt Marian and Uncle Everett.

Aunt Marian had a mindset that if you told her she couldn't, she would say, "Well, we'll just see about that." She had a round cake or cookie tin with a lid that she used to keep all of her sewing things in. She was doing some mending and I was playing with the lid down on the floor. I guess I had moved it where she couldn't see it and when she got up and started to walk she stepped on the tin lid and slid, breaking her polio leg in two places, one of which was an open, compound fracture. She held the leg together until they could get her to the hospital. She was placed in a cast from the foot to the groin.

At that time casts were only made of plaster of Paris and you couldn't get them wet. She was going to have that cast on for at least six weeks and the doctor told her she couldn't take a bath. Well, Aunt Marian wasn't about to not take a bath for six weeks! So, with a big sheet of plastic, she wrapped the cast, taped it tight, took clothesline rope and tied it to her foot, tied the other end to the bathtub faucet, and lowered herself into the tub. The getting in part was easy. It was the getting out of the tub that challenged her, but she made it! And of course, the handle end of the flyswatter worked wonders for running it down the inside of the cast to scratch the itchy leg as it healed!

Shortly after my first birthday, Mother and Daddy and I moved to many places, I guess where Daddy found employment or where my mother would be happier living. We lived in Louisville, Kentucky, and in Illinois: Olive Branch, Tamms, and several houses in Cairo. One day while we were living in Louisville, Mother was leaving work and she saw a doll lying in the trash. It had a crack in its head and someone had thrown it away. Mother brought the little doll home, washed it, and placed a bandage over the cracked head. It was a Tiny Tears doll! Tiny Tears became my one and only baby doll and the only one I wanted. I loved Tiny Tears so much and kept it for many years. It was odd that Mother would bring anything home from the trash. Maybe she did it because we didn't have much money. Or perhaps she never had a doll as a little girl. Or perhaps it was much deeper than that. Maybe she associated with that little doll on a personal level. Perhaps it was a reflection of herself: broken but still worthy of being loved, damaged but not deserving to be discarded.

We didn't live in Louisville very long and moved back to Illinois. We were back where Aunt Marian and Uncle Everett were in my life. I had a hard time saying Aunt Marian and Uncle Everett so I called them Murn and EtEt and that's how they became known to everyone. I loved Murn and EtEt more than any little girl could! I spent a lot of time with Murn and EtEt throughout my early years visiting or staying at times for a week.

They moved from Villa Ridge to Mill Creek which was closer to the GM&O railroad tracks where EtEt worked as a foreman. The house sat back from the highway on top of a hill. EtEt always planted a vegetable garden at the foot of the hill. I guess that was good planning so the water would run off of the hill to water the garden. He would come home from work and Murn would put boots that were far too big on me, then he and I would walk, hand in hand, down a path from the house to the garden and pick green beans, tomatoes, cucumbers, and green peppers. I loved green beans growing up. Murn said I even wore them: on my face, in my hair, and on my clothes. Sometimes EtEt and I didn't pick in the garden. Some days we would drive down to the little country store and EtEt would buy me a fudge bar. He would sit and talk with the old men in overalls rocking in the two rocking chairs while I finished my ice cream. Then we would get in the car and head back up the hill to the house.

I don't remember many people visiting when I spent time at Mill Creek except maybe Grandma Troutman. But I do remember one other visitor. The last time I ever saw my Uncle Charles was at Mill Creek. He lived in Wood River and didn't visit very often. He looked a lot like Daddy even though he was older. He was a carpenter at the Shell Refineries in Wood River, Illinois.

On Sundays when I wasn't visiting at Mill Creek, Murn and EtEt would pick me up and take me to Sunday school and church if Mother and Daddy didn't go. I was in the primary class that had about 20 little slatted wooden folding chairs. Murn was a Sunday school teacher for the juniors. She would have to pass by children in the primary class to go upstairs to her class. As soon as I would see Murn I would want to go with her. I would jump up from my chair, start crying and grab on to her skirt, an action that could have resulted in her losing her balance and falling. I guess this happened several Sundays in a row. The next and last time this happened, Murn stopped, picked me up, put me across her arm, gave me a swat on my bottom, and set me back down in the chair. She pointed her finger at me and said, "Don't you do that again." I never did it again and I was very happy to stay in my own little Sunday school class from that day forward.

Murn and EtEt eventually moved into town to be closer to me. It was a big, tan, two-story house with brown trim on Fifth Street. It had a big yard to play in and I had my very own bedroom when I would stay all night.

My daddy only spanked me once when I was four years old and that was when we were visiting Murn and EtEt. Daddy had parked across the street from the house and I crawled out behind Mother on her side of the car. I was so excited to see Murn and EtEt that I ran between our car and a car parked in front of us to cross the street. Of course, it scared everyone and I was lucky I wasn't hit by a car. Out of fear that I could have been hurt, Daddy was going to spank me. He had taken off his belt and had me by the arm when Mother fainted. He had to stop and get Mother into the house and lay her on the couch. Murn was pacing and wringing her hands and EtEt went to the back of the house to keep from hearing me cry as Daddy spanked me at the side of the house. I never ran out between two cars ever again and my daddy never spanked me ever again.

My favorite house with my mother and dad was on 21st Street. It had a big side yard and there were kids to play with. I had developed into quite a little tomboy. I always wanted to wear blue jeans and long-sleeved shirts with the sleeves rolled up to my forearm like my daddy's. One day Daddy had brought home a boy's English racing bicycle. It was far too big for me and Daddy told me I couldn't ride it. The seat was very high and my feet couldn't touch the pedals. I was a determined little child. One day I leaned the bicycle against the side of the house, placed a lawn chair next to it, and climbed onto it, one hand holding on to one side of the handlebars and one hand on the side of the house. I could reach the pedals, but only as long as I was standing and straddling the bar. Daddy drove up after work and there I was, riding that English racer around in the yard.

Being such a determined child, it was no surprise that my mother could not get me to wear the beautiful little dresses she would buy for me. The socks would have lace on them and they would match the dress. I would scream and yell, "I don't want to wear the dress. I wanna be the boy!" Blue jeans and shirts were my clothing of choice. Most of the time my choice was fine, but sometimes Mother wanted me to dress up for special occasions. She often had to call Murn to come to our house to help her persuade me to wear a dress. Murn would come to the house and talk me into wearing it. I didn't like it, but I did it for Murn.

I think my stubbornness about the dresses, other than not liking having to wear them, was motivated by the dislike I had for a little girl my age. She belonged to a married couple who were friends with Mother and Daddy and would visit every so often. That little girl's name was Debbie too. She was always wearing frilly dresses, with ribbons in her hair and fancy socks and shoes. Mother and Daddy would make over her regarding how pretty she looked and how cute she was in her dress. The more they said it, the more I disliked her. She always flaunted her dress in front of me and would taunt me saying, "They think I'm cute! How come you don't wear dresses?" My parents knew I didn't like that little girl and I guess they knew me well enough to know that I wouldn't put up with it very long.

The last visit that the couple made with her to our house was shocking to all. The adults were in the living room visiting when my daddy said, "Where are the girls?" I think Daddy knew how much I didn't like this little girl and he preferred keeping an eye on us. He started searching through the house and found us at the very back of the house in the utility room. I had cute little Debbie against the wall with both hands around her neck, choking her long enough that she had turned blue. Daddy had to peel my fingers from her neck after which she took a large gasp of air. Needless to say, they didn't visit us again and that was the last I heard about "cute little Debbie."

Mother and Daddy started having serious problems while we lived on 21st Street. I don't think my mother was satisfied with her life and was unhappy most of the time. She loved to spend money and buy things that we didn't have money for. Daddy worked all the time and tried to pay for all that she wanted, but she just wasn't happy. He would come home from work and bring a pint of whiskey every night. He spent his evenings painting a room and drinking highballs. When he finished one room, he would start on another. I remember Murn saying that there must have been a dozen coats of paint on the walls of each room in that house. I suppose he just didn't want to have to listen to Mother's complaining, crying, or fussing. His painting was one thing; the drinking was another.

As a child, the last place I remember living with my parents was in the housing project. Daddy was working as a welder at a machine shop and Mother began waitressing at the Town and Country restaurant at the edge of town. I was told that Daddy always looked like he came out of a bandbox, an expression that meant cleaned and pressed. Mother was meticulous about cleanliness and dress and so was my daddy. Regardless of the jobs he did, his hands and nails were spotless. I remember he always used Lava soap to wash his hands and he washed them constantly and cleaned his fingernails. He was just as particular with the cleanliness of my hands. Daddy came home for lunch each day and for some reason, I always spilled my milk. It made my dad so upset that Mother began holding my milk back until Daddy was finished with his lunch and went back to work.

Mother worked a late afternoon and evening shift at the restaurant on weekends and supper shifts during weekdays. The clientele was higher-end at those shift times and the tips were better. Mother was an excellent waitress and she flirted with the men which in return resulted in her collecting large tips. She called them "honey" and "sweetheart" or "sugar" which of course the men loved. She would throw her head back and laugh this infectious, flirtatious laugh. And the way she would put her hand on their shoulders when she would ask if they wanted more coffee or another drink made the men flirt right back. Many of the lawyers, judges, and businessmen would go there at the end of the day for drinks or dinner business meetings. Daddy would be at home with me or I would be with Murn and EtEt until Daddy picked me up or they dropped me off. Sometimes Daddy and I would go there for supper and surprise Mommy. Mother's and Daddy's problems had escalated at that point in their marriage.

One evening Daddy and I waited and waited for her to come home, but Mother didn't come home when she should have. Daddy had fixed me supper and prepared me for bed. After I was in bed he put on his pajamas, robe, and house slippers and sat at the top of the stairs with his .357 magnum lying on the stair next to him. The stairs led straight down to the landing where the front door opened. Daddy and I talked back and forth until I finally drifted off to sleep. When he heard the screen door open he picked up his pistol and pointed it at the door. The door opened and it was Mother with her ex-husband, Bob the judge, right behind her. As soon as they saw my daddy I understand Bob shouted "Don't shoot, Gilbert! Don't shoot me!" as he ran back to his car and sped off.

Mother ran to a neighbor's and called the police. At the same time, Daddy called Murn and told her she might have to get him out of jail because he had just pointed a gun at Lorena and Bob. Mother told the police that Daddy tried to kill them. What she and Bob didn't know was that there were no bullets in the gun. Daddy had been a juvenile officer in the past and had worked with most of the officers. When the police arrived, the officer told him, "Gilbert, Lorena said you tried to kill her and the judge. We're going to need to take the gun. Are you going to hurt Lorena if she comes home tonight?"

Daddy handed over his gun, "Here, you can take it; it's empty. No, I'm not going to hurt her. Our little girl is asleep upstairs. I just wanted to scare them."

From what I was told, Daddy kept drinking, Mother's behavior continued, and the marriage didn't. Here is where my story truly begins.

CHAPTER 4

Leaves of the Branches

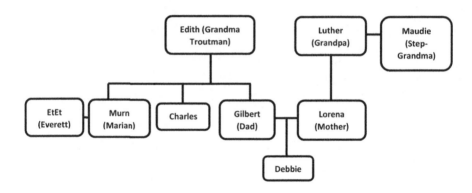

CHAPTER 4

And the Walls Came Tumbling Down
Summer 1960 - Spring 1962

I guess no one knows why two people separate and divorce except for the two people involved. The one thing everyone would agree on is that a child in that divorce can be affected for better or worse. For me, it was for worse. The people who were the walls surrounding me and keeping me safe all crumbled. I had just turned six years old the summer when my mother and Daddy separated.

Mother and I left the home where we lived with Daddy to live in a hotel. It was a typical hotel room: bed, chest, chair, lamps, and a bathroom. There was a restaurant in the basement and sometimes Mother and I would eat there. The hotel had a television lounge of sorts. It was a very large room with a few overstuffed chairs and a big, cabinet-style, black and white television. The lounge was between the lobby and the hallway of our room. In the evening, Mother would have me bathe and put on my pajamas, robe, and house slippers. The rooms didn't have televisions so she would let me go to the lounge and watch for a little while before bedtime. She had a travel alarm clock; it was tan and there were three sections to it, each hinged to the other. It would fold up as a closed case when it wasn't being used. Mother would wind the clock, hand it to me, and tell me that I could watch television until the big hand was on the 12 and the little hand was on the eight, then I was to come back to the room to go to bed.

I remember sitting in the lounge alone, holding that clock in my lap with my legs crisscrossed upon a big, comfortable chair that seemed to swallow me.

41

I constantly checked the clock to make sure I returned to our room when Mother had said. As headstrong as I had been, I was now timid and afraid of making Mother mad at me. Sometimes there would be another guest sitting in the lounge, but usually it was just me. Mother never watched television with me. I was lonely sitting in that lounge by myself. What I didn't know was how much lonelier I was going to become.

I'm not sure how long we stayed at the hotel but I don't think it was very long. While we were there, I didn't see Daddy, Murn, or EtEt. I missed them all and wanted to see them, but I guess Mother didn't want me to. We soon left the hotel and moved across the river to East Prairie, Missouri, to live with Mother's father, my Grandpa Luther. I didn't really know my grandpa. He was a very tall man, big in stature. He wasn't mean to me, but I was somewhat afraid of him. Maybe it was because I had never been around him very much, or maybe the way he looked at me. There was a piercing look in his eyes that was hard and cold, and his face was chiseled with no hint of a smile. He wasn't anything like EtEt with his full, round face and kind eyes.

The house was an old shotgun-style house. Entering the front door, you could see doorway after doorway, straight through the house to the very back, walking through every room until you reached the kitchen. It was dark inside and smelled. There was a dampness that made me feel cold even in the summer. I had to sleep in a bed with Mother. She always made me sleep next to the wall. At that age, I never understood why, but she knew why all too well. Next to the bed, we had what they called a slop bucket. There was no indoor bathroom so at night everyone had a slop bucket in their bedroom and had to use that if they needed to go to the bathroom. During the day we used an outhouse. I hated using either one of them! I had never lived in a house that didn't have a bathroom, or that smelled. My world was very different from it had ever been.

No one ever really talked to me while we lived there, not even Mother. I did become fond of Grandma Maudie. Grandma Maudie was the only one who seemed to acknowledge my presence. She had a kind voice and would hold me close to her when she would ask me if I wanted something to eat or drink. She was soft and squishy like she was made of marshmallows. She was a country woman, talked with a heavy southeast Missouri accent, and her face was very wrinkled and creased. I don't remember Mother working then but I was so young, I'm not sure what she did. There was a backyard at Grandpa's house with a small flatbed trailer holding a few bales of hay. I remember sitting on that flatbed watching kids play in the yard. To this day, I have no idea who those children were. I played with them sometimes, but mostly I would just sit on the flatbed isolated in my sadness and fear. I missed my daddy and Murn and EtEt.

Since I was six years old that summer, it was time for me to start school that fall. I remember Mother taking me to the school to register. The first year a child starts school is often stressful for the child and sometimes upsetting for the parents. It was no different for me. It was worse; I was scared and emotionally fragile and distraught. While we were at the school, Mother and another lady showed me my classroom and then where I was to eat lunch. The school cafeteria was nothing more than a lunch counter. I was given a token that I was to put up on the counter and that way the cook would know that my lunch was paid for. Then I was shown the door that I was to go out to get on what would be my bus with a specific number at the end of the day. The school had four doors, one on each side of the building. They all looked the same to me. I don't remember my first-grade teacher, nor anything about what we learned or any of the children in my class. I do remember sitting at the lunch counter, barely reaching the counter, legs dangling from the stool, and not knowing anyone. I felt so alone and scared.

My first day at school ended with a loud bell and I knew it was time to go home. I went out an exit but I didn't see the number on the bus that I had been told to look for to ride home. I ran back into the building and out another exit, still the wrong number on the bus. Soon all the kids were out of the building and there were no buses outside. I wanted to go home but I was afraid to ask anyone and more scared that I would get in trouble for not getting on my bus.

East Prairie had a population of about 3,500 in 1960, very much a country town. Most of the roads were dirt once you were off the main streets. I left school and began walking. I had no idea where we lived, our address, or what my grandpa's house was close to. It was late afternoon and getting close to supper. The sun was starting to drop and I was still wandering, trying to find my grandpa's house. Soon I saw the dime-store where the pay phone hung on the wall outside the store on the corner. I remember Mother and me walking there where she would make phone calls. I was lost and afraid to leave what was familiar. So, there I stood next to the pay phone outside of the dime-store, in a town where no one knew me, six years old, scared, crying, with the light giving way to dusk. I stood there for what seemed like hours but probably closer to 30 minutes. In a lost child's mind, scared and crying, 30 minutes were more like 30 hours. There were railroad tracks that ran through the middle of the town and in front of the dime-store where it sat on the corner of the block. I knew EtEt worked on the railroad and I thought maybe he would come by and see me. I kept looking around, hoping someone would find me or I would remember how to get home.

Suddenly, I looked down the street and across the railroad tracks and saw my mother and grandpa walking together toward me just on the other side. As they walked closer and closer, crossing the tracks, my tears of terror turned to tears of joy. Mother had been crying. Her eyes were red and she had a purple

"V" on her forehead from the veins that would light up when she was upset and crying. I soon became afraid that I was going to get into trouble, but Mother hugged me and she and Grandpa each took one of my hands and we began the walk home. I think Mother was crying because she loved me or maybe because she was afraid of what Daddy, Murn, and EtEt would do if I had not been found. I don't remember one other day living in East Prairie after that first day of school – not one day at my grandpa's, my teacher's name, or even one child that I played with. This period of my young life was the most scared I had ever been. Everything in my life was foreign to me and in many ways, even my mother. Fear stifled my six-year-old voice and made me withdraw into myself. I was alone.

It wasn't long before my mother got a waitress job at a restaurant in Charleston, Missouri, about 11 miles from East Prairie. She rented a very nice apartment over someone's detached garage in Charleston. The apartment was clean, it didn't smell and we had a bathroom! The restaurant where Mother worked wasn't far from where we lived and my new school was just a few blocks away in the same direction as the restaurant but a couple of blocks behind the restaurant. Mother registered me again in first grade but this time I knew my teacher's name, Mrs. Pannier. She was a short, round woman with glasses and a very kind face. She always wore big, round pearl necklaces. Mrs. Pannier was very kind to me and I wasn't afraid to go to school although I was still very timid and sad. Mrs. Pannier would always ask me if I was alright and would encourage me to play at recess. Instead, I would sit over by a tree in the corner of the playground and watch the others play.

Some days after school, Mother would let me come to the restaurant. I remember sitting at the counter and she would give me a piece of pie and milk or sometimes ice cream. Then, when she got off work, we walked home together. Mother often had to work late at the restaurant and would sometimes leave in the evening. I had a babysitter, but I don't remember liking her very much. Sometimes when she was at home, Mother would be in a really good mood and she would sing with the radio and we would laugh. She was so pretty when she laughed with her long, creased dimples.

When we laughed she would pull me to her and hug me, which to some degree worried me. As a child, I was fascinated with her girdle and garter belt and wondered why would anyone wear those things. But what got my attention more than anything were her bras. Pop icon Madonna had nothing on my mother! They were so pointed! There were sown circles that got smaller and smaller until there was a point at the tip on each cup! I just knew one day when she hugged me it was going to poke my eye out – maybe even both eyes with a full-body hug!

The moments were few when Mother and I had time together and enjoyed each other. I remember on a rare occasion a man would be in the apartment visiting, but I didn't know who he was. Mother was always in a good mood when he was around. I was told as an adult that there was a picture of my mother and me which sat on the desk of a man who became the governor. One of the governors had always lived in Charleston; maybe that was the man who visited our apartment now and then.

As I look back, Mother seemed to be focused on herself more than me. She didn't seem to pay much attention to me most of the time. I have a first-grade school picture that was taken when she sent me to school with the mumps. I told her I didn't feel good and from the picture, anyone could tell. My glands were swollen and my smile was that of a sick child. Murn was so upset I don't think she ever got over it.

It wasn't long before Daddy, Murn, and EtEt began coming over to see me and I got to go home with them to Cairo on the weekends. Most of the time Murn would come to pick me up because Daddy and EtEt were working.

Murn came to school one Friday and had a long talk with Mrs. Pannier. Murn wanted to know how I was doing in school and if there was anything my daddy should know. Mrs. Pannier told her that I was a very smart little girl, but a very sad one. I never knew much of the conversation after that; Murn was very careful not to talk about the situation between Mother and Daddy in front of me. I was always so happy going with Murn and EtEt for the weekend. Daddy was around their house most of that time and we would all have a good time together.

One weekend in January 1961, when I came to visit I was told that my Uncle Charles, the uncle who had visited us at Mill Creek, had passed away. I think that was my first introduction to a family member dying. He had a heart attack and left behind a wife and four children. I have one picture with me and my Uncle Charles in front of the Mill Creek house, which was the last time I remember seeing him. He was the second of eight children my Grandma Troutman had lost; the first died during childhood.

Grandma was a thin, frail, delicate little woman whose thinness made her seem tall. She suffered from osteoporosis and had a large rounded hump just below the back of her neck. She didn't talk very much but when she did, it was this quiet, sweet voice; it was as if she didn't have enough breath to talk. Even when she laughed it was this tiny push of air. She was so dainty, always dressed in shirtwaist dresses, usually with a brooch pinned at the top of the collar. Her arms were so thin the veins looked like the highways on a roadmap. I always noticed them because she always carried a handkerchief and would often dab her nose. She was a godly woman and relied on her strong faith. We often stopped by to visit or drop off groceries and Grandma would be sitting in her chair, next to the side table with the legs that had claw feet each on a crystal ball, reading her Bible. Whenever we picked her up on Sundays, out she came with her big black purse hanging from the bend at her elbow and her Bible clenched close to her chest.

Spring came and one weekend I begged Daddy to take me fishing. Murn fixed fried chicken, potato salad, milk, and cookies. She packed my special cup that was kept at her house for me to drink out of. It was a red cowboy boot with a handle that looked like the handle of a pistol with a barrel coming out on the opposite side. Daddy and I went to Horseshoe Lake and sat on one of the wooden docks that stretched out into the dark, blackish-green water. Tall cypress trees grew out in the water.

My daddy always looked clean and pressed, even when we were going fishing. He almost always wore a long sleeve shirt with the sleeves rolled up to his forearm and creased chinos. And always, always his shirt would be tucked in and he would wear a belt. While he put the bait on my line I sat and watched closely, and the breeze often blew the scent of his Old Spice toward me. When the worm was on the hook he handed the fishing pole to me and said, "Be careful, that hook will hurt if you touch it." As soon as he got his line baited and put in the water, I decided it was time to eat. He said, "We haven't caught any fish yet."

I told him, "We can catch some after we eat." So he took my pole along with his and laid them to the side. Then he opened the picnic basket and made a big announcement about what was in it.

"Oh looky here! There's fried chicken, potato salad, and milk and cookies for dessert. But I think Murn forgot to put any food in here for you."

"Oh, Daddy, she did too! I know she did," I told him.

"I don't think so," he said. "I guess I'll have to share mine with you." Then he handed me a chicken leg to start on while he poured my milk in my favorite red boot cup.

I looked up at him and said, "See, Murn didn't forget me!"

He and I sat on the dock and ate our lunch, then he smoked a cigarette. He never talked to me about my mother. He never questioned me or probed me when I would say things about my life with her. As soon as I was finished eating my cookies, I told him, "I think we should go home."

"What? I thought you wanted to fish," he said. "What will EtEt say if we come home without any fish?"

"We'll just have to go fishin' tomorrow," I told him. They all figured out that I just wanted to go on a picnic with my daddy. Saying I wanted to fish was a way to do that. Daddy picked up the poles and took the basket, then we walked back to the car for the drive home.

Sundays came far too quickly. I knew they would be taking me back to Charleston and I would spend most of my time alone. Murn had started braiding my hair on weekends when I was there, a pigtail on both sides. Murn made sure there were ribbons to match my clothes, a bow for the end of each braid. Even while she braided my hair we would talk or she would tell me funny stories. Murn, EtEt, and I would pick up Grandma Troutman and attend Sunday school and church. Sometimes Daddy would go with us. But after church came lunch and then it was time to go back to Charleston.

The joy and happiness I had been encapsulated in since I had been picked up on Friday began to unravel as the clock moved closer and closer to having to leave. It wasn't that I didn't love my mother, I just didn't feel secure or loved when I was with her. I guess I knew she didn't really want me, at least not the way Daddy, Murn, and EtEt did.

My week in school always moved so slowly in anticipation of the weekend. Finally, it was coming to the end of school, as all school years do. I'm sure my mother wasn't sure what to do with me during the summer since she had to work and the cost of a babysitter full time was expensive and more than she could afford. The easiest solution for everyone was for me to spend the summer with Murn and EtEt, the most joyous decision that ever could have been made from my perspective.

Murn and EtEt lived on Fifth Street. Around the corner from their house was a neighborhood grocery. The owner had several children and we became great playmates. My mother's brother, my Uncle James, his wife, Aunt Fay, and my cousins lived around the block on an opposite corner. Daddy was in and out of the house all of the time. My seventh birthday was close at hand and Murn planned a special birthday party for me. The large side yard at that house had plenty of room to play and have an outdoor party. Daddy and EtEt set up picnic tables that Daddy had borrowed from the VFW. Murn covered the tables with birthday tablecloths. There were balloons, a huge cake, and lots and lots of presents. Murn invited the neighborhood kids, my cousins, my half-sister and brother, and kids from my Sunday school class. There were cake and ice cream, party favors, party hats, and games. It was the best party any kid could have asked for. I had a beautiful new dress that Murn had bought for me. Mother didn't come. I guess she had to work that day. The rest of the summer was filled with true happiness in the life of a child. I knew I was loved.

The summer was filled with wonderful activities. Murn was the Vacation Bible School director for our church. Every morning for a week was spent in Bible school. I loved Bible school. We sang songs, did crafts, learned about stories in the Bible, and had cookies and Kool-Aid at morning recess. I especially remember Mrs. Davage and Mrs. Billings, two of the elderly ladies in our church; one of the ladies handed out the cookies and the other dipped up the Kool-Aid from this huge ceramic vat.

We also went to the ball diamond at the park to watch the church leagues play softball. It was exciting watching EtEt play ball and run the bases. He could run very fast; that's why he had the nickname Bunny. Murn and I would sit together in the bleachers with our church friends or I would run around and visit with my little church friends or watch with them from the sideline fence. My summer with Murn and EtEt was special. I got to be a child with no fears, no sadness, no loneliness; not until it was time for the summer to end did my anxiety increase and my happiness dissolve.

The trip back home to Charleston was never easy but this time it was exceptionally hard on all of us. I didn't want to go back to living with Mother or going to second grade. I would be alone again and sad. Murn, EtEt, and Daddy made the trip. When we arrived at our apartment I began crying uncontrollably. All of them tried to console me and assure me that they would see me the next weekend. It went on for almost 30 minutes. Finally, Daddy stooped down and was trying to talk to me when I grabbed his shirt with both hands. "Honey, let go. We'll be back in just a few days," he said.

I kept crying and pleading, "I want to go with you. I want to go with you and Murn and EtEt!"

Daddy tried to stand up and pull my hands off of his shirt. The strength of a desperate child is Herculean. I clung to his shirt so hard that all of the buttons ripped off. I screamed at all of them, "You and Daddy are going to sit on your butts and I'm going to break down."

Daddy grabbed both my arms and put me inside the apartment door where Mother was standing. I don't know for sure, but it must have been difficult on my mother knowing that I didn't want to be with her. I stood in the door crying as I screamed for them and watched them walk to the car and drive away.

Many years later, Murn told me that the ride home for them was painfully heartbreaking; all three of them cried the entire ride back to Cairo. "What are we going to do, Gilbert?" Murn asked.

EtEt said, "That little girl can't go through that again and neither can we."

"The courts won't take a child away from the mother. They'll never give a single man custody of his child, especially a little girl," Daddy said.

"Gilbert, do you want Everett and me to try to get custody of Debbie?" Murn asked.

Daddy told her, "That would be the best thing for her." That one car ride home changed my life forever.

I started second grade in Charleston again with my mother and was very unhappy. I don't remember my teacher's name or anything about school.

I had met one girl my age that walked the same way I did to go home. We soon became friends. She lived on the other end of the block where we lived. Her family had a beautiful house. Rather than going to the restaurant after school or staying with a babysitter, Mother let me go to this little girl's house. There was a game show that was on television at the time where contestants would walk on squares on the floor and would answer questions or win prizes if they were lucky enough to land on one of the prize squares after rolling the dice. We made a home version by placing sheets of paper on the floor and laid them throughout the house as the game board and then we had various toys of hers as prizes. We played for at least a couple of hours until Mother would call when she was home from work and I would have to go home.

Ever since Murn braided my hair the year before, I wanted to wear braids daily. Each morning my mother would braid my hair into two braids. Sometimes she pulled my hair as she brushed it and it would hurt. Murn never pulled my hair. I would pull away from Mother and cry out and she would pull me back to her and scold me. I hated getting my hair braided by Mother. I started to feel like she was angry with me all the time. More and more this made me not want to live with her.

I didn't see Murn, EtEt, or Daddy for quite a while. I thought they had forgotten about me. As time passed I felt resentment building inside me. What

I didn't know was that Murn and EtEt had contacted a lawyer in Missouri and were preparing to file for custody. Murn and EtEt finally came to get me one weekend. I didn't know that Mother had been served with court papers. Mother retained a lawyer and indicated she planned on fighting their request for custody. The court awarded temporary custody to Murn and EtEt until the final decision was going to be made on the court date. Mother had packed my belongings. She hugged me and told me "I'll see you soon, honey." I think she was relieved.

We drove away and Murn explained that I was going to be staying with her and EtEt for a while. For the first time since summer, I could breathe easily again, smile again, laugh again.

The court date came and later that same day, the lawyer notified Murn and EtEt that Mother did not show up to contest the request and the judge had ruled in their favor. I belonged in a home where I felt safe, secure, and loved. I could live with Murn and EtEt and my daddy and mother could come to see me. I never wanted to choose between them. I loved them both. However, I always wanted to live with Murn and EtEt. Soon the walls that had been torn down since Mother and Daddy's divorce were being rebuilt, the pain was being soothed with love, the fear was being replaced by an unquestionable sense of belonging, and finally the little adult in me was allowed to be a child again. Sometimes a child's cry as they stand amid all the rubble is heard by loving adults and the child is rescued. I was that child.

CHAPTER 5

Leaves of the Branches

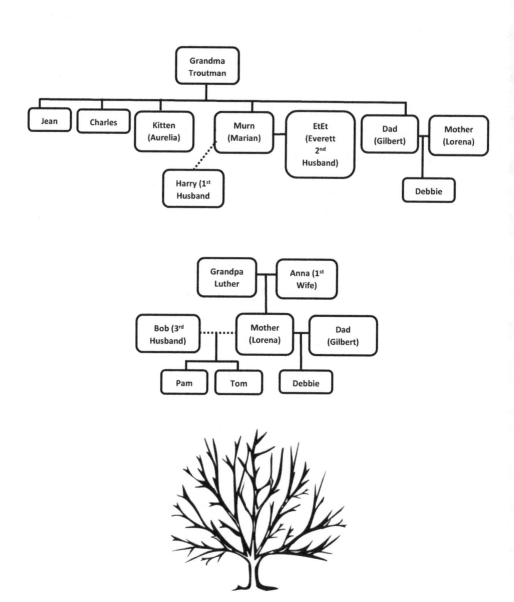

CHAPTER 5

Je Suis Content
Summer 1962 – Summer 1963

During the weeks before the judge's decision, Murn and EtEt had moved from their house on Fifth Street to another house on 19th Street that was within walking distance of the grade school I would be attending. To me, this house was a mansion. The house was in a residential area, but just off of the main thoroughfare. On one side were houses but on the other was a huge parking lot for a supermarket. The parking lot was large enough that cars never parked close to the side of our house. To make more of a separation, there was a long row of four o'clock bushes that ran the entire length from the front yard back to the backyard fence. I loved the four o'clock flowers. The deep green foliage plants were covered in small trumpet-like flowers in colors of purple, white, red, orange, and pink. Some were even multi-colored. They were so fascinating because the flowers opened around four o'clock in the afternoon and closed the next morning. They had a delicate fragrance, but because there were so many, the aroma permeated the air. During summer evenings Murn, EtEt, and I would sit on the porch and an evening breeze would softly wave the flowers and send their sweet bouquet floating in the air. Somehow they reminded me of the happiness I had with Murn and EtEt.

I loved the new house that was going to be my home. It was a white stucco one-level house with a wrap-around porch that extended across the entire front to most of the parking lot side of the house. The house had beautiful woodwork on the inside and several of the rooms had two four by eight-foot carved, sliding pocket doors that met in the center; they were almost majestic. There was a long entrance hallway where EtEt's desk sat. He would sit with his black-rimmed dime-store glasses on the end of his nose at the desk each month as he completed time cards. Murn would pay all the bills at that desk. The long entrance hall led to a sitting room, then to the dining room and kitchen. There was a bedroom off the dining room and one off the sitting room. The house had a very large living room which we entered from the long hallway and could be partitioned, allowing for a possible bedroom. The bathroom had two entrances, one from the kitchen and one from the bedroom off of the dining room. It was grand compared to the garage apartment Mother and I had lived in.

The school year had been in session for several months and I was transferring from my elementary school in Charleston, Missouri. Murn took me to my new school and to meet my teacher. My new second-grade teacher was Mrs. Whitaker. She was so nice and very kind, almost like a grandmother. She had solid white hair and her voice was so soft, her manner so gentle, I fell in love with her and my new school. Every morning Murn would fix me a good breakfast of oatmeal or cinnamon toast and an egg. She would braid my hair and tie bows on the ends of each braid to match my dress. Then we would sit at the kitchen table and have a daily devotion together and say a prayer. A hug and a kiss on the cheek from Murn and I was off to begin my day at school. I walked to and from school with children from the neighborhood. We all had to go home for lunch unless we were bus riders who lived outside the city limits. Murn would always have lunch ready for me. She would fix me a peanut butter and jelly sandwich or bologna and cheese, and in the winter I would have tomato soup with a toasted cheese sandwich. Then she would kiss me goodbye and back to school I would go.

I began to thrive in school academically. However, I was very thin and pale, which cued Murn to take me to the doctor for a physical. I was anemic and that's all it took for Murn to start me on a regimen of One A Day vitamins and Geritol Junior. (I'm not sure she knew at the time that Geritol had an alcohol content of 12 percent!) I don't think Mother had given much attention to my health, not intentionally, but by simply not observing. I had one or two cavities so Murn made sure I saw a dentist. I had a hard year that year as far as health was concerned. The dentist wanted to pull one of my teeth. Murn objected to doing it at that time because I was just getting over a cold. The dentist said it wouldn't be a problem and gave me sodium pentothal, which was commonly just called gas. I was so sick when I came out from under that I was vomiting nothing but green fluid. Within 48 hours I developed double pneumonia. Our doctor came to our house to treat me day after day.

At the end of the school year, I contracted chickenpox and measles at the same time. I was terribly ill. Once again, the doctor came to the house to treat me. During this combination of illnesses, he suggested that they keep me sedated or he said I would be miserable. Murn never left my side through either illness. She would read or sew or simply sit and think, but most of those days were spent sitting by my bedside. I completed second grade without any problems and was promoted to third grade. Daddy always signed my report cards. Mother had always sent them home on weekends with me for him to sign and Murn had him sign them as well.

After the divorce, Daddy moved into Murn and EtEt's guest room. It was so different being in a house with three adults compared to just me and my mother. Someone was always talking with me, playing a game with me or watching television with me, and sometimes just sitting in the room I was playing in. I had friends that would come to our house to play – some from our church, some from school, and some neighborhood kids.

I remember one afternoon during the summer Daddy was not working that day, and he was sitting outside on the porch in one of the two metal porch chairs, the kind with the back that looked like a seashell and you could almost rock in. Even on his day off Daddy was pressed, shaven, and handsome. One of my friends was visiting and we wanted to tie him up. We had jump ropes and for some reason, we thought tying him to the chair would be fun. My daddy was a good sport and went along with our request. While we were tying him up he fell asleep; it was a beautiful day and quite conducive to a nap. While he was napping, we found more rope and used that as well. We tied his arms to the arms of the chair and his legs to the legs of the chair. Once we had finished tying him up, our interest was on to other things and we left him sitting on the porch. A little while later he woke up only to find that he couldn't get himself untied!

"Girls! Debbie, you and Becky come back here and untie these ropes!" he yelled. He continued to struggle to no avail and Becky and I were nowhere in sight. "Marian! Marian!" he shouted.

Murn came to the front door, "Gilbert, what on earth are you yelling about?"

"The girls tied me up and I can't get loose!" Daddy told her.

They both loved telling the story of how two little girls tied him up and he couldn't escape. He always laughed and said, "I thought I was going to have to sit there until Everett came home."

At the end of each week and on weekends, Daddy would stop by a local tavern before he came home. Daddy was always a friendly guy and many of his buddies would meet there. Saturday mornings when I woke up he often would be having coffee with Murn and EtEt at the kitchen table. When I had finished my breakfast he would say, "Did you check Daddy's pockets?" I would run to his bedroom and shove my hand into each of his jacket pockets until I found the little bag of pistachios that he brought home from the tavern. He and I would sit at the table and he helped me shell the little nuts. Our fingers would be red from the dyed shells covering them, but we didn't care. He and I would eat them together; we loved pistachios.

The summer following the second grade was one of the calmest summers I had had in several years as a child. It was filled with friends at our house playing and me going to their house, Vacation Bible School, going places with Murn during the week, and Sundays after church we all, including Grandma Troutman, would go out to dinner at Bob's Restaurant where I would have my favorite: sliced roast beef, corn, mashed potatoes, and gravy. If the weather was cool enough for us to sit in the car with the windows down we would go to the What-a-Burger, a drive-in that served huge hamburgers. On Sunday afternoons, Murn, EtEt, Grandma, and sometimes Daddy would sit on the porch, sometimes read the paper, or take a nap while the delicate fragrance of the four o'clock bushes gently wafted through the air. We usually had cold-cut sandwiches for supper because we attended church every Sunday evening and Murn didn't want to have to clean up lots of dishes before church.

It wasn't long into the summer that Daddy quit going to work. Once I had my breakfast, Murn would tell me "Go wake up your daddy, but do it very slowly."

Daddy had started having convulsions. Especially if he was awakened abruptly, it would trigger a seizure. The doctor thought it was epilepsy or perhaps residual damage from malaria he had suffered in the Philippines during the war. Test after test was done. We spent weekend after weekend during the summer taking him to the Veteran's hospital an hour away and then later to Barnes Hospital in St. Louis, almost two hours one way. Those were long days; early in the morning leaving to get there and late in the evening returning home. Sometimes EtEt would go with us, but mainly it was during the week and he was working so Murn would take Daddy, and I always went along. The doctors at Barnes determined he had a brain tumor. They found a spot on his brain.

They tried many different medicines, none of which seemed to help. One medication affected his equilibrium and he stumbled a lot, another turned his hair from brown to orange, and yet another caused him to slur his speech. He wasn't allowed to drive for his safety and others, so his only alternative was to walk unless he asked Murn to take him around town when she had the car. I remember overhearing people make comments to Murn that they saw Gilbert stumbling down the street drunk or, "I saw Gilbert and he couldn't talk, he was so drunk."

Murn would get so upset when people said those things. She wasn't one to hold back, so she would straighten them out without hesitation, telling them the numerous medications the doctors had prescribed for him. Daddy always had churning undercurrents of alcoholism but this wasn't the problem. In Victorian terms, a "drunk" meant a moral failure. Daddy wasn't a drunk and his moral character was without question. My daddy did drink, but he wasn't a drunk.

As time went on Daddy began losing weight, he couldn't work, and with the gossip of people in town, he began to drink more – a lot more. This was a man who had worked all his life, served his country, and now couldn't hold a job due to his physical health, doctor appointments, and reactions to the medications. He started spending his empty days more and more at the tavern, where he began to treat his depression with alcohol. While he used to go there to drink with his buddies, now the drink became his buddy.

His drinking at the tavern spilled over into our house. I remember one day when Daddy was living with us I saw Murn in the bathroom down on her knees looking under the clawfoot tub. I asked her what was she doing and before she could answer she pulled out a pair of Daddy's shoes. In one shoe there was a pint of half-drunk whiskey. Murn and EtEt didn't drink and liquor wasn't allowed in our house. Murn was furious. I think she was more upset that, considering his condition and the trips we were making to the hospitals to make him better, he was complicating his problems and making his health worse, rather than the fact that liquor was in the house, although that was still an issue. She turned right to the bathroom sink and poured it down the drain, put the empty bottle back in one of the shoes, then put his shoes back under the tub where she found them. I'm sure my daddy got the message when he went for the pint, but I'm also sure he had a "come to Marian" meeting, although I never heard about it. But I did walk in the living room when she was telling EtEt about what she found and I caught EtEt giving a silent chuckle the way he often did once Murn had turned and left the room. I think he kind of felt sorry for Daddy because he knew the tongue-lashing he was about to get from Murn.

Murn's first husband, Harry, was a periodic drinker. Murn would tell how Harry would disappear for a whole day and she would know exactly where he had been: a local tavern. She said she could always tell he had been drinking all day by the way he shut the car door, had his hat set back on his head, and would be whistling the same tune. In the neighborhood grocery stores, there was always a small storage area where empty and full soda cases, tools, brooms, etc., would be stored. As soon as Harry would pull in, Murn would go straight to the storage area and pull out a case of empty soda bottles. Once Harry came through the door, Murn would start throwing bottles with Harry dodging them and glass shattering all over the concrete floor. Murn said she would throw until every bottle in the case was gone. Then she would turn around and climb the stairs to their apartment above the store and Harry would get the broom and the dust pan out and sweep up all the glass. One day their elderly maid, Pony, asked Murn to sit down, she wanted to talk to her. Pony said, "Miss Marian, I know you get awful mad at Mr. Harry when he's been drinkin' the liquor, and you have every right to be. But when you throw those bottles one of them could hit Mr. Harry in the temple and you could kill him! Now I know you'd feel awful bad if that would happen." Murn said she thought about it and no, she didn't want to hurt him or kill him. So many months later when Harry showed up after a disappearance, hat cocked and whistling a tune, Murn walked over to the bread rack and pulled it over in line with the door and began slinging bags of bread off the rack at Harry until every loaf was gone. She then retreated to their apartment. And, like with the soda bottles, Harry swept up the broken bags and loose slices of bread that covered the floor, took them out to the trash barrel, got back into the car, and drove up to the bakery to buy more bread to line the store shelves for the remainder of the day. Fearless and determined, Murn never gave up; when she had a point to make, she was going to make it. Daddy was just lucky all he received was a tongue-lashing instead of dodging that pint bottle or a loaf of bread!

Summer passed and within the first few weeks of school, I was pretty sure third grade was not going to be as enjoyable for me as second grade had been. Although I was now a happy and secure child at home, I didn't really like my teacher at school. She wasn't very nice and seemed like she didn't like me. I was a really good child and had never been in trouble.

One day a girl told the teacher that I had stolen her pencil, which I hadn't. The girl showed it to me, I looked at it and then gave it back to her. By the time I arrived home my teacher, Mrs. Claycomb, had called Murn and told her that I had stolen this girl's pencil. The girl went to our church and Murn knew there was always a problem with this girl, even in Bible School, but when I arrived home, Murn was waiting for me. I never really got spankings, I never wanted anyone to be mad at me, and I never wanted to disappoint anyone.

That was the worst! I pled my case, but in those days, the teachers were always right. You were guilty until proven innocent. Well, I got a spanking. The next day, the little girl told the truth, it was in her desk all along. Murn was notified that I had NOT stolen the pencil and the little girl had lied. I told Murn, "See, I told you I didn't take it."

Her response was, "If you hadn't taken it to look at, there wouldn't have been a problem." Murn always had an answer.

Another time in class we had to write letters or cards to our parents and I, of course, wrote mine to Murn and EtEt. Mrs. Claycomb took my letter and said, "They are not your parents, they are your aunt and uncle."

I looked her in the eye, took a breath, and in my deepest, slowest eight-year-old voice said, "They are too my parents." To me, they *were* my parents; I lived with them. I knew my mother and daddy but to me, the people I lived with were my parents: Murn and EtEt, my aunt and uncle. I didn't like her from then on.

Soon there was another incident. We were studying possessives and plurals and she had our class draw pictures of a business we would own with a store window that had our name on it using the correct punctuation. Well, I drew a picture of my music store, Burris' Music Store. And in the window, I drew pictures of instruments, including a cornet. I knew exactly what I was talking about and I knew how to spell it. I put a sign in the window that said, "Cornets for Sale." Mrs. Claycomb marked on my paper that it should be spelled "coronet" and wrote that a coronet wasn't an instrument and that what I had drawn was a trumpet. She was wrong and I knew it. I was a very quiet and shy child, but needless to say, Murn was not. Murn dealt with Mrs. Claycomb regarding both instances. Mrs. Claycomb and I never had another conflict again, but I still didn't like her.

Murn never had a problem dealing with situations where individuals over-stepped boundaries or did not consider the feelings of others. Murn did have a temper and you would know it if you had anything to do with releasing it. She didn't mince words and would get directly to the point. She most often became angered when something or someone was being taken advantage of, whether it was her or someone else. She often taught Sunday school and taught many different levels throughout the years. One year she was teaching the primary class with four- to five-year-olds. The minister taught the young couples' class. The primary class met in the educational wing which was on the same level as the sanctuary. One Sunday Murn went to the educational wing to where her class met and several young couples were sitting there. They told her that the minister said their class was switching with the primary class and the little ones would meet upstairs. I'm sure the minister had no idea what he had unleashed that Sunday morning. Murn found him; at five-foot-one, her pointed finger almost reached the nose on his six-foot figure as she informed him, "You're not going to push me and my little children around. They can't climb those stairs! You move your class to somewhere else but the primary class will continue to meet where they've always met!"

"OK, Marian, you're right. I'm sorry I didn't think about that," he said.

"No, you certainly didn't!" she responded as she whipped around and exited. And that was the end of that. Murn's anger was similar to that of a stubbed toe; the pain at the beginning is always excruciating but it slowly eases. Whatever you stubbed your toe on, you always make sure not to stub it on that again. The bruising and aching that followed were yours to deal with, not hers.

Fall was a beautiful season in Cairo. Walking to school with friends was always fun. On our way, we had to pass by a candy shop. They had a case full of penny candies. We stopped every day on our way back to school after lunch.

The selection was amazing: bubble gum, red shoelace licorice, caramels, strips of button candies, paraffin fingernails, Sixlets, Pixie straws, Mary Janes, and many other types of candies. As we continued our walk to school we would eat as much as we possibly could before we arrived on the playground. It was a good thing for the teachers that there was a lunch recess before we entered for the last half of our school day. The amount of sugar that was coursing through our veins was enough to have us bouncing off the walls of our classroom! The playground consisted of black cinders. The candy helped ease the pain from the embedded cinders in our knees and elbows when we fell running and chasing each other in a game of tag.

At our school, the first, second, and third graders played on one side of the playground and the fourth, fifth and sixth graders played on the other side. As a third grader, I played on the side which was across a small side street from the playground of the Catholic school which held grades one through eight. My half-sister and brother, Pam and Tommy, went to school there. Pam was in seventh grade, Tommy in fifth, and I was in third. Both schools often had recess at the same time. I would watch as the sisters played kickball with the children in their long, black habits. I often wondered how they could run so well in their "dresses" – and weren't they hot?

Now and then Pam or Tommy and I would see each other. Their playground was contained by a 10-foot cyclone fence so they would often come to the fence and I would stand on the tree lawn of our playground and we would share very simple exchanges. We knew we were related, but they always lived with their dad and grandmother. I remember one day especially when Tommy was allowed to come over to my house to play on a Saturday afternoon. We were the closest in age and I was a bit of a tomboy. We stayed outside most of the day playing football. Other than at school, we only saw each other when Mother would come for a visit and collect the three of us to

65

visit with her brother's family in Cairo or her father and stepmother in East Prairie.

As the calendar moved closer to Christmas, I was insistent that I wanted a Magnus console chord organ I had seen in one of the stores downtown. It had 32 keys and buttons on the far left that played chords while the right hand played the melody on the keys. It was in a walnut cabinet and had a stool that together looked like a miniature organ. It was $99 and I begged Murn for it. She simply said it was too expensive and I couldn't have it.

Daddy was struggling more and more, but he was a proud man and I have no doubts how very much he loved me. There was a man who needed day laborers to complete some work on his farm property. He would pull his big, flatbed stake truck into the supermarket parking lot next to our house early in the morning. Every morning, men would come who needed work and he would take so many each morning to dig ditches on his property. It was not only cold and damp all day out in the weather, but it was backbreaking work. Every day for several weeks, my daddy climbed on the back of that truck to earn some money. Christmas morning, that Magnus chord organ was sitting next to our Christmas tree with a big red bow and a tag that said, "To Debbie Girl, I Love You, Daddy."

The combination of his health problems and his increased drinking caused our family doctor to do a complete physical. X-rays revealed a spot on one of his lungs. He was immediately admitted to the TB sanitarium in Cairo. He stayed in the sanitarium for almost a year. One weekend Mother came for a visit. She and I went to visit Daddy on Sunday. We couldn't go in, but there was a beautiful back porch that overlooked a large backyard at the sanitarium and we were allowed to see him there. He came out in his pajamas, robe, and slippers and sat on the steps with Mother and me. It was a beautiful, sunny Sunday afternoon and Mother and I were both dressed up. She was so stylish with her matching skirt, jacket, and top along with her matching big brim hat. I thought she and Daddy were glad to see each other; at least they both smiled and laughed a lot. That was a special Sunday, the three of us together, but I knew I was safe because, at the end of the day, I was going back home to Murn and EtEt.

During the time he was there, Daddy's health improved; he gained back the weight he had lost and he was not drinking. Then, after spending almost a year with individuals with tuberculosis, the doctors announced that he did not have TB; they weren't sure what the spot on his lung was. Upon his release from the sanitarium, with his health better, Daddy got a job and moved out of the guest room. I don't think we ever found out what exactly was wrong with him physically. The seizures seemed to disappear and he was working again but still drinking, just not as much.

Before Murn and EtEt could move back into the guest room, which was the master bedroom, Grandma Troutman decided she didn't want to live alone anymore so she asked if she could move in with them. Of course, neither Murn nor EtEt would ever say no to her. She wanted to keep her own bedroom furniture, so Murn sold the guest bedroom suite that Daddy had used. There was always some type of movement at our house, and Murn and EtEt seemed to be the axis that kept family members from spinning out of control.

We always had people stopping by our house. Friends and family knew our home was always open. My Aunt Kitten, whose real name was Aurelia, often stopped by our house on her way to work. She was three years younger than Murn, nine years older than my daddy, and the fifth of my grandma's eight children. She worked at the Mark Twain, a higher-end steakhouse, and always looked so pretty on her way to work. She wore a pink waitress uniform that had a white collar, white cuffs on the short sleeves, a white apron, and white shoes. She wore red lipstick. Her hair was always perfect and she always smelled so good. I always knew when Aunt Kitten had been there; the scent lingered. Aunt Kitten had been diagnosed with colon cancer and had to have surgery that left her with a colostomy. I think she may have overdone it with the perfume because she was concerned that the colostomy might smell. I don't know why, but it seemed like Aunt Kitten always argued with Murn. Maybe it was because alcohol was served where she worked and Murn thought she was drinking too much, or maybe because she was the younger and Murn was the older sister and that's what sisters do; I don't know.

Cairo had a roller-skating rink and Saturday afternoons were for grade school-age children. I loved to skate, but I was afraid to use the toe stop. So, I would just extend my arms and stop myself by running directly into the bars around the walls. One Saturday I was going a little too fast and hit the bar too hard, resulting in a broken arm. It was close to Easter and we always had to dress up for church on Easter. I had my arm in a sling but it was the first time I got to wear a blazer. It was white with a crest insignia on the breast pocket. I wore a white blouse with a very thin ribbon tied in a bow and a light blue skirt.

I received an Easter card from Mother that year with $10 in it. There was a pharmacy that carried all types of holiday trinkets, including stuffed animals, across from the supermarket. I asked Murn if I could go there and spend my money from Mother. It wasn't long before I came across the parking lot with this huge stuffed Mr. Easter Bunny. He had on a tie and jacket with pants. It was almost as big as I was. What I didn't know was that Mother hadn't sent anything for me that Easter, but Murn always had a card ready as a backup for each holiday. It was Murn who signed the card, "I Love You, Mommy" and it was Murn who put the $10 in the card. Murn and EtEt always respected Mother's position in my life. I was always taught to love my mother and that she was my mother.

Murn was always committed to what she believed to be right, fair, and just. This commitment was evident throughout her life, especially with her first husband, Harry. Polio never stopped Murn from doing anything she wanted. She always drove cars and had no difficulty. During those years all cars had standard transmissions and the operator had three pedals they needed to operate. The clutch allowed the driver to switch gears, but when the clutch would slip, it could ruin the transmission. During Murn and Harry's marriage, Murn had always driven the car, but there came a time when Harry said the clutch was slipping and he needed to get it fixed before he wanted Murn to drive it. Every time Murn wanted to take the car Harry would say, "Oh Marian, I need to get that clutch fixed. I just haven't had time. I'll go get whatever you want."

This went on for several weeks when one day she was in the storage room rummaging around and Harry heard her. "Marian, what are you looking for, honey? Here, I'll help you, what do you need?"

"Harry, I thought we had a sledgehammer but I can't seem to find it."

Harry said, "Here, honey, I'll get it for you. Here it is, what do you need it for?"

Murn took the sledgehammer and headed toward the door of the storefront with Harry right behind her. Murn turned, sledgehammer in hand, and said, "If I can't drive that car, neither can you!" Then she turned and started out the door.

Harry rushed in front of her. "Wait, Marian, wait a minute! I'll go get it fixed right now! See, I'm leaving now." Murn always had a way of making her point and that she wasn't playing.

The only situation I ever witnessed close to that was when my maternal grandmother, Anna Wiles, swept into Cairo one day and wanted to meet me. I had never met her and Mother had never spoken of her to any degree. Murn answered the door and graciously welcomed her into our home. It was amazing to me how much Mother and Uncle James looked like her, especially their mouths. She was a larger woman than Murn and she spoke with what sounded like a Kentucky accent. The visit began quite friendly and of course coffee was served at the dining room table. The exchange between my grandmother and me was very superficial. What does a grandmother say to an eight-year-old grandchild that she knows nothing about and had no interest in from birth? Better still, what does an eight-year-old have to say to an adult they've never met? Murn and my Grandmother Wiles continued with their conversation as I entertained myself in the sitting room. Grandma Wiles did most of the talking, telling how she had found religion after marrying her third husband and what her life was like in Michigan. At times it seemed as if she was trying to impress Murn.

Suddenly the voices became very quiet, but I could still hear them if I listened very closely and stood by the edge of the door where they couldn't see me but I could peek around and see them. Grandma Wiles was expressing her opinion as to what a pitiful excuse for a mother my mother was because she was too busy chasing men rather than taking care of her children. Then I saw it. Murn had a smirking smile, a set jaw, a slight tilt of her head, hands clasped on the table, and raised shoulders as she took a deep breath and leaned one shoulder towards my grandmother. Then in her most controlled yet pointed voice, Murn spoke.

"The reason Lorena is the way she is, is because of you! You took your two younger sisters with you when you walked out and left Lorena with her two little brothers and a tiny baby girl alone, sitting in a corner crying, to be raised by an evil father. Not one of those four children was older than seven years old. A pathetic excuse for a mother? I'd say this is a case of the pot calling the kettle black. You may be Debbie's grandmother but you are *not* going to sit here and run down your daughter to me. She didn't have a mother to protect her or teach her how to be a mother. So now, with that said, I think it's time you be on your way." With that said Murn sat back, took a sip of coffee, and then stood up.

"Debbie! Come here and tell your Grandmother Wiles goodbye."

I don't think my grandmother knew what to say. Like Harry, she was probably thinking, "I'm going, I'm going!" Within minutes, my Grandmother Wiles was gone and that was the first and last time I ever saw or heard from her. I had my Grandma Troutman and Grandma Maudie. They were all I needed or wanted. And Mother had Murn.

During the summer we would take weekend trips to St. Louis to visit with Murn and Daddy's oldest sister, my Aunt Jean. Sometimes just Murn and I would go during the week. Aunt Jean and her husband lived in St. Louis in one of the multi-story high-rises. Each floor had four apartments, two next to each other on one side of the floor and two on the other side. There was a breezeway in the middle with a steel mesh that ran from ceiling to floor and from wall to wall. You could see for miles and the wind would blow through.

Aunt Jean and her husband, Joe Bernstein, lived on the fourth floor. There were elevators, but they were always broken and through the years they became dangerous due to teenagers stopping them or getting on with people and robbing them. Murn preferred that we take the stairs. It was hard on her with her polio leg, but she was strong and we would rest on each floor for a moment then we continued our climb.

Jean was the oldest of Grandma Troutman's children and was in her late fifties at this time, but she seemed a lot older to me. Her husband, I called him Uncle Joe, was a frontman for Barnum and Bailey Circus. He would travel and provide the city with posters and circulars before the circus arrived. They had a parakeet named Peety. Peety was often out of his cage and would sit on

Uncle Joe's shoulder and he would feed him crackers or toast. I liked watching him talk to Peety. It was as if Peety knew exactly what he was saying. Aunt Jean always had one drawer that had what adults would call junk, but to an eight- or nine-year-old, it was a chest full of treasures. I would spend the whole visit searching through the drawer. There were pencils, a variety of interesting pens and pins, key chains, magnets, and novelty items. I could take whatever I wanted. As I look back, it was Aunt Jean's sneaky way to get that drawer cleaned out.

Sometimes we would go to Wood River to visit my Uncle Charles' family. Murn thought it was important that we stay connected to his children and wife. He and his wife, Gladys, had four children who were quite a bit older than I, but three were in high school and I loved to spend time with them, especially Susan. She was the youngest and I was fascinated with how she decorated her bedroom with cardboard standups that are often used in grocery or liquor stores. They were funny signs. I think the one I remember the most was a cardboard scarecrow.

On one visit Susan and the next oldest, Cynthia, asked if they could take me with them to the city swimming pool. We were staying for the weekend and Murn had packed my swimming suit just in case. My cousins and I went to the city pool where there was a tall sliding board. I wanted to try it but I was scared; I wasn't a good swimmer and it was on the deep end. They assured me that they would both stand at the bottom and would pull me up. Well, some high school boys they knew distracted their attention. Down the slide I went into the water. They hadn't seen me come down the slide. Other kids started one after another coming down on top of me before they realized I was below them. They were so sorry, but that was the end of swimming for me!

Of course, there was Vacation Bible School during the summer. Murn had been the director of Vacation Bible School at our church for many years and she was the director again and I was the director's child. Every morning Bible school began with a processional down the aisle of the sanctuary. Each morning three different children were chosen to carry the American flag, the Christian flag, and the Bible, leading all of the children into the sanctuary. We would file into the pews singing "Onward Christian Soldiers" as the flag bearers and Bible carrier stood in the front and we would remain standing as we said the Pledge of Allegiance followed by a scripture reading. I wanted so badly to carry a flag or the Bible, but Murn said that it would look as though she was favoring me because I belonged to her. I think I finally got to carry one flag one time in all the years she was director.

I was a happy child, flag or no flag. My life was full, safe, and surrounded by people who loved me. I knew no fear. *Je Suis Content (I am content)*.

CHAPTER 6

Leaves of the Branches

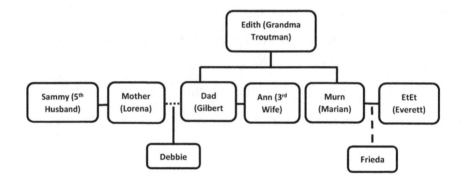

Edith (Grandma Troutman)

Sammy (5th Husband) — Mother (Lorena) — Dad (Gilbert — Ann (3rd Wife) — Murn (Marian) — EtEt (Everett)

Debbie

Frieda

CHAPTER 6

The City Mother and the Country Mom
Fall 1963 - Fall of 1964

It's amazing how happy a child can be once they feel safe and loved. By the fourth grade, my life with Murn and EtEt was settled and routine. I knew every day that I was loved and I was told daily. The only focus I had to have was to be a nine-year-old, behave, and do well in school. I loved fourth grade. I had Mrs. Stone as a teacher. She was so kind and patient with all of the students in our class. As many children often do, I loved her as my teacher. She was the kind of teacher that students remembered for good reasons. She never raised her voice at us, she never threatened, and she never forgot that we were learning.

We had music weekly with Mrs. Sullivan. Every classroom had an upright piano and a set of the *Golden Age of Song* songbooks. When she came in the door, she would have two students pass out the songbooks while she would tell us about the songs we were going to sing that day. Then she would sit down at the piano and we sang for 30 minutes. We learned the songs that were historical in the American culture. While some of the songs would be frowned upon today, Mrs. Sullivan taught us history through the music of our culture: the taming of the frontier, the hardships of the slaves, politically motivated songs, folk songs that recorded life through the years, the songs of Stephen Foster, and popular music from the 1800s that our grandparents grew up with. And of course we sang and learned all of the patriotic songs and folk songs from our Golden songbooks.

We also had art weekly with Mrs. Rust. Mrs. Rust was a practicing artist and I loved to see her come through the door of our classroom; art was also one of my favorite subjects. She limped like Murn, but instead of the limp being caused as the result of polio, she had been in a car accident when she was younger and her hip had been damaged. She was all about business. It seemed as if she never smiled; she wasn't mean, she was just serious during her time with us. She was a wonderful art teacher and taught us to be true artists. We learned a different medium each year. This year we were drawing with pencils. When parents bought supplies for the year, there would be specific requirements for art. This year we had to buy specific lead grade artist pencils and an art eraser. Those erasers were fun to play with; they stretched like rubber, similar to Silly Putty. Classmates were always getting in trouble for playing with them, in and out of our art time.

Then there was Mrs. Gilhoffer, the district nurse. She wore white stockings and shoes, a white nurse uniform with nursing pins on the collar, and a nurse's cap. I believe she only came once a month to deliver a health lesson for the class. I knew Mrs. Gilhoffer better than most students. Murn used to say, "If there's a hole in the ground, Debbie will find it." I had close to a clubfoot when I was born and as a child had to wear laced-up, high-topped shoes when I began walking. That along with holes in the ground made me a prime candidate for twists, sprains, hairline fractures, and torn tendons in my ankles. Mrs. Gilhoffer would put me in her car and take me home. Her car was an old Nash. It looked like a big, grey bug with its long, curved top that started at the windshield and then curved down to the back bumper. The headlights looked like a bug's big eyes. Murn could easily see us driving up to the house and she would meet Mrs. Gilhoffer and me at the door. Murn would shake her head and Mrs. Gilhoffer, in her most serious voice, would explain whether my ankle needed a doctor's care and x-rays or simply an ice pack and rest.

Fourth grade was when a child could begin to play a band instrument. I'm sure Murn was a little skeptical about another instrument, but I think she was so happy it would be one that I could carry in a case myself rather than hiring a small army to move it in and out of the house, that she was open to the idea.

When I was seven, I wanted to play the piano, so she and EtEt purchased an upright piano. The old uprights were monsters. They weighed what must have been a ton. It took several men, a small army, to load it onto a truck and then unload it, take it upstairs to the porch, then move it to the room where it was to reside, all without scratching or damaging the piano and the same for the doorways and floors! Well, I didn't practice, so Murn sold the piano. The next year I begged again, please let me take piano lessons. My friends were taking lessons and of course, I wanted to as well. And once again, the hunt, purchase, and moving of another upright piano ensued. Again, I wouldn't practice. Murn finally figured out that I just liked spending time sitting next to my teacher on the piano bench. My teacher was our pastor's wife and she played beautifully. She played for our church and Sunday school classes and was like another grandmother to all of us. And once again, I didn't practice so Murn sold the piano.

I'm sure when I came running home with the information concerning the band instrument display meeting during that fall Murn and EtEt wanted to roll their eyes and say, "Here we go again!" But I think they knew there was something different about this, other than the smaller and lighter design of band instruments compared to the piano. Our pastor's son often played the trumpet in church. He was in high school and was an amazing trumpet player. I'm sure they noticed how I would move to the edge of the pew when Richard played a solo or duet with his sister playing trombone, or how I would run up to him after the sermon as he was putting his trumpet in the case. He would let me hold it and talk to me about how to play it and answer my questions. Just holding it was thrilling. It was beautiful: long, shiny, gold with a rose gold bell. It was the most beautiful thing I had ever seen!

After two piano failures, Murn and EtEt still took me to the elementary school where all the different instruments were laid out on display. A salesman from the local music store was there along with the school district's band director. There was no question in my mind, I was going to play the trumpet. After the presentation, Murn and I walked up to the front of the room and she signed a rental agreement. We walked out with my very first cornet. Most beginners started on the cornet due to its smaller size and then graduated to a trumpet once they learned the fundamentals and physically grew into a size more conducive to holding up the length of a trumpet. This was the beginning of my love affair with music. I practiced every day. I was still able to spend time with my piano teacher because when I could play well enough, I would play hymns for church and she would accompany me, which meant we would have to practice. I also begged to take private music theory lessons with Mrs. Sullivan. In addition to being the school music teacher, she taught private piano lessons and agreed to give me music theory lessons. I just couldn't learn enough about music and Murn always encouraged me.

Thanksgiving was approaching and Daddy's birthday was a few days before. Murn helped me bake a cake for his birthday. He liked chocolate cake with white icing. He was supposed to come for dinner but never came. Murn said not to worry, we would cut the cake when he arrived. Well, it wasn't long before Daddy walked in, wearing creased chinos and a beautiful black flannel shirt. I was so excited to show him the cake I had baked. The cake had two round tiers of devil's food chocolate, with creamy, white buttercream frosting with peaks like meringue all over the top. Daddy sat down at the table and I placed the cake in front of him with one lit candle for him to blow out. He had his head lying in his hand with his elbow on the table then he put his other arm around me and said, "You didn't bake that, did you? I bet Murn baked it." Daddy always liked to tease me. Murn said, "Let's get some dishes out and you and your daddy can have a piece of cake."

I turned around to go get the plates when I heard Murn. "Gilbert! Honey, your daddy's fallen asleep in your cake." The white icing was smeared all over his sleeve on the underside of his forearm. Murn grabbed the dishcloth trying to wipe off the icing and told me, "Debbie, help your daddy into Grandma's room to lay down. He can have his cake after he takes a nap."

While she didn't show it, Murn was disgusted. Daddy had been all day at the tavern and the guys had been buying him drinks for his birthday. I helped Daddy from the kitchen into what was now Grandma's room, which was the closest to the kitchen, where he laid down and went fast asleep, or…passed out. When I went to the living room where Grandma and EtEt were sitting, Murn had been expressing her feelings to them. Murn always handled everything. I could tell Grandma was embarrassed by it and as was common, EtEt just chuckled to himself. He knew yet again what Daddy was about to receive from Murn and it wasn't going to be a birthday present!

A few days following my daddy's birthday, President John F. Kennedy was assassinated: Friday, November 22, 12:30 p.m. I'll never forget; the school was in a flutter. We had just returned from lunch and settled down for the afternoon subjects. Televisions were rolled into each classroom. There we sat as we watched Walter Cronkite telling America what had happened and giving a moment-by-moment description of what was occurring. I remember the exact moment when he announced that the president had died. Everyone was in shock. Our teacher cried and many of my classmates cried.

All Cairo schools were dismissed at the regular time and as we all returned home, there was an eeriness on the streets. My friends and I were scared as we walked home. I guess we weren't sure what was happening. It was so quiet and it seemed like there was hardly any traffic. Like most, our family was glued to the television for the next few days. I think this was my first real awareness of the office of the president of the United States. Murn, EtEt, Grandma, and I watched the replays of the motorcade through Dallas as he was shot, the mourners as they passed by the casket at the Rotunda, Mrs. Kennedy with John Jr. and Caroline as they walked behind the casket in the funeral procession, and then the funeral. At that time, I had never really been exposed to death and funerals other than when I was told my Uncle Charles died. Perhaps it was this tragedy of the assassination of our president that taught many children my age about sadness and death.

My daddy and Mother had been divorced for about three years by this time. Daddy finally found someone he was interested in. He reconnected with a woman named Ann, who he had known when he was in the service. She had lost her husband to cancer and was left with five children to raise with the help of her father. She lived an hour away from us but she and Daddy started seeing each other. Soon, they were married and Daddy moved from Cairo to her house an hour away. While I missed seeing him daily, I wasn't too upset by it. My happiness and safety were found in my life with Murn and EtEt. He would call regularly and Murn and EtEt would make sure we visited him once or twice a month. My stepbrothers and sister ranged in age from five to 12. The youngest was a girl, Lisa, followed by Roger, Steve, Jeff, and Allen. Jeff and I were the same age while Steve and Allen were on each side of us by a year, and Lisa and Roger were a year apart.

When going to Daddy's house to visit, the day was filled with playing ball with my stepbrothers, Daddy cooking out, and Murn visiting with Ann while

Ann's father, Grandpa Treese, EtEt, and Daddy chatted about politics and sports.

My mother was living in Kansas City, Missouri, around this time. While she would call often, send cards and write letters to me, and visit one or two times a year, I didn't know much about her life, and probably shouldn't have at my age. I just knew that she was my mother and I loved her, but I didn't want to live with her. That's all that mattered. She too had married again and I think she had been making comments about wanting me to live with her. I didn't know exactly, but Murn had told me to call her if my mother ever came to my school. I thought, why would she come to school? Why wouldn't she come to the house like she always did? I soon found out why.

One day we were in class silently reading at our desks. I sat by the windows on the side of the room farthest from the door in front of the class and at the back of the row farthest from the door in the back of the room. Mrs. Stone was at her desk in the front of the room grading papers. Suddenly I looked up and saw my mother standing in the front doorway. There she stood, a beautiful woman dressed impeccably. She had on patent leather spike high heels, a pencil skirt with a kick pleat and matching jacket, a soft cream shell under the jacket, and a coordinated wide brim hat with a patent leather purse hanging from her arm. She was striking with blonde hair, very tasteful makeup, and long, red-painted fingernails.

I couldn't breathe. I started hyperventilating and scooting my desk backward, farther away from the door. It was as if I was in a spinning tunnel like that of the *Twilight Zone*. I immediately knew that something was wrong; Mommy was coming to take me with her. Where was Murn, EtEt, or my daddy? Mrs. Stone must have heard the commotion made by the sound of the desk scraping across the floor as I panicked. When she saw my eyes glued to the doorway, she immediately got up from her desk and moved to the door. I began to cry and my classmates were asking me what was wrong, why was I crying. Mrs. Stone and Mother talked at the door for a very short time and then Mother came inside the classroom.

Mrs. Stone came over to me and said, "Debbie, your mother's here to visit and I'm going to show her some of your work. Why don't you go down to Mrs. Brown's classroom, call your Aunt Marian, and let her know your mother has come to visit?"

Mrs. Stone guided me to the back door. Our elementary school had three floors. Our classroom was on the third floor and Mrs. Brown, the principal, taught sixth grade, which was located on the second floor. I flew down the steps. I'm not sure my feet ever touched a consecutive step. I ran into Mrs. Brown's room and up to her desk sobbing, "My mommy's here, I need to call Murn!"

I didn't know it, but the school personnel had been forewarned by Murn that my mother might try to take me. Murn and EtEt always made sure that I was consulted as to who I wanted to be with. It was always, "I want to be with you and EtEt, then Daddy and Mommy can come to see me."

Mrs. Brown called Murn and then told me to wait with her until Murn arrived. We stood out in the hallway as she tried to calm me down and still keep an eye on her class. Shortly Murn arrived, pulling herself up the steps as fast and hard as she could. When she reached the landing, I threw my arms around her waist so hard, I almost knocked her down. She was out of breath and stood there a moment while she thanked Mrs. Brown. Then Murn and I climbed the steps to the third floor. I held on to the skirt of Murn's dress. She was in one of her sleeveless, shirtwaist house dresses that she never wore out in public, only when working around the house.

When we reached the classroom, Mrs. Stone had my folder open at her desk showing Mother my school work. Murn moved closer with me holding on tight. Mrs. Stone looked up and said, "Oh, Mrs. Lipe and Debbie are here now," as she motioned for Mother to move toward us.

Murn smiled and said, "Well Lorena, we didn't know you were coming to visit. When did you get in town?" Since she lived in Kansas City, Missouri, it was obvious this was a trip she had planned and not informed anyone. Murn and Mother hugged each other as Mother laughed then said to Murn, "How are you, honey?"

The two of them standing next to each other were like the characters in the story "The City Mouse and the Country Mouse." But it was more than that. Mother came to impress and Murn came to rescue. Mrs. Stone shared that she had been showing my mother some of my work. While the three adults exchanged pleasantries, I stood behind Murn, clutching her skirt. Suddenly Murn said, "Debbie, did you give your mother a hug?" Then she promptly took my arm and pulled me in front of her guiding me to my mother.

Mother leaned down and put her arms around me, "Hi, sweetheart, it's so good to see you. Please don't cry, Mommy doesn't want you to cry." I loved my mother, but the fear of having to live with her and leave Murn, EtEt, and Daddy was terrifying to me. But I hugged her, knowing that Murn was right behind me.

"How long are you staying, Lorena?" asked Murn.

"Honey, I'm just here for the day," said Mother.

The bell rang and we waited until all the children cleared the stairways before we started to leave. As we stood there waiting, Murn said, "Lorena, you're coming to the house for dinner, aren't you? Everett will want to see you and you can spend more time with Debbie before you leave." Mother thanked Murn and agreed that she would like that. They both thanked Mrs. Stone and proceeded down the stairs. Murn knew what Mother had come to do, and

Mother knew that Murn knew, but no one would ever have known watching it all unfold.

As we walked out of the school, Murn must have realized she didn't have a car. That was one of the few days EtEt had taken the car to work and when she got the call from Mrs. Brown she had called a cab. Mother said, "Marian, where's your car, honey?" Murn chuckled and said, "Well, Everett has the car and I took a cab here so I guess we need a ride home." They both laughed, and I wasn't sure what was so funny. I was still latched on to Murn's skirt and just knew I wasn't letting go. We approached Mother's car and I tried to follow into the back seat behind Murn as she was getting inside. Murn once again took my arm and moved me to the front passenger door and sternly said, "You sit up front with your mother. She's come a long way to see you. Go on, get into the front with your mother," as she took my arm, turned me around, and moved me to the front. So I reluctantly climbed into the front seat and sat as close to the door as possible.

Once we were at home, Mother took off her high heels, hat, and jacket, then sat at the kitchen table drinking a cup of coffee as Murn prepared dinner. Their conversation was lighthearted and full of laughter. She asked about Grandma. Mother loved "Mother Troutman" as she called her, probably because Grandma never criticized her, was loving, and was always glad to see her. It wasn't long before EtEt came home. He came into the kitchen carrying his lunch box, smiled, and said, "Well, look who the wind blew in from Kansas City!"

Mother threw her head back as she always did, let out a big laugh, jumped up, and gave him a big hug. "Everett, you old sweetheart!" It was obvious that Mother loved Murn and EtEt and by the way they reacted to her, they loved her too. When I was older, Murn used to always tell me, "Honey, I love your mother. I just don't love the things she does." EtEt cleaned up, Mother helped set the table, and we all sat down and enjoyed a family dinner. I was happy. I was with the people I loved, safe in the arms of Murn and EtEt.

We finished dinner and Mother said she needed to get on her way. I never knew if she had come alone, or if someone was somewhere waiting for her, or exactly where she was going. What started as a potential kidnapping ended up as a family reunion. Why Mother changed her mind that day was never discussed. As much as she may have thought she did, I don't think Mother wanted to raise me. I don't think she wanted to raise any child; she didn't know how to. After all, she never had a mother to show her how. When she saw my reaction at school, I'm sure she knew I would grow up unhappy if I lived with her. And I'm sure she knew she would have the fight of her life from Murn and EtEt, and my daddy would have tracked her wherever she went.

As I look back on that day, I think what really stopped her was not only my happiness but hers. I think she knew if she had taken me that day, eventually, she would have lost my love. There was no question of the love she had for Murn and EtEt. She needed them, their love, their kindness, and their support just as much as she knew I did too. Murn, EtEt, and Grandma had always given her something priceless, something others hadn't given her, something that she couldn't afford to live without: her dignity.

I wonder what the conversation between Murn and EtEt was like in bed that night. Murn must have been so afraid, knowing what had almost happened. EtEt, although he did not know about what had transpired at the school, knew Mother had come intending to take me away. It was a possibility they had expected and feared. How close it could have been to a previous nightmare he and Murn had suffered through many years ago!

Years before I was born Murn and EtEt had fostered a little girl named Frieda for over a year. They adored the little girl, especially EtEt. No one knew where the mother or father were and after many months, they decided to adopt her. Murn had miscarried two times before when she was young and married to Harry. The doctors told her she couldn't carry a child full term, probably due to having had polio. This little girl was a gift from heaven. The adoption was in the early stages but progressing. Every Sunday they attended Sunday school and church. Murn or EtEt would take Frieda back to the educational wing where the preschoolers had their Sunday school class. There was nothing different that Sunday. Once she was dropped off, Murn and EtEt went to their Sunday school class. That morning, with no warning, Frieda's mother came in the back door of the church into the educational wing and took Frieda. By the time Murn and EtEt were told, there was no sight of the two. Murn and EtEt were devastated and heartbroken. Murn said it took years before they could talk about it. They never saw or heard what happened to Frieda. Murn always said Frieda's mother came like a thief in the night. She said she didn't think EtEt ever entirely got over it. Murn's fear that day my mother came must have rekindled those memories of Frieda.

When I was little, Murn would rock me on her lap and sing a song called "Babes in the Woods."

> Oh don't you remember a long time ago,
> Two little children their names I don't know
> Were stolen away on a bright summer's day.
> Poor babes in the woods, I've heard people say.

I would always cry when she sang it. I remember she always had a faraway look in her eyes as she sang. I wonder if she was thinking of Frieda. When I was older, she told me they had always been afraid that Mother would take me and they would never see me again. That's why they were always so protective of me, yet wise enough to know that my mother had to be a part of my life for my sake, for Mother's sake and theirs. I don't think Murn or EtEt ever told my daddy about Mother's attempt, at least not that year. He would have gone crazy! Murn probably just told him Lorena dropped in for a visit.

Mother returned later that year in the spring, this time for a pre-announced visit. The day we were expecting her this big red and white convertible drove up to the house with the top down. As she exited the car, Mother looked like the actress Grace Kelly. She wore a headscarf over her hair then wrapped around her neck and big sunglasses. This time her husband Sammy was with her. Sammy dressed like a flashy country singer. He wore a cowboy hat, cowboy boots, a suit with the piping across the front and back and down the sleeves, and a bolo tie. I had never seen anything like him except on television when we would watch a country singer on *The Ed Sullivan Show* or maybe the *Grand Ole Opry*. He drove what I think was a 1959 or 1960 Cadillac Eldorado convertible with fins. Every time I saw him with my mother, even in pictures, they had the top down. I didn't like Sammy and I don't think Murn, EtEt, or my daddy did either. I heard them talking one time about Sammy; they said he had a metal plate in his head. I didn't know what that meant, but I knew he had a long scar across one side of his forehead. I could tell they weren't fond of me being around him, but they wanted me to be around my mother and, well, he was part of the package.

When Mother came to visit, she would often pick up my half-brother and sister, Tom and Pam. That day she and Sammy took us across the bridge to East Prairie, Missouri. Our Grandpa Luther and Grandma Maudie still lived there and that was the only time we would see them. Then, at the end of the day, she would deliver us all back to our respective homes. I often wonder if she ever tried to kidnap Tom and Pam. They were older and their dad was a county judge. Maybe that made the difference. Or maybe since she had tried to kidnap me, Mother had decided she didn't want to raise any of us, especially the three of us! Or maybe she just realized she didn't know how. But I'm sure Murn and EtEt did and I'm sure they waited anxiously for my return home.

CHAPTER 7

Leaves of the Branches

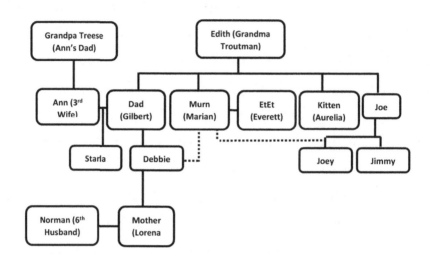

CHAPTER 7

Fiddlesticks and Pick-Up Sticks
Fall 1964 – Summer 1965

When fifth grade approached I decided I was too old to have braids any longer. Murn announced to my daddy and mother that I wanted my hair cut. I never understood why she bothered to tell them, but I guess she thought it would be such a change that she should prepare them. I'll never forget the day we cut off my braids. Murn carefully placed a rubber band at the top of each braid to hold it together once it was cut. At the bottom was a rubber band but also a red ribbon tied in a bow. I remember the sound of the scissors cutting through the hair above the top rubber band. I held it in my hand and asked, "What are we going to do with them?"

Murn, as she was working on cutting the other one, said, "Well, we'll give your mother one and give the other one to your daddy. What do you think about that?" I thought that would be just fine. I later heard her tell EtEt, "I hope Gilbert and Lorena are happy with the braid they asked for. It's a poor excuse for a child!"

My braids were gone but my hair was very straight and I needed a permanent to give it some curl. Murn never went to the beauty parlor. She always gave herself a Toni home permanent and for as long as I could remember, if Murn was going somewhere special like to church or out in public, she would curl her hair herself. She always stood at the stove with a curling iron lying in the flame from the gas burner and without a mirror, she curled her hair. However, I was often sent to the beauty parlor to have my hair cut and styled.

The fifth grade was somewhat of an adjustment for me. I had to go to a new school. During the summer we moved from the house where we lived on 19th Street to Elmwood Place, a housing project. At the time, people referred to it as the white housing project. There were eight long rows of brick two-story buildings, each row with three individual sections. Each section had about six apartments. Our apartment was in the 700 row and the first section, 703 Elmwood Place. Each section had two one-bedroom apartments on each end. Those were primarily for older individuals. One was an upstairs apartment and the other downstairs. The other apartments in each section had a kitchen, utility room, and living room downstairs and three bedrooms and a bath upstairs. The section we were in was very nice. We all kept our yards cut and trimmed. Most of the people around us were elderly. On one side of us was Mrs. Pulley. She lived with her son. On the other side was an elderly couple a little older than Murn and EtEt who were raising their grandson. He was in high school and I believe I had my first crush on him.

At the opposite end of our eight-apartment section was where EtEt's mother had lived before she passed away. It was odd that our apartment was just a few doors down from where she once lived. I called her Grandma Lipe although she wasn't actually my grandmother. I often would go with EtEt to get her groceries each week. She was 90 years old and still lived alone at the time.

EtEt was a foreman on the GM&O Railroad and made good money. It's a good thing he did because Murn and EtEt took care of so many of our family members. In addition to Grandma Lipe, they supplemented Grandma Troutman's income, had the full support of me, often sent money to my mother when she asked, had started assisting Aunt Kitten, and constantly sent money to my Uncle Joe who just couldn't seem to take care of himself even though he was a grown man. Because of all of their dependents, we ended up having to move into the housing project. EtEt made far too much money to qualify us to live in the housing, but when Murn and EtEt's application was reviewed, it was obvious that their monthly costs diminished their income tremendously and therefore qualified them.

As if sending him money wasn't enough, Uncle Joe would show up like a bad penny although he never seemed to have one. He never had a job, always needed money, and did whatever he needed to get money for alcohol. He always blamed his condition and situations on being born late in Grandma's life and being the baby of all Grandma's children.

EtEt decided to go hunting one day after Joe had been visiting and went to get his gun but it was gone. Uncle Joe had pawned it. EtEt went down to the pawnshop and bought it back. Another visit from Uncle Joe and the gun was missing again. EtEt knew where to look and he bought it back again. The third time EtEt just shook his head and said let it go.

The episode that made Murn the angriest with him was what he did when he was staying with his mother. One Saturday Grandma Troutman was preparing to iron her dress for church the next day and the iron was gone. As Murn would tell it, "I'll be darned! Joe was so ornery he pawned his own elderly mother's iron for $10!"

We hadn't heard from Uncle Joe for a while, but one day he called and was hitchhiking from San Antonio, Texas, to Cairo with his two little boys and wanted to know if Murn would wire him some money so they could eat. Murn and EtEt sat at the kitchen table deciding whether or not they could afford to wire him the money to get bus tickets and get the children off the road. It wasn't too long after that phone call that the money was wired to him and the next thing you know, Uncle Joe and my two cousins, Joey and Jimmy, were staying with us. More dependents.

Not long after they arrived, Uncle Joe got a job delivering furniture and could only afford a room for himself, so Joey and Jimmy stayed with us. Joey was a year younger than me and Jimmy was about two or three years old. It was summer when they came to stay with us. Joey and I became great companions. We also got in trouble more together than I ever did alone. Nothing ever serious, just kid stuff. Murn used to send us to our rooms when we misbehaved. She would stand at the bottom of the stairs waiting as we ran past her and swatted us on our bottoms with the pancake turner as we ran up the stairs with her close behind. I was faster, so Joey usually got it more often since she was right behind him. One day we were upstairs in my room giggling about how the pancake turner didn't hurt because it bent when it touched us. We didn't know that Murn was upstairs and heard us. A few days later we were into mischief again and once again Murn called us in and told us to get in our rooms. As always, I led us up the stairs when all of a sudden I heard Joey howl "That hurt!" Murn had traded the pancake turner in for a wooden spoon. As you can imagine, the cup of the spoon didn't bend and created suction on contact with one's bottom. Murn's only comment was, "Now let's see if you think that's funny!"

At our house, every time the church doors were open, we were at church. Sunday morning and Sunday evening, Wednesday evening prayer service, revivals, Bible school, youth group, and any other occasion that was held at the church. Murn had been the church clerk for 16 years and EtEt was a deacon, and I might as well have been a preacher's kid. As the church clerk, Murn always took her stenographer's pad to monthly Wednesday evening business meetings. I watched as she made squiggly lines, which I learned was shorthand, on one column of the paper. Then during the sermon, she would also make similar marks in the margins of her Bible. I asked her one time why she wrote in shorthand. She said she wanted to keep her skills up in case she ever needed to use them again in a job. She was always prepared for what might come.

Murn was very young in her thinking but if there was something she was firm about, bulldozers couldn't have moved her! She didn't do any housework on Sunday and if she had to do something I would hear her saying, "It's pitiful that we can't give the Lord just one day a week!"

I remember a crisp, rainy fall Sunday afternoon when Joey and I begged Murn to let us play Monopoly on the kitchen table. She didn't like the game because it used dice. We begged and begged her to let us play. Even EtEt said, "Oh Marian, let the kids play the game." She finally gave in and out came the Monopoly board, dice and all. EtEt was watching a ballgame on television, sitting in his favorite overstuffed chair which gave him a perfect view out the large front window. Murn was lying down on the couch resting while Jimmy was taking a nap next to her. The game moved pretty fast with just Joey and me playing and we had houses and hotels all over the board.

At the housing complex on our end, all cars had to park on the street and people had to walk up a long sidewalk that ran parallel with our section and would then follow a long sidewalk that was perpendicular leading up to our front door. Suddenly I heard EtEt say, "Marian, there comes Evelyn and Earl."

Murn must not have heard clearly what he said and asked, "What did you say?"

EtEt answered, "I said, there comes Brother and Mrs. Travis."

I had never seen Murn move so fast! She flew into the kitchen, scooped up all of the Monopoly money and cards onto the game board, grabbed the board, and threw it into the utility room. Game pieces went everywhere. "I told you I didn't want you playing that game!" she exclaimed.

About that time our pastor and his wife knocked on the door. Murn immediately changed gears answering the door and welcomed them with a warm and hospitable smile. Joey and I were still sitting at the table trying to process what had just happened.

Jimmy was quite a handful. He was a sweet little boy but had a habit of holding his breath when he didn't get his way. I can't tell you how frightening it was. He would hold it so long, he would turn blue. Murn was so worried about it she talked to the doctor. He told her not to panic or worry about it. He said just to leave him alone. If he passed out, he would start breathing again on his own and he did. My cousins stayed with us that summer and through the fall. During that time Uncle Joe had reunited with my cousins' mother. They rented a house in town and Joey and Jimmy were with their mother and dad. Our life was a little quieter after they left and the wooden spoon wasn't needed any longer.

December that same year, Daddy and Ann had a baby. Starla was a New Year's Eve baby only because she came three months premature. It was odd for me because I had always been the baby.

Just before she was born, Daddy's appendix burst and peritonitis had set in. He had to have a colostomy for a few months until the infection was out of his abdomen.

Months before Starla's birth Ann had been diagnosed with pancreatic and liver cancer. She had turned almost a blackish olive. She had beautiful black hair and wore sunglasses most of the time to protect her eyes, which were sensitive. I remember Daddy telling Murn that the woman in the bed next to Ann in the hospital told her family that "That negro woman is married to a white man and she had a white baby!" Daddy just laughed and I don't think they ever told the woman the truth.

Starla had to stay in the incubator for weeks before she could go home with them. When she came home, Murn, EtEt, Grandma, and I made the trip to see the new little family member. My daddy seemed so proud as he placed this tiny little bundle in Grandma's arms. We all thought she was a cute baby. She was just so little!

While all the adults were being entertained by Starla, I went to the kitchen and watched my daddy as he fixed dinner. He was a lot thinner and was still using crutches due to abdominal surgery. "How's my big girl doing in school?" he asked. I told him about my cornet and what we were studying in school. Daddy was always serious about school and expected me to do well.

The conversation on the way home in the car was focused on Ann's condition and how was Gilbert going to raise that little girl. I think they both knew who was going to raise her but just didn't say it out loud.

I passed fifth grade with flying colors and summer once again had bloomed. I had learned how to paint with watercolors from Mrs. Rust, sang new songs with Mrs. Sullivan, and continued lessons on my cornet with my band director.

That summer I noticed Murn began hanging a calendar above the wall phone in the kitchen. She wanted a calendar that showed the phases of the moon. There were big, red "Xs" on days with a full or new moon. I wasn't allowed to answer the phone on days with an X on it. On full moons, my mother would be very aggressive and hateful. She would start an argument with whoever answered the phone. I answered it one time before the calendar was hung and Mother had me in tears. On days with new moons, Mother would be depressed and crying. When either of these phases occurred, Mother would have a blue V-shaped vein line that would appear above her nose on her forehead. Murn would always be the one to answer the phone on those two phases of the moon during the month. Even when Mother visited, we would always watch for that V. Daddy told Murn and EtEt that the phases of the moon were watched by police officers because the crime and domestic violence increased during those phases.

It seemed like Murn knew exactly how to deal with Mother. She could calm her down on either phase. Even when Mother visited and would spend the night with us, in the wee hours of the morning she would be up pacing like a caged animal from one open door to the other, clawing at her arms. Murn would get up and make some tea or coffee and get her to sit down at the table and just simply talk calmly with her. After they had finished their drink, Mother would be like a different person, calm and collected, and they would both go back to bed.

One day during the summer, Murn sat down next to me on the couch and said, "Debbie, how would you like to visit your mother this summer?" I started crying, "I don't want to go." Mother had asked that I come to stay a week with her during summer vacation. Murn pulled out her best enticements. "You'll have fun, just you and your mother, eating out, doing things together, letting her show you places in Kansas City," she said.

"I don't want to go! Don't you want me anymore?" I cried.

"Of course I want you, sweetheart. I just think it might be nice for you to spend some time with your mother. It's okay, let's talk about it later on and see how you feel."

I knew exactly how I was going to feel later on; I didn't want to go. I wasn't an adventurous child, I liked to be in my own home, in my bed, with Murn and EtEt in the next room. I didn't even want to go on sleepovers at my friends' houses.

After many discussions, I ended up going to visit my mother in Independence, Missouri, for a week's visit. Murn and EtEt drove me to St. Louis where we met my mother and Sammy, the cowboy.

We all met at my Aunt Jean's in St. Louis on a Saturday. I didn't want to leave Murn and EtEt, but Mother said we were going to the zoo and a picnic before we left for Independence. Going to the zoo seemed to minimize my sadness with the excitement of the potential fun for that day. Mother seemed happy that day, which also made me more open to leaving with her. She always had a camera with her, a Kodak Brownie Hawkeye. She had that camera for many years. Most of the pictures I have with my mother and even those with my Daddy were taken with that camera. Later that day we made the trip to Independence. Mother was in a good mood on the first day or two. Sammy wasn't around and we just spent time together.

Mother was working at a dry cleaners and I went to work with her during the day. There was a man named Norman who drove the delivery truck and he and Mother seemed like they were very fond of each other. He was nice to me and Mother always laughed when he was around.

One evening on our way to dinner we were driving on the highway and someone shot at our car, twice! I was scared and so was Mother. She drove to the nearest police station. I remember sitting in the station as they interviewed my mother. From what I could hear, Mother said it was the wife or maybe it was the ex-wife of a man she was seeing. I never knew who the man was, but it must have been someone other than Sammy; looking back, I'm pretty sure it was Norman and Mother must have been involved with him.

The next day, Mother's mood turned. She had been crying all night and that morning. She wasn't very communicative with me and seemed very sad. I remember she went to a phone booth and called Murn. I didn't know at the time, but when I was older I found out that Mother had told Murn that she and EtEt needed to come and get me. When I asked Murn why, Murn said Mother told her, "I can't get a man with a kid hanging on my coattail." So, Murn and EtEt drove back to St. Louis and Mother took me to meet them at Aunt Jean's apartment.

I wasn't sad. I was always much happier when I was with Murn and EtEt. Never again did Mother ask me to come and stay with her. I do remember Murn, EtEt and I went to visit Mother at Raytown, just outside of Independence, Missouri, one summer following my three-day visit. Sammy was out of the picture and Mother had married Norman. He had three children; the youngest was closest to my age. This time Murn and EtEt stayed in a hotel nearby and I stayed with them at the hotel. They probably figured it was easier to just stay close than to have to turn around and come back. I stayed with them and during the day we visited with Mother.

Some of the time Murn, EtEt, and I would eat out, just the three of us. The song "The Pink Panther" was popular because the movie had recently come out late in 1963 and I remember it seemed like all the restaurants were playing it and it was played over and over on the radio.

It seemed that Mother had her hands full with Norman's three children, two who were high school teenagers and the son who was close to my age. He was a little odd and Mother kept a tight rein on where we were and what we were doing. As it turned out, it became clear there was reason to be concerned about him. I guess my mother's experience as a child provided her the foresight as to the characteristics which could allow her history to repeat itself on me.

Our lives seemed to be consumed with taking care of family members. It was as if Murn was the solver of all problems; everyone looked to her for help. EtEt was always supportive regardless of who, what, or how much. When the seas began to calm down, another tsunami appeared to be rolling in.

My Aunt Kitten had done well for several years, but she eventually had to quit working at the Mark Twain restaurant and begin drawing disability. She was placed in one of the upstairs apartments on the end of the first section in the second or third row of Elmwood Place. She was losing weight and not well. I don't know if her cancer had returned or what exactly was wrong. Murn would often check on her and we would get her groceries. She also had a gentleman friend for many years named Charlie who would look in on her and spend time with her. After a while, Murn began checking on her more frequently by phone and spending more time with her at her apartment.

That spring my Aunt Kitten began getting worse. She needed someone to stay with her overnight. She couldn't sleep and was taking so much medication that she would take too much or too little or the wrong medicine. Murn began staying nights with her. So every evening after supper, after my homework was done, Murn would kiss EtEt and me goodbye, then she would leave to spend the night taking care of Aunt Kitten. She would return home before EtEt had to leave for work, wake me up, fix my breakfast, send me off to school, do laundry, clean the house, sleep for a few hours before I came home for lunch, fix my lunch, catch another nap, then be up when I arrived home from school. For me, nothing was different in our home; Murn kept everything in the house running smoothly. She still took care of all of the household business, checked on Grandma Troutman, attended to church commitments, and shopped for whatever was needed for us, Aunt Kitten, Grandma, or anyone else who needed her help.

As the summer progressed, my daddy's wife, Ann, and my Aunt Kitten both seemed to be struggling harder with their respective cancer battles. Ann was now confined to a bed in their living room where she stayed 24/7. She wore sunglasses constantly. When we visited, I remember Murn having to sit close to the bed while Ann would lie on her side, raised by a pillow or holding

99

herself up on her forearm. She was always smiling and glad to see us. Daddy's health was still not good and he still had a temporary colostomy. Daddy and Ann's dad, Grandpa Treese, tried to corral the older children, care for a baby, and tend to Ann's growing needs. Starla was just seven or eight months old and spent much of the time with Grandpa Treese in his room on his bed. He had a television in his room, read books constantly, and most of the time stayed to himself. He had been an architect during his career and was a very bright man. Grandpa Treese had a solid white head of hair cut in a crewcut. He was part American Indian and you could see it in his face. He walked with a cane and when the kids became rowdy and out of control, he would come out of his room with the cane and with a loud, gravelly voice yell, "You kids calm down, now!" Things would get quiet very quickly.

Once Starla began to sit up by herself, she began to bang her head on the floor when she didn't get what she wanted. She would beat it so hard, she would have a bruise or a knot on her forehead. Daddy talked to the doctor about it and they told him not to worry; when it started to hurt, she would stop. The doctor told them to put her in a room alone and let her have at it. Murn didn't think much about the doctor's response, but Daddy and Ann continued to let her cry and beat her head on the floor.

It was rare that I ever heard Murn or EtEt use a swear word, although I'm sure there were many times they felt like it. I heard substitutes like "shoot! darn!" or on occasion when she was really mad, I'd hear a hiss-like sound, "ssssht!" followed by the word "fire!" What I thought was the most interesting word that Murn used when she was frustrated was "fiddlesticks." She often used this when she didn't believe what someone was saying, when she was frustrated, and at times disgusted with something. What I learned was that regardless of what had happened or was occurring, Murn always followed "fiddlesticks" with an action of picking up sticks – always someone else's sticks and there were always sticks to pick up.

CHAPTER 8

Leaves of the Branches

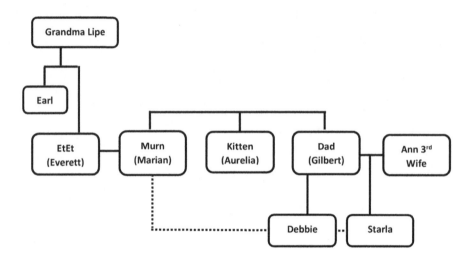

CHAPTER 8

The Rock Will Wear Away
Fall 1965 – Winter 1966

Sixth grade came and the school principal was also now our teacher, Mrs. Crabtree. She was nice enough, but like Mrs. Rust, she didn't smile very much. She had black hair that was pulled back into a bun. She wore black cateye glasses and bright red lipstick. She put up with absolutely no nonsense. During sixth grade, several of us played in the junior high school band. Three of us walked about 19 blocks from our houses, passing the elementary school on our way to the junior high in the mornings, and then after band, we would walk back about 15 blocks back to our elementary school.

During the fall and spring, it was beautiful to walk through the magnolia-covered island medians that lined Washington Avenue but the winters in Cairo were ice cold. There was often ice hanging from the magnolia trees and they would be thick with mistletoe. Because Cairo lies between the Ohio and Mississippi Rivers, the moisture in the air made the winter feel like the cold cut through our clothes. We weren't allowed to wear pants to school in those days and although we could wear tights and knee socks, I remember how cold my knees and hands would be.

The elementary schools all began at the same time in the mornings but the junior high started 30 minutes earlier. After band was over, we still had to walk back to our elementary school, so the three of us were always about an hour late coming from band. I don't think Mrs. Crabtree liked the situation but she never said anything to us. There was always a disapproving look on her face when we walked in late.

While my life was steady and stable, Starla's was about to change and so was ours. Starla's first birthday came and, sadly, Ann was losing the battle with cancer. Ann was getting to the point that she knew she had to make plans for her children. She began interviewing individuals who might want to take each of the children. People would come to the house and meet with Ann and they would discuss the children and their needs. If Ann and the child liked them, she would arrange for a weekend visit with the people. One by one she found a home for each of her children. It was heartbreaking for everyone watching them pack their belongings and say goodbye to their mother, grandfather, and my dad.

Starla was my daddy's child so he had a say as to where she would be. He was not in good health and couldn't care for a little one. He talked to Murn and said he guessed he would have to put Starla in an orphanage. I think he knew that would never happen. As Murn and EtEt had anticipated when she was born, they decided that they would take Starla to raise. I remember Murn talking to Daddy on the phone, "No Burris is going to an orphanage. Everett and I will take Starla to raise if you want us to."

In July of 1966, when Murn was 58 years old and EtEt 60, she and EtEt took a 19-month-old Starla to raise. Ann and Daddy moved to Cairo. Grandpa Treese stayed in the house where they all had lived together in Carbondale. Murn and EtEt made sure that Starla visited her mother as often as possible for Ann's sake and Starla's, just as they had my mother and me.

That fall I was beginning junior high school. Murn took me to the Dottie Shop, a women's clothing store, to buy my new clothes for school. She bought me Ship and Shore and Bobbi Brooks oxford shirts, box pleated skirts, V-neck sweaters, and coordinated argyle knee socks. Then we went to the shoe store where she purchased my very first pair of oxblood Bass Wejun penny loafers. This year was the first year I could wear loafers and I felt so grown up. In previous years I had worn Hush Puppies or saddle shoes, which were fine, but the older kids wore loafers. Murn and EtEt always made sure that I had everything I needed. Murn wore the same winter coat for seven years, but each year I had new school clothes and a new winter coat.

Murn was this tiny package of a woman but a force to be reckoned with. Her complexion was clear and soft as it covered her prominent cheekbones. She never wore makeup other than a little face powder, a little rouge, and a faint amount of lipstick that she wore only to church or a special occasion such as a funeral or special function. Her smile was always a closed-mouth smile and her laughter was always silent and tight-lipped, with a gentle fist covering her mouth. I realize now that she was probably embarrassed because she had lost so many teeth and those she had left were in such bad shape. She always carried a roll of Clorets breath mints in her purse. Murn was so particular as to cleanliness and personal presentation. She always smelled of Clorets or Red Cross toothache medicine with its strong cinnamon smell. She would use that medicine when a tooth was hurting, until it fell out or she pulled it herself.

EtEt never had teeth from as far back as I can remember. According to him, he couldn't tolerate wearing false teeth but I wasn't sure that he ever had them. You never really noticed that he didn't have a tooth in his head until he got so tickled and would then open his mouth, throw back his head and laugh. I never understood how on earth he could eat all the things he did without teeth, even steak! Murn said he just gummed it to death. The money that could have been used to have the dental work Murn needed, to be followed by securing a set of false teeth, was used for taking care of all the people who depended on her and EtEt financially. They sacrificed so very much for so many.

Murn was still staying nights with Aunt Kitten. The regimen was still the same. Every evening after supper, after my homework was done, after Starla was put to bed and I went to bed, Murn would kiss EtEt goodbye and leave to spend the night taking care of Aunt Kitten. She would return home the next morning before EtEt had to leave for work, get me up, fix breakfast, send me off to school, get Starla up for the day, do laundry or clean the house. Once she had taken care of all of us, she would send Starla over to our neighbor, Mrs. Pulley, then Murn would sleep for a few hours before I came home from school. Then Starla would come home, I would come home, Murn would start supper, EtEt would come home, and everything would start all over again. This went on for several months from fall into winter. Murn was tired. She never said anything or complained, but you could see it in her eyes. Our pastor knew it too. He told EtEt that he could see in her eyes that she was heading for a heart attack. She had to slow down.

It got to the point that Murn couldn't take care of Aunt Kitten any longer. Cancer had taken control. She needed more intensive care and assistance to bathe and go to the bathroom. I know it broke Murn's heart, but that winter, Aunt Kitten was placed in a nursing home in Murphysboro, about 55 miles away.

Murn's previous nightly regimen with Aunt Kitten changed to a weekly regimen. Almost every Saturday, early in the morning, we made the trip to Murphysboro to see Aunt Kitten. Her small room had windows alongside her bed and two chairs. She had a portable television that sat on a table in the corner at the foot of her bed. The building was a large, two-story house with many sections that had been converted to a nursing home. We got to know the staff and they seemed to be good to Aunt Kitten. Murn would spend the

106

whole day with her, fixing her hair, rubbing her arms and back with body lotion, and making sure there were no bedsores or signs of neglect.

In the beginning, Starla would go with us, but it was too long a day for a toddler, so she would stay with church friends who would babysit her at their house for the day. At first, Aunt Kitten would visit with all of us, but it wasn't long before she was in so much pain that EtEt and I would leave.

Murn gave us spending money and EtEt and I would go to the Woolworth store downtown and sit together at the lunch counter for lunch sometimes, but always we would order this wonderful, cold, three-inch-high lemon cheesecake. EtEt and I loved that cheesecake. It was like a Jell-O sponge. They cut the pieces about three inches square, which seemed huge, but it was as if it was filled with air! I would take a bite and it crackled down to nothing, so one piece went unbelievably fast. Sometimes we would take extra pieces back with us so Murn could have some, but I think it was more so I could have some later. EtEt would sit at the counter and have coffee and smoke a cigarette while I shopped.

EtEt's brother Earl and his wife lived in Murphysboro and now and then EtEt and I would go to their house and visit. It made for a long day for EtEt and me, but even longer for Murn. It must have been hard for Murn to leave her younger sister after each visit and harder to be so far away.

In addition to the Saturday trips to see Kitten during the fall and winter, Starla was in the hospital several times. She kept having high fevers. Murn would stay up nights watching over her until it would become evident that Starla needed to go to the hospital. The fever would go so high the hospital staff would have to place her in ice water. The doctor didn't know why the fevers were happening. Murn stayed at the hospital with her almost all day. Daddy would come to the hospital often to check on Starla and relieve Murn. Eventually, Starla's fever would drop and the doctor would send her home.

We never really knew what was causing the fevers, but as a three-month preemie, the doctor said it was not uncommon for there to be issues as she grew up, especially since Ann had carried Starla when she was so ill and all of the bile and fluids had also circulated through Starla.

Commitment is demanding. It often requires more from people than they have to give, and those who live a committed life take on superhuman armor. Murn had that armor. She wore it every day that I can remember. Murn beat the unbeatable, conquered the unconquerable, and loved the unlovable. Perhaps commitment is fed by love, love that is tested over and over again. If it is, that explains Murn; her love was ever-present.

There are many times when people don't pass the test and other times when they ace the test every time. Life has taught me that the latter is rare. Murn was rare. There are also times when love is letting go and other times when love is holding on, either of which can be difficult and either of which can be the right thing to do. Love is complicated, but commitment most definitely requires love. Love was never complicated with Murn, but love always, always has a price.

CHAPTER 9

Leaves of the Branches

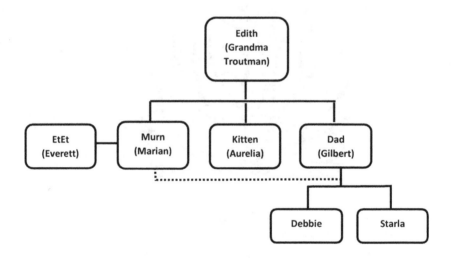

CHAPTER 9

The Rock of Gibraltar Crumbles
Spring of 1967 – Fall 1967

The past year had been full of physical and emotional pressure on everyone, but especially on Murn. I was getting accustomed to having a little sister and not being the baby in the family. Starla was a cute little toddler. I would watch her for Murn as she played outside when I came home from school.

She had more of a stubborn streak than I ever had. I remember one Sunday morning in church when Starla started kicking her feet on the back of the pew in front of us. Murn had given her the "evil eye" as only Murn could do but Starla continued to kick. About the second kick after the evil eye, Murn picked her up out of the pew, took her hand, and marched her up the aisle to the entrance, out the door, turned Starla over her arm, and spanked her bottom! I have a feeling it was similar to the spanking I received when I was about her age at Sunday school. Then, Murn took her by the hand, marched her back in and down the aisle into our pew, and sat Starla between her and EtEt. Starla never kicked the pew again…ever! You could say that Murn had a way of impressing behavioral expectations on both of us.

Between Murn and EtEt taking Starla to raise, Murn staying during the summer with Aunt Kitten night after night, then traveling every weekend to visit with her once she was placed in the nursing home, Starla's hospitalizations, continuing her church duties, taking care of our home, and the loss of Grandma Lipe, Murn was exhausted. One day during the early spring our pastor's prediction came true. What he had seen in Murn's eyes turned out to be a massive heart attack.

I don't remember how or where it happened. I simply remember being at the hospital with EtEt. Our church friends, Mary and Les, took Starla during this time. I wasn't allowed to see Murn because I was under 18. EtEt was with her in the room and I was in the waiting room. The prognosis was not good. The heart had been extremely damaged and the doctor wasn't confident that she would recover.

EtEt would come to the waiting room and check on me. I could see how worried he was; he always ran his hand down over his face. Our pastor, Daddy, Uncle Wayne, and several church friends were there once the word spread. Daddy couldn't leave Ann very long and Uncle Wayne had to get back to work.

One of our church friends was there and sat with me for several hours. I remember her talking to me about how Murn would probably not make it and that she would be going to heaven where she would be with Jesus. I was crying uncontrollably and she made it worse. I'll never forget it. She was sitting next to me with her arm around my shoulders, bent down looking up into my face. Why was she saying these things? I became angry. Murn would never leave me. As a child I never felt such anger and fear. I hated her for saying that. How did she know? She didn't know whether Murn was going to die or not. EtEt walked into the waiting room at that moment and I jumped up and ran to him, throwing my arms around his waist. He hugged me and told us that Murn was stable and awake. The next few days would tell us more.

As the days passed, Murn grew stronger and stronger. I didn't get to see her as long as she was in the hospital. The rules at St. Mary's Hospital were very strict during those days, with specific visiting hours and the Catholic nuns enforcing every rule. EtEt had taken off of work to be with Murn and I went to school just like she would have wanted. EtEt and I ate out and many friends sent food to the house for us. Starla remained with Mary and Les. Murn had always been a worrier and it was important that she was assured everything was under control and we were all doing what needed to be done. I'm sure she was concerned about Aunt Kitten, but Uncle Wayne and Aunt Ilene were checking on her and looking in on Grandma Troutman.

EtEt always brought his paycheck home and laid it on the table for Murn to deposit during the week while he was working. When Murn came home from the hospital, EtEt ran the errands that Murn always did, including depositing his paycheck. One day the bank called, the same bank they had always done business with. They were concerned because someone had forged EtEt's signature and tried to deposit his check. The situation was cleared up when Murn admitted that actually, she had been the forger for many years! She had always signed his checks and this time he had endorsed it himself.

Murn recovered sooner than anyone expected her to. She was a strong, determined woman. When Murn came home, almost everything went back to normal. There were certain things she wasn't allowed to do like carry Starla and vacuum, so EtEt and I did those things and helped with other chores as she directed. Climbing the stairs was hard for her because she had lost so much strength due to the time in the hospital, so she slept on the couch downstairs for a while, but it wasn't long before she was doing everything she always did. That was Murn.

Summer arrived and I had finished my first year of junior high school. I was turning 13 within a few weeks and EtEt was letting me cut the grass with our power mower. He would sit on the porch and watch as he kept a close eye on my technique but mainly to make sure I didn't run over my foot or something more dangerous. I could never get the mower started by pulling that rope. He always had to get it started, then let me take over. Pretty soon I thought I could make some money cutting the neighbors' grass. Murn wasn't in favor, but EtEt assured her I could do it and he would sit on the porch and watch me as well. I made 50 cents for each yard. One yard had a pipe that protruded about three inches up in the middle of the yard. I ran over that pipe on two different occasions, damaging the mower, and each time EtEt would take it and get it repaired. Of course, each repair cost more than the 50 cents I was making running over the pipe. But I was making money cutting grass!

Murn was well enough that we returned to visiting Aunt Kitten in the nursing home each weekend. She was getting so much worse. While Murn had been recuperating, Aunt Kitten had lost more weight, wasn't eating, and was in pain all the time. Bedsores had developed and she was nothing but skin covering bones. I remember Murn telling EtEt on the way home one Saturday that she didn't know how much longer Kitten could last. At 13 I began to learn how vicious cancer was. Starla's mother, Ann, was also struggling more with her cancer and Daddy couldn't care for her; it didn't help that he was drinking more.

I'm not exactly sure what happened, but I know she wasn't with Daddy any longer. Ann returned to her home in Carbondale not only to leave Daddy but also to be with her aging father. Without Ann, Daddy was alone and his drinking increased even more. I think he was lonely, his health was not good, and the alcohol was a numbing agent. He picked up odd jobs and became the maintenance person at the apartment building where he and Ann had been living. Daddy could never sit still. He always had to be doing something and this job gave him a purpose.

Early in the summer, Murn had received in the mail a flyer about a new recreational community called Cherokee Village in Arkansas. It offered three-day and two-night lodging with access to the community lodge and all of the facilities free for a family. Of course, they were trying to sell people lots for building houses and all you had to do was to attend one of their sales pitches in return for the lodging. We had never taken a vacation so Murn and EtEt decided this was one way they could afford it. I was so excited! After Murn's heart attack I think she and EtEt knew we all needed to get away as a family. Early one morning I helped EtEt load up the green Ford Falcon station wagon. We put the back seat down so Starla and I could sit, play, and lie down in the back if we got tired. What an adventure! Murn was dressed in one of her best shirtwaist house dresses, EtEt was in his summer camp shirt and felt brim hat, and Starla and I were in the back with luggage and a big bag full of snacks. I don't think I had ever seen all of us at one time as happy as we were.

The trip on the way down was filled with reading the huge billboards enticing travelers to stay here, visit here, or stop here. We listened to the radio, played "I see something you don't see," and stopped every so often to use the restroom at Stuckey's. I loved to stop at Stuckey's! They not only had food and candies, but they had souvenirs and gifts. We weren't in a hurry so we would spend time looking at all of the interesting trinkets. I remember this one small wooden plaque that Murn bought. It read, "Houses are made of brick and stone. Homes are made of love alone."

We arrived at Cherokee Village that afternoon and our excitement was visible on each of our faces. The lodging was like a long row of apartments, much like a motel. EtEt checked us in at the main lodge and got the key, drove us down the hill, parked in front of our assigned unit, and began unloading the car. The unit wasn't fancy, but it was clean and fine for a free vacation. There were a swimming pool, a restaurant in the lodge, and a lake, and they were in the process of building a golf course.

I asked if Starla and I could walk up to the lodge and see what the pool was like. Murn said okay but I was to hold Starla's hand and not let her loose. To get to the lodge, you had to walk up the hill at the side of the gravel road. We made it up the hill, looked at the pool and tennis courts, then started back

115

down the hill. Starla didn't want to walk and wanted me to carry her. Trying to keep her from throwing a fit, I picked her up. I had on sandals and the loose rocks were difficult to walk on, especially when walking downhill. As luck would have it, I fell and to protect Starla, I held her up and went down on my knee. The blood started running and I started crying. I had a deep gash just below my kneecap. When Starla and I reached our unit, Murn immediately grabbed towels and started cleaning the gash and trying to stop the bleeding. It was obvious I was going to need stitches.

EtEt called the lodge desk, explained what had happened, and asked where the hospital or medical center was. Shortly a manager knocked at our door. The closest medical facility was 40 minutes away and he was going to drive us. Murn stayed with Starla while EtEt and I with my towel-wrapped knee, tears and all, got into the man's car for the trip to get my stitches. Hours later we returned with four stitches, bandages, and orders not to swim for a week. Needless to say, that put a damper on the vacation. We stayed that night but we decided to leave the next day. I couldn't swim, the lodge was hard for Murn to access, and there wasn't much left for us to do there.

So we headed home. We made the best of the trip home by stopping along the way to visit different tourist attractions, but we arrived back home on the second day of our vacation. Between the gas, food, souvenirs, and the hospital bill, the trip wasn't free! It turned out to be our overnight family vacation.

Summer passed and another school year was beginning. I was now in junior high school, basically grown up! Once again it was time for school supplies and new clothes. And like always, Murn saw to it that I was dressed and prepared for a good start. The most exciting thing for me this year was that we had a woman band director! She was beautiful. I remember thinking she looked a lot like Jackie Kennedy and her name was Jackie too. I was in awe! I had no idea women could be band directors; I had always seen men as directors.

As really good seventh-grade musicians, a few of us were allowed to play in the high school band. There was one bright spot for me during the seventh grade: band. I had many musical opportunities that year that I had never had. I marched in a football half-time show, she took us to march in a parade at the state capitol in Springfield, Illinois, and in the spring I played in the pit orchestra for a musical, the first musical I had ever seen.

The school year progressed and Christmas break was shortly upon us. At Christmas time we always had a 10- to 12-foot fresh-cut tree in our house on 19th Street, which fit nicely with the tall, high ceilings. When we moved to Elmwood Place the ceilings were much lower and after the first few years Murn said maybe it would be best if we purchased an artificial Christmas tree. It would be safer, less of a mess and we wouldn't have to buy a new one every year.

Daddy caught wind of Murn's plan and told her he would get us a tree. He said there was a beautiful tree at Woolworth's and he thought he could get the manager to come down on the price. Daddy took me to look at the tree. There it sat, high upon a display case as tall as my daddy, almost touching the ceiling. When I saw it I could feel my eyes open as big as silver dollars. The lights were bright with every color of the rainbow with huge ornaments covering the tree and gold garland circling it from top to bottom; it was beautiful! Daddy told me that we were going to get that tree.

A week or so passed until one day a truck pulled up in the alley behind our unit. One of Daddy's buddies was driving the truck and there was my daddy and the Christmas tree in the back of the truck. It was the exact tree that had been on display at Woolworth's, complete with ornaments, garland, lights, and a beautiful star with an angel in it on the top. My daddy and his buddy carefully moved the tree into the special corner Murn had prepared for our new Christmas tree. It almost touched our ceiling and it was beautiful. Daddy hugged me and said, "I told you Daddy was going to get you that tree."

Murn was a little skeptical as to what he paid for it and if it came with all of the decorations. My daddy was excellent at bartering and holding people to their statements. Daddy gave Murn a detailed account as to how he bought the tree. The display that he and I had looked at had a sign that clearly stated the price of the tree. When the salesman asked if he could help him, Daddy asked, "Is that the price of *that* tree?"

The salesman confirmed the price and Daddy began to barter with him and the salesman dropped the price $10. They both agreed on the price and Daddy told him he would take it. They went to the cash register where Daddy paid for the tree and was given a receipt. The salesman then told him he would go to the back and bring up his tree. Daddy stopped the young man and said, "No, I bought *that* tree," pointing to the display tree.

The salesman, shocked by my dad's statement said, "Mr. Burris, that's a display tree, it doesn't come with the decorations."

Daddy countered reminding him, "I asked you specifically if that was the price for *that* tree and you told me it was. The sign doesn't say anything about not including the decorations."

The young man tried to explain that there were over $100 worth of ornaments on that tree and he couldn't possibly sell that tree completely decorated for the price he paid.

Daddy stood his ground and said, "Son, I have a receipt that shows I bought *that* tree. I asked you if that was the price for *that* tree and you said yes, then agreed to lower the price by $10. My little girl is expecting *that* tree. Now are you going to help me get it down and load it into the truck or am I going to have to get my buddy to help me? Because I bought *that* tree and *that's* the one I'm taking." He even made the salesman give him the empty boxes that went with the ornaments!

I would have loved to have seen that truck moving through the streets of Cairo from one end to the other, ornaments and all, with my Daddy standing in the back holding on to it as they drove to our house. Needless to say, Daddy was quite pleased with himself and each year when we put up *that* tree, we reminisced about the story of Daddy purchasing *that* tree.

I was beginning to understand why Murn had purchased the simple little plaque at Stuckey's on our short summer vacation and why she always hung it in our kitchen wherever we lived. It served as more than a souvenir from our trip. It became our family's mantra. My mother, daddy, and I always had a house, and even Mother and I had a place to live, but there was always something missing. Murn and EtEt never worried about fancy houses, new cars, new fashions, or yearly vacations. I'm sure they might have liked to have had a little more enjoyment of material things in their life than what they had. But what they did have was love. Our family was their priority. Everywhere they lived they made it a home. It didn't matter where we were, what the buildings were like, or how long we were in one place; when I was with Murn and EtEt our home was where we were, being together. Our love was what made it a home.

Houses that are made of brick and stone and even the Rock of Gibraltar may wear away or crumble. But homes and people filled with love can withstand the greatest disasters.

CHAPTER 10

Leaves of the Branches

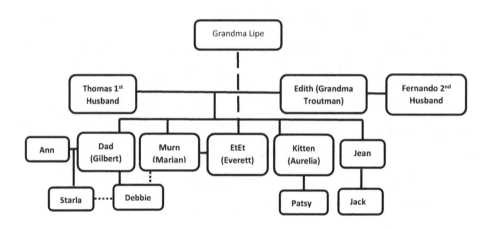

CHAPTER 10

A Chain Reaction
Fall 1967-Winter 1968

G rowing up in Cairo was wonderful. It had the charm of a southern town where the seasons each had their beauty. At the north edge of town was a bowling alley and a roller skating rink where young people spent weekend afternoons. The people had a slight southern accent where certain vowels were stretched and consonants were lingered on before the word was completed. Children, mainly white children, rode their bicycles from one end of Cairo to the other. The northwest residential section, predominantly white, was divided by the main street, Washington Avenue. Washington Avenue was primarily lined with the grander homes of the Antebellum. The street was made of brick and when you rode your bicycle across it, it was such a bumpy ride it was more comfortable to stand up and pedal rather than sit down. In the middle of the road were what we called islands but were properly known as boulevards. The boulevards were lined with magnolia trees that smelled wonderful in the spring and summer, dropped their cones in the fall, and held balls of mistletoe and ice in the biting winters. The streets on each side of the boulevards were one way. As children, we walked on the boulevards with cars passing on each side. The black children seemed to confine themselves to the southwest and northeast areas of Cairo. While Cairo had the charm of a southern town, it also had southern biases.

St. Mary's Park was a place where picnics, baseball, and softball games were held. A large gazebo sat in the middle where people could relax and the park was surrounded by large two-story homes from the turn of the century. Magnolia Manor and what now is called the Riverlore House sat directly across from each other on the street which enters the park.

In the 1960s, there were 17 churches in Cairo with the largest denomination being that of Baptist. Our church, the Washington Avenue Baptist Church, sat at the south entrance of Washington Avenue and 22nd Street. One of the most architecturally beautiful churches was St. Patrick's Catholic Church, which sat on the corner of Ninth Street and Sycamore, the main highway on which one entered and exited Cairo.

Along that same highway were the three-story police station, the three-story federal post office, and the beautiful Cairo Public Library.

The downtown area on Commercial Avenue was lined with clothing stores, Woolworth, S.H. Kress & Company, department stores, a music store, and various specialty shops. Just outside the P.N. Hirsch store, called Blum's, was an old streetcar chuck wagon. An elderly black man wearing a white paper hat and a white butcher apron would sit on a stool beside the wagon waiting for a customer to place an order. The smell of those burgers and fries would draw people to him as they walked by. Those burgers were the best in town and he was entertaining and engaging with his customers.

The major street that connected the two main thoroughfares, Sycamore and Commercial Avenue, was Eighth Street. It boasted a lunch counter drug store, shoe store, the Gem movie theater, a jewelry store, the brokerage where my aunt Fay worked, and a novelty store. Restaurants, banks, barbeque restaurants; a bakery, drugstores, printing shops; The Cairo Evening Citizen office, car dealerships, gas stations; motels, Dairy Queen and Dixie Cream ice cream shops; dry cleaners, grocery stores, a city swimming pool; and numerous other specialty shops lined both sides of Sycamore, the four-lane major highway that entered Cairo from the north and exited south to the bridges crossing the Mississippi River to the state of Missouri and the Ohio River to the state of Kentucky.

I was now starting eighth grade and I was finally a teenager. My year started with anticipation, excitement, lots of friends, and youthful happiness. The drama seemed to have calmed down with Mother. Daddy was working, which kept him busy, which meant he wasn't drinking as much. Murn was physically back to her energetic self, and EtEt, like always, went to work every day.

One of my friends in the neighborhood was the daughter of the sheriff but her parents were divorced and she lived with her mother. Her mother drove her and four of us to school and picked us up each day. She smoked cigarettes and had a raspy, growling voice. That combined with her dry humor, followed by a coughing laugh, always let us know she was teasing us. We all loved her; she was loud, had a terrific laugh, and had a sense of humor that made her seem like one of us. Murn would give me money to give to her every month for gas and told me to make sure she knew how much we appreciated the rides. We always paid our way.

For some strange reason, the schools had scheduled the junior high band period against the high school period and we had a new band director. I had played in the high school band since seventh grade. Due to the schedule conflict this year, the director couldn't be in two places at once and after he took attendance of the junior high band, he gave me a whistle and left to work with the high school band. With the director's whistle in hand, my directions were to rehearse their marching and playing. On the streets that surrounded the block that held the junior high and senior high school, I marched the junior high band like a drill sergeant giving corrections regarding marching technique and musical performance. That was my first experience as a band director and

I was bitten by the band director bug. From that time forward, my focus was on becoming a band director.

I also started private trumpet lessons with Stanley Thomas that fall. He was the principal at a small high school about 12 miles away from Cairo. He always reminded me of Sammy Davis, Jr. He was a small black man with close-cropped hair, a little mustache, and a chiseled face. He was an outstanding trumpet player and teacher. I loved taking lessons from him. EtEt would take me on Saturday mornings and Mr. Thomas would meet us in the gymnasium. The gym made me sound amazing and taught me to breathe correctly and fill the trumpet with air. EtEt would sit in the bleachers and listen or if there was a baseball game being broadcast, he would be in the car listening to it on the radio.

We still were visiting Aunt Kitten most weekends, but I don't even know if she knew we were there. Sometimes we went after my trumpet lesson on Saturday and other times on Sunday after church. Murn didn't understand why the Lord just didn't take her. Her skin had now become like a piece of brittle cloth that was wrapped around bones. There wasn't an ounce of fat or muscle on her. The bedsores had gone so deep that Murn could see the hip socket move inside a large, open sore. Aunt Kitten would scream when anyone tried to move her. It was heartbreaking for Murn. Aunt Kitten just kept breathing. Murn would sit on her bed and stroke her hair as she softly spoke to her and I'm sure prayed silently that God would free her from her misery.

One day in October while I was at school, Murn had a phone call and was visibly upset when I arrived home. I was sure that Aunt Kitten had passed away. When I asked her what was wrong, she just said that Aunt Jean had died and she had to go to St. Louis the next day. Aunt Jean? We all had been expecting to get a call saying Aunt Kitten had died, but not Aunt Jean. No one was prepared for this. When EtEt came home they had a private conversation and the evening was very solemn.

Aunt Jean was the oldest of my grandma's children and only two years older than Murn. Murn and she always tried to talk every other week, especially since Aunt Jean's husband Joe had died five years earlier, but sometimes a month would pass. She hadn't called Jean for several weeks and I think that was the hardest for Murn.

The call had come from a Missouri state police officer. He asked Murn if she knew a Jean Bernstein who lived in St. Louis, and if so, what was her relationship to her. Murn told him she was her sister and asked why. The officer told her they had found many letters and cards in her apartment addressed to Jean from a Marian Lipe in Cairo, Illinois, and were trying to locate a next of kin. Murn asked what had happened. The officer told her that she had passed away and he preferred not to go into the particulars over the telephone. He thought it would be best if she could meet him at the apartment the next day. I don't remember her making calls to tell anyone Jean had passed away because I think she wanted to first find out the circumstances. EtEt agreed that was probably for the best.

By herself, Murn left for St. Louis the next morning. When she arrived at the apartment and met the police officer there was yellow tape across the door. He explained to her that it appeared to the police that Aunt Jean had been afraid of living alone in the high-rise and the apartment had been closed up for some time. It had been a very warm October and he wanted to prepare Murn before they entered the premises.

As they walked into the apartment the smell of death and decay hit Murn in the face. As far as the police could tell, Aunt Jean must have been standing at the bathroom sink and had a heart attack. She then must have fallen over into the bathtub. Since she didn't know any of her neighbors and didn't communicate with anyone on her floor, no one noticed anything was wrong. The maintenance office for the buildings received a call from the residents below Aunt Jean's apartment complaining that their bathroom drain was not draining and must be stopped up. The coroner estimated that Aunt Jean had died several weeks before that maintenance call. Due to the heat and length of time, she had decomposed to the point there was nothing but bones and sludge. Murn wasn't allowed to go into the bathroom.

It must have been the most horrific, gut-wrenching moment of Murn's life. A glance around the apartment revealed the last moments of Aunt Jean's life. A half cup of dried coffee remained on the kitchen table where she must have sat her last morning, a small dish with crumbs from her breakfast of toast had been placed in the sink, and her bed was unmade after her last night's sleep. Murn gathered Aunt Jean's personal materials, purse, and financial information before she left with the officer.

When she arrived home, Murn first called Jack, Aunt Jean's son who lived in California, to give him the terrible news. Then she began calling the other brothers. She then left to tell Grandma Troutman. Jack and his wife came and Murn met them in St. Louis days later. I don't think there was a funeral. Her remains were laid to rest next to her husband Joe; she always called him "My Joe." The date on her headstone reads October 24, 1967. That was the date they found her but no one knows the day when she actually passed away.

I often thought of how hard it was for Grandma to hear that her first child had died, not to mention the conditions. I also thought how hard it must have been for Murn to have to tell Grandma that Jean was gone and that there wasn't going to be a funeral and why. There were so many questions that would never be answered. Did she die immediately? Was she alive and in such bad physical condition that she suffered a long, slow death? Counting little Margaret who died not long after birth, and Uncle Charles who had passed away six years prior, Grandma had outlived three of her children. Murn was quiet those days that followed in October, but life moved forward and as always, she kept life normal for all of us.

Just as the rawness of Jean's death had begun to heal, the day came in November when Murn's prayers that the Lord would end Aunt Kitten's suffering were answered. Aunt Kitten was 54 years old and Aunt Jean was 61. The oldest and the youngest of Grandma's girls were gone; now there was just Murn. The funeral arrangements were made by Murn with Aunt Kitten's daughter Patsy's blessing. Patsy, her husband, and their four children had to come from Ohio. We didn't get to see them very often, but I liked Aunt Patsy. I always called her that only because I had been so young and she was so much older than I that I was told to call her Aunt Patsy. She was really my cousin and her children were my second cousins. Murn had raised Patsy for a while when she was in junior high or high school when Murn and Harry had the grocery store; I never really knew why. But Murn and Patsy had a special relationship.

Aunt Kitten's funeral was my first personal experience with death and the ceremonies of a visitation and a funeral. I was awestruck with the flowers, the casket, and how a dead person looked. Aunt Kitten was so emaciated and white. She had red lipstick on just like she wore when she would stop by our house on her way to work years ago. I watched as Patsy, a much taller woman, towered as she stood between Murn and Grandma at the casket. Murn consoled Patsy, patting her back, while Patsy had her arm around Grandma, holding her close. While there were certainly sadness and tears, everyone knew that Aunt Kitten was finally at peace and her suffering had ended. Murn spent the hours that evening introducing Patsy to various people who attended the visitation. I spent most of the visitation that evening with my cousins in the funeral home's coffee room. Patsy frequently sat down next to Grandma, placing her arm around her, comforting her.

About halfway through the visitation Daddy came. He was dressed nicely but was staggering and I was pretty sure, and I know Murn knew, he had been drinking. I watched from the back as Daddy stood at the casket. Murn stood next to him and was rubbing his back. Daddy held on to the side of the casket and wept so hard. Next thing I knew he was kneeling in front of the casket as if he couldn't stand up, with one hand on the casket edge. He began crying uncontrollably. My Uncle Wayne and the funeral home director helped Daddy up and took him to the coffee room to try to sober him up with coffee. I followed them into the room and sat with Daddy as he drank the coffee and tried to pull himself together.

I'd never seen my Daddy cry and I don't ever remember seeing him cry again. I think Ann leaving him and losing his two sisters within a month was more than he could bear. EtEt came in, sat and talked with him for most of the time. EtEt was such a kind, empathetic man. He and Daddy were close and as he treated Mother, EtEt never judged or criticized Daddy. His compassion was the essence of who he was. The coffee seemed to have helped and Daddy left the funeral home before the visitation was over. I think he was a little embarrassed and overwhelmed emotionally. He had sobered up just enough to begin to feel something again and I'm pretty sure he was leaving to medicate himself with alcohol.

During the funeral I watched everyone; I particularly watched Murn. EtEt sat with his arm across the pew behind Murn with his hand often patting or rubbing her shoulder. During the past year and a half, Murn had spent more time with Aunt Kitten than anyone. The conversations and the intimacies between two sisters from all the quiet hours they spent together must have played over and over in Murn's mind. I wondered if Murn was thinking about those missed conversations with Aunt Jean and what things would have been said.

After the funeral, we had an hour's trip to the cemetery. I had never seen the Burris plot. For the first time, I saw the headstone with my grandfather's name: Thomas Scott Burris – 1878-1933. Grandma Troutman was 46 years old when my grandfather passed away at 55 years old. I realized my daddy was only 11 years old when his father died. None of my cousins nor I ever knew our grandfather. In fact, we never knew our step-grandfather. Grandma remarried in 1941 to a man named C. Fernando Troutman who was a farmer. There were never any stories about him and oddly enough, I don't think as grandchildren it ever entered our minds to ask. It's odd that I never asked why Grandma's last name was Troutman. I vaguely remember Murn saying something about Dad Troutman one time to Grandma, but never did I hear about his marriage to Grandma or Grandma talking about him. After six years of marriage, C. Fernando passed away in 1947. Grandma was just always known as Grandma Troutman. I knew that she was my daddy and Murn's mother, along with my Aunts Jean and Kitten and Uncles Charles, Wayne, and Joe, but I never thought to ask why her name was Troutman. It just wasn't important. I guess by the time I came along Grandma had been alone so long that all of the conversations regarding him were long past but there were stories of my Grandpa Burris.

Grandma's name was already on the headstone where she would lie next to her first husband and father of her children. It was odd watching Murn, Daddy, Uncle Wayne, and Grandma standing there surveying the Burris plot where a husband and father, a daughter and little sister they barely knew, and now daughter and sister Kitten, would be waiting for other family members to join them.

Christmas that year seemed to be clouded by the difficult events of the year. In addition to our family's difficulties, the country seemed to be experiencing pains of change, expressions of opposition, and fights for the oppressed. The Vietnam conflict was beginning to swell; the hippies were holding sit-ins for peace and to protest whatever needed to be protested; and marches, boycotts, or riots demanding equal rights between blacks and whites were becoming commonplace in various cities and towns. Cairo, Illinois, was no exception; the residents were experiencing the cold and biting winds of change. While culture was beginning to develop tornadic winds, I was more concerned with the wind of change blowing in our family.

Early in the spring, the GM&O railroad tracks needed repairs done on the rails about 70 miles away and EtEt was being temporarily transferred to oversee the work until it was completed. It was too far for EtEt to drive daily, so he and Murn decided he would rent a room close to where he would be working and come home on weekends. EtEt made arrangements to ride with one of his workers who was staying there as well, which would allow Murn to have the car during the week. Every Sunday in the late afternoon, a horn would sound and EtEt would walk out to the car with his suitcase that Murn had packed with clean clothes and his lunch box. We wouldn't see him again until Friday night.

Race relations in Cairo became increasingly more tense as the spring brought in the warm and stormy weather. The tension in Cairo rolled in like an early morning fog off of the two rivers, slow and ominous. In the beginning, just the outer fringes of the city lost sight. Then the fog became denser from the Ohio River on the east and the Mississippi River on the west until the sides merged, covering the entire city, leaving the vision of the residents limited to only that which was in front of their own eyes: their personal views.

130

The rivers represented much about the people of Cairo. The Ohio River was a crystal blue, steady flow where all the boating and swimming occurred in the summer. The Mississippi was dark and muddy with undercurrents that churned as it pulled a person down and never let them surface for air. Where the two rivers converged and the waters mixed, there was still a very visible line that divided the two.

Protest marches were occurring downtown and there were boycotts at various stores. Violence and fear were growing on both sides of the community – black as well as white. There were many on both sides who weren't active opponents but simply bystanders. They too became victims of the violence. Fear was growing out of anger and anger growing out of fear. And hate was just growing.

EtEt became more nervous each week leaving us alone. There were fire bombings and break-ins all over the city; no area was off limits. I remember Murn sitting up watching out the upstairs bedroom window late into the night when threats were being made and Molotov cocktails were being thrown into houses.

One night Murn woke me up and told me to be quiet. She thought that someone was trying to break in downstairs. EtEt had purchased another shotgun and during these turbulent times, it was kept loaded in his and Murn's bedroom. She handed me the shotgun and told me to follow behind her. To walk down the stairs, because of her crippled leg, she had to hold on to the rail and the wall. So in my groggy state, carrying the shotgun, I followed behind her holding the gun in the ready position. Luckily, there was no problem downstairs other than the fact that I had just come down a flight of stairs, half asleep, with a shotgun pointed at the back of Murn's head. It wasn't until she took the gun from me that we realized that the safety was off! I don't remember ever seeing that shotgun again.

Eighth-grade graduation came and I was one of two students selected to perform. We each played our contest solo. What an amazing performance opportunity! Graduation was held in the gymnasium. The place was packed and in my blue cap and gown, I stood up and played my best in front of everyone. EtEt was there to see me. Murn stayed at home with Starla. Maneuvering the distant parking, the long walk to the gym, and climbing bleachers would have been too taxing and difficult for her.

EtEt was at our eighth-grade talent show earlier in the year when I played "Spanish Flea" along with the recording by Herb Alpert and the Tijuana Brass and won first place. EtEt's eyes would always get really big and he would just grin and say, "You played well! That was good!" And that alone was enough; it always made me smile. EtEt and I didn't talk very much, but we were buddies.

EtEt always loved to tease or tell a joke. Anytime we were in the car and passed a cemetery, he would ask me his favorite question in some form or another. Murn always knew what was coming and would crimp the corners of her mouth and roll her eyes as she turned her head to look out the window, knowing what was coming. And every time I would take the bait! "Debbie, do you know how many people are dead in that cemetery? Debbie, do you know how many people are buried in that cemetery?"

And as any inquisitive young person would say, "How many?"

With such glee that he had caught me again, his eyes would get big and he'd turn and look at me as I hung over the front seat between him and Murn and say, "All of them!"

"Aw EtEt! That's not funny!" I'd exclaim. He would just laugh and Murn would always roll her eyes and shake her head.

One Friday EtEt came home as usual, but he was dragging one leg as he walked up the alley. Murn thought he had fallen or hurt himself working. Murn was waiting for him at the door and when he walked in she reached up and kissed him and said, "Honey, what's wrong with your leg?" Starla and I were in the living room and watched as he walked by her and sat down in his favorite chair. Murn followed him in and kept saying, "Everett? Everett! What happened to your leg?"

He wasn't answering her. He looked confused and it appeared that he was trying to talk but couldn't. I began asking, "What's wrong with EtEt? Why won't he answer?" Starla crawled up into his lap and laid against his chest. Murn and I went into the kitchen where she told me that she didn't know what had happened, but she was going to call the doctor. She was told to bring EtEt to the hospital the doctor would meet them there to examine him.

When they returned home, Murn said EtEt had had a stroke and the doctor was sending him to the transportation hospital in St. Louis. At that time the railroads and transportation companies had their own hospitals. That night, Murn and I took EtEt to the Missouri Pacific Hospital in St. Louis. Our church friends, Mary and Les, picked Starla up and said she could stay with them as long as Murn needed. Murn had packed a bag for us to stay a couple of nights just in case.

Once the doctors examined him and had run their tests, they told Murn he had had a stroke, that both of his carotid arteries were 90 percent blocked, and that he needed surgery immediately. In the 1960s, this surgery was very serious and some individuals did not survive it. They scheduled the surgery for very early the next morning. I could see the fear in Murn's eyes. I knew she was praying as the doctor was talking.

Murn found a motel close to the hospital where we stayed all night. I remember how foggy it was that morning and how far the hospital was from the parking lot. Murn held on to my arm like she always held to EtEt's. We stopped a couple of times to let her rest a bit, catch her breath, and then we would continue. I could tell she was nervous because her jaw was set and there was a slight furrow in her brow. That was Murn's worried look; I had grown to recognize it. She took the elevator up to see EtEt before the surgery and I waited in the lobby. When Murn came back down, we sat together quietly and waited. I had been in so many hospitals by that time in my life: the Missouri Pacific and Barnes Hospitals in St. Louis; Veteran's hospital in Marion, Illinois; St. Mary's Hospital in Cairo; the TB sanitarium (outside of course); and the nursing home with Aunt Kitten. It seemed as if I was growing up in healthcare facilities.

After a long morning wait, Murn was told EtEt was out of surgery and was in recovery. They told her to go up to his room and the doctor would meet her there. I could see the relief on Murn's brow and she let out a heavy sigh that had been building inside her since he came home on Friday. Murn took the elevator to meet with the doctor in EtEt's room. Murn was very practical; once she spoke with his doctor and EtEt was back in his room where she could see for herself that he was okay, she then came back to the lobby and let me know that he was fine. The doctor told her that one of the arteries was worse than he had anticipated. One artery was completely blocked and the other was at about 90 percent. He said they had cleaned the arteries out; EtEt did very well and he should have no problem recovering. He also told Murn that they would keep him sedated for the rest of the day and if she wanted to leave and get some rest, she could leave a number where she would be staying and they would call if there was any problem. The doctor didn't know Murn. We stayed until visiting hours were over.

We were going to stay in the same motel that evening, but before we went to the motel, Murn decided we had to go shopping for clothes for the next day. Not just clothes, but clothes appropriate for Sunday school. Yes, I had perfect attendance in Sunday school and Murn was determined I was going to get my fourth-year bar to hang from my Sunday school pin. When we arrived back at the motel, Murn started going through the phone book looking for Baptist churches close to the hospital. Since visiting hours didn't begin until after lunch, Murn said I was going to Sunday school. I'll never forget the experience of attending the particular Baptist church she decided on that she found in the Yellow Pages. As Murn and I walked up to the church doors, men were standing at the front door greeting people and smoking cigars. Once we entered the sanctuary we were taken aback by the sight of standing ashtrays placed at the ends of various pews! I thought Murn was going to have another heart attack! I knew her disgusted look and it was all over her face. I got my fourth-year bar that year, but each time the story was told about that Baptist church by me or Murn, that same disgusted look came over Murn's face. A church with ashtrays!

EtEt recovered; his walk improved to the point that you couldn't tell it had initially been affected and his speech returned. There would be times that he would hesitate with what he was starting to say, but he always got it said.

After several trips back to the hospital for checkups, the doctor recommended him for a disability pension. EtEt was 63 and the cold winters and hot summers were just too hard for him to continue working on the rails. So EtEt became a retiree. No more lunch boxes, no more green Dickie work pants and shirts, and no more work caps; now it was just casual clothes and his felt-brimmed hat, everywhere he went.

While I know without a doubt that Murn was so grateful he had recovered, I think she was having to adjust to him being home all day. I heard her tell one of her friends on the phone one day, "Every move I make Everett wants to know what I'm doing. If I'm in the kitchen, 'What'cha doin', Marian?' If I go upstairs, 'Where ya goin', Marian?' Sometimes I just want to tell him

I'm running away! I love him but I'm not used to him being underneath my feet all the time!"

Summer was well underway and Murn and EtEt's new life began. I think EtEt adjusted to retirement as the weeks passed by taking me places, visiting with the men at the gas station, visiting his sister who lived a few blocks away, watching television, taking Starla for walks, reading the paper, and his new vice, smoking a pipe. The doctors stopped his cigarette smoking. I think retirement was good for both EtEt and Murn. Her having had a heart attack and EtEt now with her 24/7 seemed to slow her down just a little. They still had their early mornings together but now she would take time to fix and eat lunch with all of us or have him help her do something in the house. I imagine they got to know each other more than they ever had. Many couples never get to enjoy each other's company at that age. I'm glad they had that time together to become acquainted in a whole new way.

I spent the summer that year with two other neighborhood friends skating, bowling, and on a rare occasion going to the movie show. I remember one weekend in particular that I wanted to go to the show with my friends. Murn said, "No, your daddy wants you to spend the afternoon with him and I told him that would be fine." I was not happy and like a teenager, I pouted until he came to pick me up.

I had been asking to buy a press for my tennis racquet. I think it was only about 50 cents. I asked Daddy what we were going to do when I got in the car with him. He said, "You'll see." When we arrived at his apartment building we went to the basement where he had all of his tools and a workshop. There were what looked like pieces of molding lying on the work table. Daddy started placing tools on the table and handed me sandpaper and told me to begin sanding the pieces of molding. Then I realized what we were doing that afternoon. He opened a sack and laid out four springs, four bolts, and four wing nuts. We were going to make a tennis press. During those few hours, that afternoon Daddy taught me how to measure, mark and cut wood, use a miter box, glue, and set lock braces, chisel joints, and drill holes. And when I cut a piece of wood incorrectly, I heard over and over, "Measure twice, cut once." Two new pieces of wood would appear in front of me to begin again. By the end of the day, I had a press for my racquet.

I used that press for many years and it was probably more expensive than the 50 cents one I had wanted to buy. It was certainly more valuable. I wanted so badly to be with my friends at the movie show that day. Little did I know many years later I would be willing to give up anything to spend that afternoon again with my daddy and hear him say, "Measure twice, cut once."

Starting high school was somewhat more unsettling than it should have been. Cairo had always had two high schools: Cairo High School where the white students attended and Sumner High School where most of the black students attended. The Sumner building had serious problems and students were to be merged into Cairo High School. With the societal conflicts whirling in Cairo, the merger was creating a microcosm of the same conflicts within the now only-existing high school. Some of the white students felt like the black students were intruders, some of the black students didn't want to be there, and the incoming freshmen didn't know anything but what they were experiencing. Police were standing in the hallways, teachers were nervous, fights were breaking out between the races, and a level of discomfort impeded learning among most of the students.

The band was the most uncomfortable for me. Blending two bands to form one when each band had students occupying placement seats potentially would create major conflicts. With the re-seating, someone had to be seated above the other who would essentially be demoted from where they sat in their previous band. The students from the black high school sat in the first chair seats, I sat second chair first although I had been first chair first before the merger. They had lost their school and tensions were high. Looking back, it was probably a wise decision on the director's part and comforting for the black students.

Not long after school started the call came that Starla's mother had been admitted to the hospital in Carbondale and within days, on September 11, 1968, the call came that Ann had passed away. Starla was only three-and-a-half years old. Murn and EtEt decided that they wouldn't take Starla to the funeral. She was so young and I think Murn felt it would be more traumatic than comforting and best that she remembered her mother alive, not in a casket. I don't think Daddy went to the funeral since they had separated on difficult terms. I don't think he could have made the hour trip if he wanted to; he chose to spend that day at his favorite tavern instead.

It had been a hard year for my family; this was the third death, a heart attack, and a stroke. When Ann died, I don't think anyone had the strength to face one more visitation, one more funeral, or one more burial. Death and illness had robbed us of our lives that year. I think Starla's older half-brothers may have felt angry that Starla wasn't there for their mother's funeral, but they had no idea what we had been through mentally, physically, and emotionally. We had no more to give.

Life as a high school freshman became more uncomfortable as the school year progressed. The daily emotional drain was increasing. The class that had always made me happy became more uncomfortable. We had our third new band director in four years. This man was nice enough but was easily intimidated by the racial tensions. If it hadn't been for my private lessons with Mr. Thomas, I would have been miserable. It was rumored that they were going to cut band from the curriculum next year and that too infused anxiety into the tension.

138

My seventh-grade band director, Jackie, had stayed in contact with me after she left. I was a very talented young musician and an excellent trumpet player for my age. When she heard about the issues within the band in Cairo, she invited me to come on the weekends and play with her high school band where she was now teaching. She spoke with Murn and told her that if she and EtEt would put me on the train scheduled for Carbondale on Friday afternoons, she would meet me and I could spend the weekend with her at her mother and father's house and she would put me on the return train to Cairo on Sunday afternoons. That way I could perform with her band for basketball games. Murn and EtEt decided that they would allow it. They knew how very much I adored her and how much I missed playing with a good band. So once basketball season began, EtEt would put me on the Friday afternoon train headed toward Carbondale. Jackie would meet me at the train station and we would go out to eat, then head to her school for the ball game where I got to play. After the game, we would go to her parents' home where I would spend the night Friday and Saturday. Just about every weekend that winter I played with her high school band.

I loved spending weekends taking the train and playing with Jackie's band at ballgames. However, Murn and EtEt were disturbed that during those weekends I was missing church and Sunday school and were considering not allowing me to go any longer. But they also knew that my heart was filled with music and it was important for my education. With the growing tensions in Cairo, losing the band the next year, and my missing church on Sundays, they began to explore moving. EtEt was retired and we were free to leave Cairo for me to have the education I needed. Jackie had remarried during the year and her husband was a businessman in the Carbondale area. He made some calls and connected Murn with the individuals to speak with to secure housing they could afford on EtEt's disability retirement pension.

December entered sadly for EtEt. Grandma Lipe passed away on December 5, 1968, one day past her 92nd birthday. I don't know where she was when she passed away, but she had moved from Elmwood Place before we moved there. She was a tiny little woman but was made of steel. She had been a farm woman and worked hard all of her life. Even in her 90s, she would rake the leaves in her little yard and those that the wind blew up in the air she would knock down with the rake. I knew I would miss going with EtEt to visit her and deliver groceries. There wasn't a funeral as I remember, only a graveside service. At her age, only her children, great- and great-great-grandchildren were left who knew her. She was buried at a little church cemetery at the Dutch Ridge Missionary Church. EtEt's father was buried there and it wasn't far from where EtEt and his brothers and sisters grew up. Her children stood together with their spouses at the grave and I watched as EtEt took his handkerchief from his back pants pocket, dabbed each eye then wiped his nose and returned it to his pocket. EtEt was so very soft-hearted. I had seen him do the same sequence during a sad story or when he saw something that touched his heart. How blessed he was to have had his mother so long, and she had been even more blessed that he had been such a good son.

Christmas soon passed, Starla had her fourth birthday, we were entering a new year, and we were soon going to be moving when there was an apartment available. Perhaps this year would bring good times rather than the last two years' emotionally draining events we all had survived. Until now, loss to me had only been understood in the loss of a game by defeat, an item that had been misplaced, or the loss of weight the adults always talked about. This year I learned another definition and what loss truly meant. While my previous engagement with loss may have resulted in disappointment in losing a game, aggravation or frustration in losing an item, or even happiness in losing weight,

I learned the true meaning of the word loss when used to reference death. I saw the pain of loss in my family's eyes, the absence of someone's presence in our lives, and the fear that loss in its cruelest definition would appear and steal the people you love, leaving you with a hollowness for that person that no one or nothing could ever replace. Once you experience this unforgiving loss, the other types of loss seem unimportant or insignificant. I realized that what's most sad about this type of loss is that, unlike the others, this one can't be avoided; it will come to each and every one of us. And when it comes, roaring or slithering in, a loss will steal your very desire to breathe.

CHAPTER 11

Leaves of the Branches

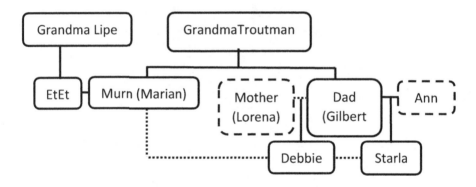

CHAPTER 11

Two Men and Their Daughters
Spring 1969 – Summer 1969

I was lucky to have two men in my life growing up. Even though Murn and EtEt had raised me and had custody of me, my daddy was always in my life. This is probably why I never called EtEt Dad. The relationship between my daddy and EtEt was as close as brothers even though they were brothers-in-law. There were periods when I was growing up that Daddy stopped by every day. I was a lucky girl; two men loved me with all their hearts. And my little half-sister Starla had the same after she was born.

On Valentine's Day, 1969, during my freshman year in high school, we moved from Cairo to Murphysboro. This is where EtEt's brother lived and we certainly knew the 55 miles to and from Cairo very well. The Cairo school district confirmed their decision to cut band from the high school curriculum beginning the next school year. Murn and EtEt recognized how important music was to me so they decided we would move in order for me to be in a high school with a band program. We still attended our church every Sunday in Cairo and of course visited our family while we were there. We often left home on Saturday and stayed until Sunday afternoon.

Nineteen-sixty-nine was a very interesting time in history: Vietnam, the draft, hippies, drugs, patchouli oil, and some of the greatest music reflecting the culture at the time and the life-songs of the youth. I was soon to be 15 and like most teenagers, I was trapped between being a child and being a young adult.

Moving during the middle of my freshman year in high school was somewhat uncomfortable for me. It's bad enough being a high school freshman, much less entering late in the year. I was lucky. Our next-door neighbor had a daughter who was a year older than me and she was very kind to acclimate me to the school and various new friends. Being in the band also helped me to develop new friends quickly; it gave me a home.

I had completed my freshman year and survived the move, and now summer was upon me. The next big event was my birthday. Turning 15 was a teenager's relief! No longer a freshman, and a year closer to having a driver's license! I was a typical 14-year-old turning 15. I thought that I was grown up. I had more freedom and with that, a new sense of responsibility. I also had the typical aloofness and was too grown up to have my family hug on me. I was beyond what I thought at the time were childish actions. The days before my birthday were filled with activities with friends: movies, picnics, hiking, listening to music together, and talking on the phone connected to the wall. My birthday was on Tuesday. Since we still attended church on Sundays in Cairo, we planned to stay a few days extra to visit our friends and family and spend my birthday with my daddy.

There were four of us: Murn, EtEt, Starla (who was four-and-a-half years old at the time), and me, the mature, soon-to-be 15-year-old. There wasn't any family who had enough room in their house for all of us to stay, so EtEt was going to stay with his sister and her family, I was going to get to stay with my older half-sister Pam, and Murn and Starla were going to stay with Grandma Troutman and Daddy. I was excited to stay with Pam. She was married, but her husband was in the Army. She had a baby and it would just be us girls. She was four years older and I was feeling quite grown!

We had dinner that evening at Grandma's house. I think I remember having fried chicken with all the fixings. Daddy seemed to have a cold. He had a cough and kept wiping his nose with his handkerchief. Grandma seemed so happy that we all were there. She had one of the little senior citizen housing apartments. They were brand new when she moved in. A kitchen, living room, bedroom, and bath. It was perfect for her. There were seven apartments in a row and they had the alarm buttons in each room that could be hit in the event of an emergency. An alarm would sound and a red light would flash outside their door. She only received about $78 a month from old age assistance and her rent was based on her income. This was a perfect, safe place for her to be. The hospital was only a block or two away and my Uncle Wayne, her son, lived about three blocks away. I loved my grandma, but for a soon-to-be 15-year-old in 1969 with no cell phones, tablets, computers, electronic games, cable television, well, I was bored and couldn't wait to go to my sister's house. FINALLY, dinner was over and EtEt was going to take me to Pam's house. I told everyone goodbye and out the door we went!

Sunday morning came much earlier than expected. Murn called early and said that EtEt was coming to get me. Why? "I'll tell you when you get here."

Shortly, EtEt was knocking on the door and we were on our way back to Grandma's house. When we got there, Daddy was lying on the couch. "What's wrong? Why couldn't I stay longer?"

"Your daddy is sick," Murn whispered. "He needs to go to the VA hospital in Marion; he has the flu or something." Murn said he had been up all night and had been running a high fever. She told me, "I tried to get him to drink some orange juice and lie down, but he kept saying he was afraid to lie down; he was afraid he was going to die." She said she told him, "Oh Gilbert, you're not going to die!"

Murn called the ambulance and was going to take him to the veteran's hospital in Marion. She had planned on riding in the ambulance with him, getting him checked in and settled, and then she would come back with the ambulance. We would go back home and the next day she would go over to Marion to take care of him. Daddy seemed much weaker. He was lying on the couch and Starla was leaning up against the couch in the bend of his arm when the ambulance came. Daddy looked up at me and said, "Honey, I'm sorry I'm going to miss your birthday."

"That's okay Daddy, I'll come with Murn to see you tomorrow in the hospital." He already had my card propped up on the side table between the two living room chairs.

The EMTs helped him to the stretcher and as they started to take him out the door, Grandma patted him and kissed him on the cheek. He held out his hand, grabbed mine, and said, "I love you, honey. You be good." Murn gave them time to get him in the ambulance. She had convinced him to go to the hospital so they could push the fluids and give him an antibiotic. She told us he would be fine and she would be back in several hours. During the day Starla and I stayed with Grandma and EtEt went back to his sister's and filled her in on what was happening and picked up his things.

Daddy and Murn had about an hour's ride to the hospital. During the ride, Daddy shared with Murn some things he wanted her to know about his feelings and wishes for Starla and me. Years later, Murn told me that Daddy had said to her that he "…just wanted to put his arms around Debbie and hug her, but she's just not that way." Murn told him it was just my age; lots of teenagers go through a period where they tend to be aloof. He also told her not to let me go to Julliard School of Music for college. He said I had been too protected growing up and I was too naïve; something would happen to me in New York. I didn't go to Julliard, I didn't even apply – and even if I had been accepted, I wouldn't have gone for my daddy.

It was about 2:00 when Murn returned from the hospital. She said she had gotten him into his room and he had changed into his pajamas, robe, and

146

slippers. Murn told us she had hated to have to leave him so quickly, but the ambulance had to leave and she was at their mercy. She told him she would be back first thing the next morning. She had not had lunch so Grandma made her a sandwich and a glass of tea. "When I left him he was sitting on the side of the bed with his lower lip quivering," Murn told us. "Let me finish this sandwich and we'll head back home and maybe I can get over there tonight and see him."

Suddenly the phone rang. Grandma answered then said, "Marian, it's for you." Murn took the phone and after saying "hello," there was a loud cry, "No! Oh no! That can't be! I just left him! I'll be there as quick as I can." She hung up the phone and broke into tears and screamed this broken, "Gilbert's dead!"

I'll never forget Grandma, this sweet little 83-year-old wailing! It was a sound I had never heard and at a volume I had never heard from my grandma. It must have come from the deepest part of her soul. Starla was clinging to Murn as they both cried, and EtEt couldn't believe it! He covered his mouth and started to cry and walked out the back door. It was surreal to me. I couldn't feel anything! All of them were locked within their own grief and disbelief! It was as if a cloak of death had surrounded each of us.

I didn't know what to do. I grabbed Daddy's keys and I went outside to his car. I sat behind the steering wheel and cried. I remember holding on to the steering wheel and laying my forehead against it as I watched the tears drop one after another. I couldn't get the picture out of my mind of him lying on the stretcher as they took him out the door. How could he be gone? How could that have happened? I could smell his Old Spice cologne in the car. It was mixed with the smell of Pall Mall cigarettes. How many times had I watched him drive up to our house in this car? I just held on to the steering wheel and cried, and cried. I finally thought "I can't sit here any longer. I have to do something and I just can't go back into the house right now."

The local hospital was a block away. I started walking over there. I knew there was a pay phone in the emergency room. All I could think to do was to call my mother. I called her collect and she accepted, "What's the matter, honey? What's wrong?"

"Mother, Daddy died!" I cried out through a stream of tears.

She had been married to him and loved him at one time and he was my daddy. I knew she would care. I needed someone's comfort and compassion at that moment. Her response changed our relationship forever. Not only was my 15th birthday a rite of passage for a teenager, but my mother's response was going to thrust me into adulthood. "What do you want me to do about it, honey?" Mother asked.

That question took my breath away. It was as if I had been hit full force in the chest! I staggered back from the phone, dropped it down from my ear, and fell back against the wall. How could she say that to me? Didn't she care? It took everything I had to pull myself together and all I could say was, "Nothing, I just thought you would want to know." I couldn't talk anymore. I had nothing to say. I couldn't even cry; the breath had been knocked out of me. I didn't want to talk to her anymore. "Okay, I'll talk to you later," I said and hung up the phone. There I stood, alone in the emergency room waiting area. It was now as if there had been two deaths.

I had nowhere to go, so I walked back over to my grandma's apartment. I went in the back door; I couldn't bear to walk by his car parked in the front where I would have to pass by to enter the front door. Murn was packing our things. Starla was sitting on Grandma's lap patting her as a child often does when an adult is crying. I wondered whose lap Grandma sat on as a little two-year-old when her mother died. Grandma was heartbroken. As I look back, her loss was greater than any of ours. This was the fifth child she had outlived and she had already lost two husbands. She must have felt cursed. I had heard people say that the worst thing for a mother is for her to outlive her child. I learned what that meant that day as I watched my grandma's lower lip quiver the way I imagined Daddy's did when Murn left him.

It was a quiet ride in the car as we returned home to Murphysboro that afternoon. It was so quiet you could hear each of us breathing.

When we arrived home, Murn began packing our clothes for the return trip to Cairo the next day. Murn handled as many of the arrangements with the funeral director as possible on the phone. We were to meet with him the next morning, on my 15th birthday, to finalize the arrangements. Then she left for the VA hospital to get his belongings and arrange for the funeral home to pick up his body. The hospital did an immediate autopsy due to the sudden death. We learned that he had died from what at the time they then called walking pneumonia with complications from cirrhosis of the liver.

Daddy didn't have a lot at this point in his life. He was renting a room in a hotel that rented to individuals for long-term stays. The one thing he did have was a ring that he treasured. Starla's mother had purchased the ring for his birthday one year. Every year for his birthday, Father's Day, and other special occasions, she would increase the diamond size. Daddy wore that ring proudly. When Murn arrived at the hospital, they had already moved him to the morgue and had his personal belongings in a bag. There was no ring. It's hard to imagine someone stealing a ring off of a dead man's finger. There's something unique about a ring. It's a symbol of something special, that which can't be seen or explained, and sometimes a symbol of pain and perhaps bad choices.

Daddy had a Japanese wedding band that he had given to my stepbrother. I remember being upset that he didn't give it to me because I was his oldest

149

daughter. At the time, Murn explained to me that he had told her why he didn't want me to have it. When he was in World War II, he had been stationed in the Philippines. He never talked about his time during the war, but I guess Murn had told him I was upset about the ring. She told me the story.

His unit was moving through the jungle where the bodies of dead Japanese soldiers had lain for days in the heat and the dampness of the jungle. It must have been horrible. As so many soldiers do, men in his platoon were taking valuables – souvenirs – off of the soldiers' bodies. He told her the bodies were so bloated from the heat and days lying there that it was often difficult to take jewelry. My daddy admitted to Murn that he had cut off a finger of a soldier to take the ring. He said after that, he never took another thing. He was embarrassed, sickened, and ashamed of his action. That's why he didn't want me to have that ring – it was unclean. Daddy was a good man. He carried that guilt and shame of taking that ring with him for the rest of his life.

I've often wondered if it was karma, someone taking Daddy's ring from him after he had died. Was it "an eye for an eye, and a tooth for a tooth"? Was the price we paid equivalent to the price the soldier's wife had to bear not getting back her husband's wedding band? I've always heard that "karma is a bitch." I learned…it is.

Early Tuesday morning we drove back to Cairo, dropped EtEt at Grandma's along with Starla, and Murn and I went to the funeral home. It was the first time I had ever been in a casket display room. It was cold there in the basement. Caskets were lined up in a diagonal arrangement. I'd never seen a wooden casket with flocked material covering it. Then there were steel ones and very expensive polished caskets in walnut and mahogany. The funeral director knew our family and moved us quickly past the flocked caskets. It was my birthday; I wasn't supposed to be here! I was supposed to be celebrating with Daddy, Murn, EtEt, Grandma, and Starla. Instead, I was picking out a casket to bury my Dad.

Murn was a rock. How did she do it? She held herself together and helped me understand that finances were limited. I think she had a small life insurance policy on Daddy, but the rest would be on her and EtEt's shoulders. She guided me to the caskets which would be appropriate and what we could afford. I picked a beautiful light blue steel casket. They showed us burial garments. Although Daddy was always put together well and always clean and pressed, he didn't have a suit. When he wore a tie, he either didn't wear a jacket or he simply wore a golf jacket, although he never played golf. I picked out the suit but I wanted one of Daddy's own ties on him. The rest of the planning was in Murn's hands.

I hadn't been in Daddy's apartment since we had moved to Murphysboro. When we went to check on it and check for important papers after he had passed away, I noticed a wastepaper can. Daddy didn't play an instrument but I know how proud he was of me. The wastepaper can was one of the oval-shaped metal cans that often had embossed pictures on one side. Daddy had bought one that had a French horn with sheets of music around it. Seeing that somehow let me know that Daddy had chosen that one to remind him of me. I would never do away with that wastepaper can.

The visitation was difficult. As we walked down the funeral home aisle toward the casket I noticed the beautiful casket spray. I had picked out roses and carnations. As we moved closer I saw the ribbons hanging out of it; one said "Dad," one "Son," and another "Brother." And then I saw him.

Daddy was only 46 years old. A teenager may feel like that is old. As an adult, I realize how very young he was. He hadn't changed much through the years. There I stood, looking down at my daddy. He was the first dead person I had touched. How cold and hard his hands were. I patted his chest and it felt like patting a brick. His sideburns had turned white but the rest of his hair was dark brown. He never was a large man – slim, medium height, he only wore a size seven-and-a-half shoe. Drinking and poor health had taken some of his weight. He had been infected with a disease from simply living, contracted through a combination of life events that eventually ravaged his entire body. He had so much long, straight hair on his hands which led up his arm. I remember as a little girl I would gently pull the hair straight up and then smooth it on his forearm. He always wore long-sleeved shirts and rolled the sleeves up midway between his wrist and his elbow. I couldn't see his arms there in the casket, but I would never forget how they looked; tanned with long, soft hair.

So many friends of our family, church friends, and those who knew and worked with Daddy throughout the years came to the visitation and funeral. Grandma cried and cried. She was so thin and delicate. Her vein-aged hands clutched her white laced handkerchief she sat in the front row; people would bend down and hug her while offering their condolences. Murn stood by the casket greeting and thanking all of those who came to pay their respects. I remember how strong she was – warm and smiling. I would move between Murn and Grandma. Starla was scared, and at one point she cried, "Daddy looked at me!" EtEt walked her towards the back and different people would sit with them and try to occupy the little, now orphaned four-and-a-half-year-old.

I don't remember much about the funeral; I don't remember much of anything about that week. We buried Daddy in the Burris cemetery lot. The cemetery was about 45 minutes away. I do remember seeing Grandma's tears as I watched her look around at the headstones of her children and first husband who were buried there. And now my daddy, her sixth child. We were in the front row at the gravesite: me, Murn, Starla, and Grandma. EtEt had

152

been a pallbearer and was standing with them. Our pastor officiated the funeral and the graveside service. Daddy was a member of our church but wasn't an attendee. I remember when he did attend when I was young…especially the day he walked down the aisle to be saved at the altar call. I remember Grandma and Murn crying then too. Except those were tears of joy. My thoughts were interrupted as the funeral director stood before me and knelt with the folded American flag that had draped the casket. "This flag is presented on behalf of a grateful nation as an expression of appreciation for the honorable and faithful service rendered by your father." There was a 21-gun salute; seven of the men he had often visited with at the VFW together fired three shots. BAM! It echoed through the cemetery. BAM! BAM! I jumped at each firing.

The salute was followed by the playing of taps. It was bewildering to me how those four pitches which make up the melody to taps that I had played for services and funerals as a young trumpeter had brought such joy and pride to my daddy when he would hear me play, and now brought such unbearable pain and heartache for me when it was played for him. As the first notes were played, my thoughts were taken back to when I started playing trumpet in fourth grade. Daddy said it was a boy's instrument. Murn told him, "Gilbert, leave her alone and let her play whatever she wants to."

A couple of years after I began studying, I was asked to play taps at a Memorial Day service. Daddy was there, beaming like a proud peacock! Nothing negative was ever said about me playing trumpet after that Memorial Day service. And now, nothing would ever be said again. He'd never see or hear me play taps again. He wouldn't see me graduate high school and attend college. He wouldn't hear my recital, watch me conduct, or witness the many achievements and life events I will experience. And I will never again hear him say, "I'm proud of you, honey."

I wonder what conversations he and I would have had as I grew older. I wonder what he would have looked like at 60 or 70. Starla would never have the years I had with him. She'd never know her Daddy past the memories of a four-and-a-half-year-old and I would never know him beyond the eyes of a 15-year-old. Through the years, I've often looked at my last birthday card from him, "I love you always, Dad." Always is a long time to be without your dad. Every birthday brings with it heartache; his death can never be separated from my birthdays that would follow. Every birthday will always bring back that one, unforgettable birthday.

The days following Daddy's funeral were spent with Murn cleaning out his room in the hotel, notifying Social Security and the Veterans Administration, sending death certificates to the insurance company and businesses he may have owed, writing thank-you cards for the flowers at his funeral, and going through his papers to distinguish what needed to be saved and what could be done away with.

Since we had moved from Cairo to Murphysboro five months earlier, I had grown accustomed to not seeing him daily. Starla and I both had days where his death and his absence from our lives seemed to haunt us more than others, but Murn made sure our lives continued with consistency yet gave us time to grieve, each in our individual way. Starla would often cry at different times: a show on television, at night before falling asleep, or when someone would say something about Daddy. I was sullen and would hole up in my bedroom. Murn and EtEt kept our family life moving forward as they always did. I played in the municipal band and had rehearsals and concerts weekly. Starla went to Vacation Bible School with one of her little friends. Murn cleaned and cooked and washed clothes daily.

EtEt made his daily trip to the grocery store, often with Starla by his side. The store gave game stamps that you would collect and stick to a playing card of sorts. Once you filled a card you could get a plate, book, or pan, depending on what the grouping was at that time. The stamp also might show that you won a dollar amount. He loved getting home and putting those stamps on the collection card and to see if he had won anything. I don't think he ever did but I think his joy was in the hoping.

About a month had passed since we buried Daddy. Things were starting to calm down emotionally for us. Death is never easy, but Murn seemed to understand that routine helps when learning to cope with loss.

That day in July was like every other day. We didn't have an air conditioner and all of the windows were open. It was warm and Murn was wearing one of her sleeveless housecleaning dresses. I always noticed how defined her arms were from using her upper body all her life due to polio. Murn was sitting in a chair at the kitchen table putting a new bag in the vacuum cleaner, I was in my room listening to music, Starla was playing in her room, and EtEt had just returned from his daily trip to the grocery store and was on the opposite side of the kitchen table standing between the table and the sink counter, placing the new stamps on his card.

Suddenly I heard Murn call my name and as a teenager, I yelled back "What?" She screamed again in a bloodcurdling cry, "Come here quick! It's Everett!"

As I came out of my room I heard this loud gurgling, snorting sound. Murn was crying and standing up from the table as I ran past her and went out the back door. On the outside of the house between the kitchen and the living room was a long, narrow window that cranked out. EtEt had planted flowers under that window and often would be down on his knees weeding and forget the window was there and would rise and hit his head on the corner – something I had done as well. I don't to this day know why, but that horrible sound I heard made me think he had hit his head much harder on that window and was badly hurt. I didn't see him outside. Then I heard Murn scream, "He's in here!"

I ran back in through the living room door and Murn was standing up, looking across the table to the floor. There he was, flat on the floor between the table and the cabinets and refrigerator where he always stood checking and pasting those stamps. He had urinated on himself and the snorting sound had stopped. I pushed the table out of my way and knelt on the floor beside him. I started compressions. I had never been trained, I just didn't know what else to do; it was a spontaneous reaction! I put the heel of my hand on his chest and my other hand on top of it where I thought his heart was and with all my might began pumping. I must have broken every rib in that area. "One, two, three…one, two, three."

Murn called the ambulance and they arrived shortly. She stayed on the other side of the table holding Starla. I'm sure Murn didn't want Starla to see it. Murn was sobbing and Starla, in her little four-and-a-half-year-old way, was trying to console her. Everything happened so fast. I kept pumping the entire time until the ambulance arrived, then EMTs began working on him. Murn was helped into the back of the ambulance with EtEt while Starla and I rode in the front with the driver. I'll never forget the driver telling me that I had done a good job. He was alive and I had brought him back by doing the compressions. I later learned that his heart had stopped and that's why he had urinated on himself, and the gurgling, snorting sounds I had heard were the death rattles. I never, ever want to hear that sound again. To this day I can hear it; it's a sound you can't reproduce or explain.

When we arrived at the hospital the EMTs and nurses rushed EtEt into the emergency room and told Murn to come with them. I stayed in the waiting room with Starla. The room was a very small area with the staff person at the ER desk looking on. It was hard for me to keep Starla occupied. My thoughts were on what had just happened and what was happening right then. What if it was my fault? Maybe I hadn't done the right thing. Maybe I should have done something differently. What if I hadn't run outside when the death rattles were sounding, maybe he would have had a better chance.

Starla and I walked the hallway, looked at magazines, sat quietly, and other individuals in the waiting room talked with Starla and entertained her off and on. About three hours later Murn came out with a plastic bag holding his clothes. There was no expression on her face. Her eyes were glassy. She sat down on one of the chairs next to us. "He's gone," she whispered.

We just sat there for what seemed like hours, quiet, tears rolling down our cheeks. Murn finally broke the silence, "We need to get a ride home." I don't remember how we got home; I think she called a cab. How could this be happening? Why us? Why EtEt? What were we going to do? Hadn't we already been through enough with Daddy? All these thoughts were running through my head yet I couldn't think, couldn't talk, couldn't feel. I was emotionally and cognitively paralyzed.

Once we walked into the house, Murn told us she needed to make some phone calls but she first needed to get some paperwork in her bedroom. I heard her door close; she seldom ever closed that door. I straightened up the table and chairs in the kitchen and Starla went to her room and crawled up on her bed and curled up in a fetal position, sucking her thumb. I wondered if Murn was alright, if she was going to be alright. Are we all going to be alright? I paced from the kitchen to the living room, up and down the hallway, and in and out of my bedroom. Behind that closed door, I imagine Murn was grieving alone.

After a few minutes, once she had pulled herself together, she opened her bedroom door and asked me to bring her a glass of water. Starla ran to her and when I brought back the water, she told me to sit down. She hugged both

157

of us and told us everything was going to be alright. Murn said, "Debbie, you did everything right, honey." I needed to hear that from her. I never asked her what happened in the ER. I don't know if she got to talk to him, to tell him goodbye, or tell him that she loved him. She never offered that, and I never asked. I guess I felt whatever occurred in his last minutes was private between her and EtEt. Or maybe it was just too painful for me to know the answer. Had I told him I loved him? He was such a quiet man. Did he know I loved him?

Once again, I watched as Murn held herself together and did what needed to be done. She called the funeral director in Cairo and made arrangements to have his body picked up and moved to Cairo. Then she called our pastor at the church in Cairo asking him to preach the funeral of course and telling him she wanted the funeral to be held in our church, but the visitation would be at the funeral home. Then the long, drawn-out, painful telephone calls were made to our family – Grandma, EtEt's sister, Uncle Wayne, church friends, and many other friends of EtEt and those he worked with. She was so calm, so controlled. One by one she would tell the whole story and answer their questions. Now and then I would see her wipe the tears from her eye under her glasses. How could she hold herself together? She must have been operating simply on adrenaline. I sat in the living room as she made each call.

Murn had me call my mother. I was hesitant based on the response I had gotten when I told her Daddy died. What would her response be now? I knew she adored EtEt. He was always supportive of her, kind and caring, and never criticized her. He accepted her unconditionally and even if at times he didn't agree with some of her actions or behaviors, he never said a word against her. When I called and told her what had happened, she broke into tears. Her voice broke and I knew to lose him touched a very tender part of her heart. She and her husband were living in Montana and she didn't have the money to come for the funeral. Even if she had, I think it would have been too painful for her. So we left it that she would try to come home later. She wanted to talk to Murn so I handed her the phone. Murn had always been like a sister to Mother rather than a sister-in-law. I saw once again Murn trying to comfort Mother rather than the other way around.

The calls finally were made. It was evening and there we sat; it was now just Murn, Starla, and me. There was EtEt's pipe on the end table next to his chair. This wonderful, kind man was gone from our lives. He was such a quiet man but his absence was like the roar of a tornado. The silence was excruciatingly loud and it felt like my heart was being slammed by the debris of the hours since it had struck this morning. Murn helped Starla get ready for bed and I just sat there, waiting for the calm after the storm and dreading the next few days of the harsh reality. That night was very quiet. I didn't think of it then as a teenager, but now I wonder how broken Murn's heart must have been lying in their bed alone, knowing that she had to raise Starla, who was not yet five, and me, a teenager, alone. I never heard a sound that night coming from her room, not even a whimper. I wonder if the loss was so intense and the burden so unbearable that it took her voice, or maybe her voice left with him.

The next morning was filled with packing for the days to come. Murn laid out EtEt's suit, shirt, and tie for us to take to the funeral home. When we arrived in Cairo, we dropped Starla off at Grandma's house and Murn and I went to the funeral home to prepare everything. It had been only a little over a month ago that Murn and I stood in the casket display room selecting my daddy's casket. This time I wasn't there to select a casket, I was there to support her. She selected a beautiful bronze-rose steel casket. She arranged the details for the funeral, including the music, the songs that would be sung by their good friend Juanita who was also a member of our church, and made the financial arrangements. The funeral director had handled most of our family's prior funerals so of course there was no problem. I wasn't sure if Daddy's funeral had been paid off, yet here was another.

When we returned to Grandma's many of our church friends dropped in to visit and brought food. I watched as Grandma puttered around her little kitchen taking care of the food, trying to let Murn rest and visit with her friends. Grandma had a pang of sadness on her face, thin and sallow, and again her little chin and lower lip quivered as it had a little over a month ago, just like Daddy's had when Murn left him sitting on the side of the hospital bed. Her eyelids were so heavy they covered her eyes that occasionally released a tear that would roll over her pronounced cheekbone and into the hollow of her cheek. She always had a handkerchief or tissue tucked inside her dress under her bra strap, or in the belt of her dress. Every so often I would see her reach for it and wipe her eye or nose. Her face was drawn and she was hesitant in her movements. Her thin, frail, skin-draped little arms would slowly and carefully arrange and rearrange the dishes as she placed the food on the table. This was too much.

EtEt was so good to Grandma. He called her Mom and would take her wherever she needed to go when we lived in town and the time she lived with us. I'm sure she was worried about Murn being left with Starla and me to raise alone, 50 miles away. Here was a mother who had lost so many of her children. Within a month a son had passed and now a son-in-law who was like a son was gone. Now she must have been worrying about the only daughter she had left and not knowing how to help. Murn had already had a massive heart attack a few years earlier. I'm sure Grandma must have been afraid of how the stress and pressure would affect Murn, along with her fear that she might lose her daughter too.

160

As we had many times before, we made the journey down the funeral home aisle. This time Murn was holding on to my forearm, not EtEt's as she always had. The casket spray was beautiful. It was deja vu. The ribbons on the spray now said "Husband," "Uncle," "Brother," and "Son-in-Law." Once again, we were standing next to a casket. We had just done this, we had just felt the intense pain and heartache of loss, we had received most of these same people a month ago. How much emotion and loss could we bear? What did God want from us?

EtEt looked just like he was sleeping. His face was full, peaceful, and had the gentle expression that I had loved and known from the time I was a little girl. That was the same look I had seen on his face when I delivered the compressions there on the kitchen floor. Lying there in the casket he looked like he was ready for church: his black suit, white shirt, one of the two ties he owned, and of course, his favorite tie clasp. He always wore a tie clasp. He also always had a pack of Wrigley's Doublemint gum in his suit coat pocket. I stood there wondering if there was still a pack of gum in his pocket. On Sundays during church, I would start to get hungry around 11:00 and I'd always ask him for some gum. I hated Doublemint gum. It always seemed to make me hungrier, but something is better than nothing. I wonder if he had lived, would we have laughed about how he always had Doublemint gum because he knew I didn't like it? If he had had Juicy Fruit gum he never would have had any when he wanted it!

Many of the mourners that evening were our friends: family friends, church friends, and most of the men he supervised on the rail in his job as a railroad foreman. Many of the men he worked with were black and called EtEt "Mr. Bunny," his old high school nickname. As they came through the line, they all called Murn "Mrs. Bunny." She thanked each of them for coming and shared how highly EtEt thought of each of them.

One of the last men in the group had worked with him as his assistant foreman. He had his hat in one hand and offered his other hand to Murn with tears in his eyes and said, "Mrs. Bunny, I just don't know what to say. I can't believe Mr. Bunny is gone." Murn took his hand then reached up and hugged him. The two people EtEt had spent much of his daily working life with – one white, one black, one female, and one male – embraced for a moment in the shared loss. When they released the embrace, they both wiped their eyes with one hand then nodded as he patted Murn's hand enclosed between both of his. I realized, watching that quiet moment, that loss, grief, pain, and sadness know no color, no race, no gender, no difference.

Starla seemed more affected by EtEt's visitation than she did at our daddy's. She had spent most of her days around EtEt since his retirement. She kept wanting to look at him and would peek over the side of the casket. Maybe she thought he was just sleeping; I was wishing he was. Murn, once again, told the story over and over to those as they passed by the casket. How did she do it? How could she stand there and be so gracious at a time when her heart must have been breaking?

She always woke up with EtEt around 5:00 and had coffee with him before he went to work. Later I learned that was the time they did all of their decision-making and had the talks that husbands and wives have without children around. I woke up early one morning and caught them before he left. He was much taller than Murn; she only came up to his shoulder, so he leaned down while she held on to his arm reaching up and they kissed each other goodbye before he walked out the door. I had never seen them display affection, although it was always apparent there was deep love between them. I remember how sweet it was. Each day, out the door he went with his black metal lunch box in his hand, his work cap on his head, Murn standing at the door, one hand on the door frame and the other on her hip, watching him walk to the car. He always walked with a slow gait and his shoulder tipped lower on his left side; probably from all the many years he leaned over for Murn to hold on to his forearm. They had stood by each other all those years together. I guess that's what gave her the strength to stand there that whole evening, holding on to the casket, that and her faith.

I remember walking into our church the day of the funeral. The pulpit area was filled with flowers that extended from and circled the casket. The red carpet on the center aisle between the pews seemed to stretch longer than it ever had as it led us on the walk to the front. How many times EtEt had walked up and down that long aisle as an usher collecting the offerings or as a deacon serving communion on Sunday morning. He was solid, humble, dependable, and compassionate. He said very little with his words but much with his actions.

Many years ago our minister approached him about becoming a deacon one day and EtEt told him he couldn't do that because he smoked and he just couldn't give it up. That was his one vice and I guess working with the men in all kinds of weather, day in and day out on the railroad just made having a smoke make the day easier. As the foreman, he wasn't supposed to help with the work nor was he to sit down. Knowing the kind of man EtEt was, the minister went to Murn, knowing the kind of woman she was. He told Murn, "I would rather have one Everett that smokes than 100 other men who don't smoke. Can't you convince him to become a deacon?"

It was no surprise that EtEt became a deacon. Every first Sunday of each month until he died he served communion and as soon as church was over he was in the car lighting a cigarette before his stroke or his pipe after. I'm pretty sure God was okay with that. I know the preacher was.

The scent of the flowers permeated the sanctuary. We never sat in the front pew, but today Murn, Starla, Grandma and I sat in the front, as close as possible to EtEt. We were on one side and the pallbearers were across the aisle from us.

Once again our pastor officiated at the funeral. As a deacon, EtEt and our pastor had worked closely together throughout the years. This must have been hard on Brother Travis. His family and ours were very close.

EtEt's favorite hymn was "In the Garden." One of Murn and EtEt's dear friends sang this during the funeral. I didn't think she was going to make it through the first verse, "I come to the garden alone, while the dew is still on the roses." Her voice began to crack as the tears rolled down her cheeks and that was when Murn began to cry. Murn held a handkerchief in her hands covering her mouth, head bowed. Starla crawled under her arm, laid her little head on Murn's breast, and patted her on the chest. I just sat there with the tears bubbling up, trying not to sob.

The service ended and the organ played as the mourners were guided out of the church, aisle by aisle. Before they closed the casket, we told him goodbye one last time. Murn patted his chest and leaned down and kissed him on the cheek as she had every morning as he left for work all their years together. I lifted Starla so she could see him. Then Murn turned around and placed her hand on my forearm as she always had on EtEt's to help her walk, took Starla by the hand, and we walked out of the church.

The funeral car was directly in front of the church doors to make it easier for Murn. It was the same place EtEt parked every Sunday morning, Sunday evening, and Wednesday night for the prayer service. So many people were standing outside the church when we came out the door; many waiting to say their goodbyes to us, but most began heading to their cars as part of the funeral procession to the cemetery. The hearse was parked just in front of the funeral car. We stood just outside the funeral car and watched as the pallbearers along each side guided the casket up the aisle and then lifted it off the wheeled cart and carried it to the hearse with our pastor following behind them. How gently the pallbearers slid the casket into the hearse and each stood peering into the hearse as if they were suspended in time as they in pairs released the casket. We didn't have that long to travel, only about 15 minutes. My memory of the graveside service was focused on Murn. Maybe somehow my brain and heart were protecting me; 15 years old and losing two dads within a month was the most tragic thing that I had ever had happen to me. The two most important men that had ever been in my life were gone forever.

The rest of the summer was the same as it would have been, but there was an empty chair. His chair in the living room with his pipe beside it, his chair at the dinner table with his special glass for iced tea, his shell-backed metal chair on the patio where he had sat at all our houses for as long as I could remember, and his seat in the car where he drove us everywhere we went. Murn carried on her daily chores, prepared full suppers, and made sure Starla and I had the same routine as we always did. And without EtEt, every Sunday we returned to Cairo to attend church and to spend time with Grandma.

One Sunday on our way out of town as we were returning home, Murn said she needed to make a stop. She turned down a street I had never been on. It was where many of the black folks lived on the northeast side of Cairo. We pulled over in front of this one particular house and she honked the horn. A black gentleman, the same one she had hugged at the visitation, came out and walked over to Murn's side of the car. It was EtEt's assistant foreman. He and EtEt always exchanged rides to work. He leaned on the window sill and placed his hand on Murn's shoulder and said, "How you doin', Mrs. Bunny?"

They spoke for a while about how EtEt died. Then Murn reached in her purse and pulled out EtEt's gold pocket watch. It was a beautiful watch. Its cover had an intricate engraving of a scene depicting a train engine traveling through the countryside. A railroad man had to have a really good timepiece and Murn had bought him that watch when he became a foreman. "Everett would want you to have this and so do I," she told him. He teared up and wiped his eyes and said, "Mrs. Bunny, I can't take that."

Murn said, "Yes, you can. I want you to." I remember seeing how touched he was and how I couldn't believe she had given EtEt's pocket watch away. How gracious, how kind, and how strong she was to be able to give away such a prized and beloved possession. I guess it was with that one act that I learned that physical things are not where memories are found; memories are imprinted on the heart.

Time moved forward and I started my sophomore year in high school and Starla started half-day kindergarten. The days must have been lonely for Murn. EtEt had been retired for a couple of years and had been at home with her all day. She must have gathered his clothes and given them away while we were in school. She protected us so very much. One time when I was much older, I said to Murn, "How come you never cried after EtEt died?" She looked at me and said, "Oh, honey, I cried. I cried in the bathroom, I cried at night when I went to bed, I cried during the day when you were gone to school and Starla would take a nap. I just didn't cry in front of you. Don't you remember at times I would go to my bedroom and shut the door? You or Starla would come to the door and ask me, 'What are you doing? What's wrong?' and I would tell you I was taking care of some business. Those were times when I needed to cry. I had two little girls to raise and I had to keep things as normal as possible. I couldn't let you girls see me break down. I didn't want you to worry or be afraid. You had been through enough."

As our lives moved forward, I was drawn even closer to Murn and helped her in ways EtEt always did when it came to lifting, taking care of the yard, going to the store, and helping with Starla. But Murn made sure I lived my life as a teenager. She never took that away from me, I think she thought I had already lost much of my young adult life through the deaths that had made me more mature in my heart and my mind. She was right; I had grown old inside my 15-year-old body. As hard as Murn tried to allow me to be youthful and carefree, I became an emotional adult, a parental figure rather than a sister to Starla, and a helpmate in many ways to Murn. As the summer was ending and another school year was beginning, we embarked on our journey together without EtEt. Looking back, Starla and I were lucky to have had two men who loved their daughters. Some kids never have one.

CHAPTER 12

Leaves of the Branches

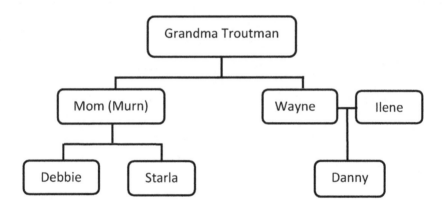

CHAPTER 12

Shadows of Summer and Darkness of Winter
Fall 1969 – Summer 1970

The cold, dark shadows of the losses of summer followed me into my sophomore year of high school. I don't remember telling anyone at school what had happened during the summer, but perhaps Murn had notified the school or maybe my closest friend had told people. I walked through my classes mechanically, with no energy, no expression, no interaction. The shadows weighed heavily upon me and made me feel very different from my other classmates. As hard as Murn tried to keep our lives normal, for a teenager, mine wasn't normal. I wasn't spending time thinking about who was going to win the next football game, what I was going to do Saturday night, or what I was going to wear to the homecoming dance. I had aged emotionally far beyond sophomoric interests. I became a worrier that fall. I worried about everything: Murn being alone, her taking care of a soon-to-be five-year-old, picking me up from high school in the winter, Murn having another heart attack, and so many things that most 15-year-olds never think about. I became old in my young mind and very serious. It was as if the shadows had swallowed my sense of humor, my ability to laugh or smile, my happiness. There were days at school that fall semester when I couldn't bear sitting in class.

All my teachers knew I was struggling deep within my soul. I was trying with everything within me to hold back tears. Most of the teachers knew I was very fond of the librarian and the attendance secretary. I couldn't go to the band room where I would have found the most comfort because my band director was only there one hour a day. I'll never forget the kindness of those insightful teachers I had in several subjects who would come over to my desk and ask, "Would you like to go to the library and check on the schedule for the filmstrip projector?" Or, "Debbie, would you take the attendance down to the office?" How did they know I was ready to burst into tears? How did they know I wasn't hearing anything they were teaching? Each teacher would then follow me to the door and into the hallway. Then, with a compassionate smile, they would tell me to take as long as I needed. I would spend the remainder of the period, sometimes into the next, hiding in the library or attendance office crying until I could pull myself together and go to my next class. As the days went on, I sat in my class and watched all the students around me, but it was as if my sadness covered me to the point that I was invisible. I was a voyeur of teenage life.

The only place I was a participant was in the band. There was a sense of comfort during that hour. Maybe it was because my dad was proud of my trumpet playing or because years ago, EtEt took me to my private lessons and would sit and listen; maybe I felt close to them when I was playing my trumpet. I loved music, I loved playing my trumpet and I took it very seriously. Perhaps because I was in the moment during band I was alive. I could express my sadness musically in a lyrically, beautiful phrase or my anger in a loud, rhythmic motif. It was as if when I walked into the band room the cloak of sadness fell from my shoulders. I could just be Debbie, a normal 15-year-old, a good musician, a good trumpet player. It was very fortunate that not only was I a good student but a good kid in general. After the events of the summer, I could have taken some pretty dark roads as a teenager, but that wasn't in my raising or my nature. Music was my drug of choice. My band director began to fill that fatherly void in my life through music. He allowed me to stretch beyond the trumpet and learn other instruments. He let me help him set up the chairs and stands for daily rehearsals and concerts and file music. As we worked together, we talked about music. He challenged my musical skills by playing duets and exercises after school with me on my trumpet and him on his saxophone. I don't think he ever really knew how important he was in my life that year as well as the years that would follow. I hope he did, although we never talked about what I had been through and how important he was in my healing.

Every morning at our high school, a student would raise the American flag on the pole that stood in front of our school and someone would say the Pledge of Allegiance over the loudspeaker. Each day when they raised that flag, I thought of the flag that covered Daddy's casket, how it was presented to me at the gravesite, and how it lay folded in a plastic bag in my closet. After a few weeks, I asked Murn if I could give it to the high school to fly every day in front of the school. That way somehow I would feel my daddy was close to me. Murn thought that would be a wonderful idea.

I took the flag one morning to the principal before school started and told him I wanted to give it to the school. When I handed the flag to him I could see in his eyes that he knew how difficult it was for me to part with it, even though I had chosen to do so. His eyes teared up, then he hugged me and told me how grateful the school was. I walked up the stairway and I stood in the hallway on the top floor that morning at a window that faced the flagpole. I don't remember what class I was supposed to be in but I just know that I was going to watch from that window as it was raised.

No one was in the hallway and it was absolutely silent, you could have heard a pin drop – rare in a large high school with three floors and three large sections on each floor. The principal came over the loudspeaker and announced that my sister and I had donated the flag to the school and that it had covered the casket of my father who had passed away that summer. He

171

explained that our dad had been a World War II veteran and the American flag covering his casket had been part of the military honors at his funeral. He thanked our family for the donation and asked for a moment of silence as they raised his flag. I stood at the window and watched the raising of his flag as a tsunami of memories and tears washed over me. It was as if the raising of that flag was the volcanic eruption of all of the emotions I had held down since the summer and an enormous wave of tears flooded my eyes.

One of my favorite teachers, my English teacher, suddenly appeared by my side. As she stood next to me, she put her arm around my shoulders and never said a word. She just made sure I wasn't alone. She was a young, first-year teacher who was very popular with her students. She had a dry, sarcastic sense of humor and made learning in her class like watching your favorite television show. She was the perfect teacher for high school students. Once the flag had been raised, she walked me down to the faculty lounge and told me to stay as long as I needed to. I sat there, alone in a dark, dingy and smoky room gasping for the emotional air to return to class. All in all, I think I somehow knew that if Murn could share EtEt's watch, then I could and should share Daddy's flag.

I was relieved to some degree when the weekends came. I didn't have to hide my feelings in front of so many for such long periods. I felt comforted, as always, by just being with Murn. She always made me feel like everything would be alright. Saturdays we spent shopping, I cleaned my room, and just helped Murn with anything she had a hard time doing alone.

We drove to our church in Cairo each Sunday and back home before evening fell. One Sunday Murn pulled off the highway just outside of Cairo on to a road known as the "seven-mile graveyard." I don't know why it was called that, there wasn't a graveyard; there were just seven miles of nothing but fields and farmland. We were on a gravel road, no one in sight, and Murn pulled over to the side and put the car in park with the engine running. Next, she said, "Get behind the wheel." I was stunned. She said, "Come on, get out and get behind the wheel," as she scooted over towards me in the passenger seat. I got out and walked around to the driver's side and slid in under the steering wheel. "You need to know how to drive in case I need you to," she said. I didn't have the driver's education class until the spring semester. Every Sunday, from that point forward, on the way home, Murn would stop at the seven-mile graveyard and let me practice each week until she was confident with my driving ability. I know now that once again, Murn was planning for any emergency. I know she was concerned that she might have another heart attack or be sick on the road, and she didn't want me to feel helpless. If I knew how to drive, I could get us to help.

As the semester moved closer to the end, the holidays brought another wave of the shadows. We spent Thanksgiving in Cairo at my Uncle Wayne's house. Grandma was there, Murn, Starla, Uncle Wayne, his wife my Aunt Ilene, and my cousin Danny. There could have been an army of people but it would have still been obvious that two were missing, EtEt and Daddy. We had had Thanksgiving at their house before, but this time it was somber: not much conversation, no family stories, no laughter, just chit-chat to fill the silence, to hold back the pangs of loss. Every so often Murn would come into the living room and with her best cheerful voice say, "What'cha doin', sweethearts?" or "Are you all about ready for dinner?" I knew that was just her way of checking on Starla and me. She knew it was hard on us, but like always, she did her best to move forward and keep things as normal as possible. But what about her? Did she decide to come to Cairo for Thanksgiving to help all of us by being surrounded by family?

Making it through Thanksgiving should have given us some emotional relief, but all it did was highlight the upcoming Christmas holidays without the two men we loved.

The Christmas concert came and went for me. Murn never got to attend our concerts at school, only at church while I was growing up. She never got to see Starla's school concerts. The schools were not handicap accessible and the parking was always a nightmare. This was many years before there were handicap parking spaces or hang tags. There was no way that Murn could maneuver the walk from the parking lot to the schools and the many stairs to the buildings and the auditoriums. The combination of polio, age, and heart attacks had limited what she once did without a bat of the eye. EtEt had been the one to attend my concerts. From now on, I would be alone at Starla's and my concerts, but Murn would take us and pick us up.

Murn's main means of shopping for presents at Christmas was ordering from the catalogs we received in the mail: Sears, J.C. Penney, Montgomery Ward, and Fingerhut. Lack of parking spaces in front of the stores, snow and ice, fighting the crowds – all were difficult for her to do alone and quite dangerous for her with her crippled leg. As soon as the catalogs arrived, Starla would go through each one over and over, marking the things she wanted.

This Christmas didn't seem that important to me. Murn decided that we would stay home for Christmas this year. I think she realized that being home together would be more comforting than being at someone else's house. She woke up early as she always did on Christmas and the smells from the kitchen brought back Christmases from the past. Instead of a turkey this year, we had a hen for just the three of us. She fixed dressing, candied sweet potatoes, dumplings, and that jellied cranberry sauce that came in the can. That morning we gathered around the tree, Starla and I on the floor, and Murn sat on the end of the couch beside us. There were presents for Starla under the tree and the presents that Starla and I had shopped for were there for Murn. Hanging on the tree was a felt Santa Claus with a zipper on the front and it said "Santa's Money Bag." Murn said, "Debbie honey, that's yours. I know there are things that you want like records and music, and I wouldn't know what to buy, so this way you can pick them out for yourself."

In Santa's bag was $100. I started to cry. Murn knew it wasn't because of disappointment or the fact that it was money instead of presents; she bent down and hugged me and we both started to cry, then Starla jumped up and put her little arms around us and we just held on to each other and cried. We hadn't done that together since the emergency waiting room right after EtEt died.

After a few moments, I felt this familiar quick "pat-pat." Murn had a way of transitioning from a difficult or tender moment with a double pat. It sounds odd, but she would just pat you twice, very quickly, and then we would move on. We both laughed, she lifted her glasses, wiped her eyes, and said, "Let's get dinner on the table, girls. I'm hungry!" We made it through our first Christmas without EtEt and Daddy. Somehow I felt EtEt's presence sitting in his chair smoking his pipe that Christmas day, along with Daddy's spirit sitting on the couch smoking a cigarette as they watched television together and talked about baseball or politics, shadows from the past. At least that's what I wanted to believe.

The holidays passed and Starla had her fifth birthday. She was a New Year's Eve baby. So we made a cake and celebrated. When she blew out her candles she wished that Daddy and EtEt were here. How hard it would be for her to grow up without really knowing those two men. All she would have would be tiny memories like the missing pieces of a huge puzzle.

A few days following her birthday it was time for me to return to school during the first of January, a new year. It seemed easier emotionally. The band

175

played for basketball games, we were preparing for band contest, I started looking through trumpet solos for solo and ensemble contest later in the spring, and Murn and Starla and I settled into a routine with just the three of us. It wasn't that we had forgotten or didn't think of EtEt and Daddy, we were just adjusting to life without them and living with their memory and their shadows.

Our kitchen table became a very sacred place. Not only was it where we came together for meals, but it was where Murn taught us about life, talked to us about things we needed to know as we were growing up, and shared with me the business side of becoming an adult. She never said it then, but I realized years later that she was making sure if anything happened to her I would know what to do, where things were, and what to do if something did happen. She always covered every base, never dropped a stitch.

The winter was very cold and we had a lot of snow. The snow and ice made it very hard for Murn to go anywhere. I didn't have my driver's license yet so she had to take us wherever we needed to go. My friend who lived next door had her license so we rode to and from school together, which helped tremendously. Starla had learned how to walk to and from home the two blocks from kindergarten. But there were still errands that needed to be run and shopping to do. My job was to keep a path cleared from the back door to the car so Murn could get in the driver's side door. We would all go to the grocery store together, Murn, Starla, and me. I would help her from the car to the store, reach items too high for her, and load the groceries into and out of the car on our return home.

But every Sunday, rain, snow, or shine, we went to our church in Cairo. We started going down on Saturdays to visit with Grandma so Murn could help Grandma do whatever she needed help with. Then we might stop in and see Uncle Wayne and Aunt Ilene or some of Murn's friends, and sometimes I would visit my friends. Then we would stay all night at a small family-owned motel. We knew the owners and it was a very nice motel and Murn could drive up right in front of our room. Those Saturday evenings in the motel became special times. Murn would make sure we had snacks and sodas, and we would watch television together: *The Jackie Gleason Show*, *My Three Sons*, *Green Acres*, *Petticoat Junction*, and sometimes *NBC Saturday Night at the Movies*. Not only were those special times together, but they put fun, laughter, and happiness back into our lives and helped heal our wounded souls. Sunday morning, we would check out of the motel and go pick up Grandma at her house, then to Sunday school and church. Usually after church, we would take Grandma out for Sunday dinner or pick up food and take it to her house. Then we would start the trip back home. I swear there were times that winter I thought we were going to slide the whole way! Murn was never afraid, or at least she never showed it. I think she enjoyed the challenge of driving on ice and snow!

Late in February, Uncle Wayne called to tell Murn that Grandma had climbed on a stool to get something off of a high shelf and had fallen and broken her pelvis. She was in the hospital in Cairo and was okay but he thought Grandma wanted Murn to come. Murn was her only remaining daughter and while Uncle Wayne and Aunt Ilene certainly looked after her, they were working every day and, well, a mother wants her daughter with her at times like these.

I was in school during the week, so Murn made arrangements for Starla and me to stay with her dear friend Edna and her husband, Doc. This was the couple that had taken Starla's half-sister to raise. Grandma's prognosis was not good. Grandma had osteoporosis so bad. Her bones were full of holes like a honeycomb which meant there was little chance of the bones healing.

Murn came home just before the weekend to pick us up and then return to Cairo. She looked tired and worried. Looking back, I'm sure she knew that

Grandma would never return to her little home. I'm sure she was concerned too, that we were an hour away and it was going to be difficult for her to be raising us and tending to Grandma.

As the days passed, Grandma developed pneumonia which is common following a break like this in the elderly when confined to a bed for many days. Grandma was transferred to the nursing home wing of the hospital, St. Anthony Hall. Starla and I were never allowed to see her in the hospital because visitors had to be 18 to visit the patients at that time. Once she was moved to the nursing home wing, we could visit her. I remember seeing her in the hospital bed; she was so thin and in so much pain. I never remember ever hearing my Grandma complain or say anything negative. She was such a demure, kind, and gentle soul. She would flinch every so often and her eyes didn't twinkle like they once did. She would try to talk to us but the phlegm in her chest and throat made her cough, and it was difficult for her. It was difficult for us to watch her struggle.

I watched Murn as she would lift Grandma's shoulders and pull her over to the side and hold her in her arms so she could spit out the phlegm; Murn's face reflected the pain that Grandma felt. She then would lay her back down, wipe Grandma's mouth, and give her a drink of water. Grandma would cry out with the slightest movement of her hips and legs. "Mom, are you in a lot of pain? Do you need a pain pill?" Murn would ask.

Grandma would shake her head no as she grasped the bed rails on each side of her. Her tiny hands and arms now had large veins that looked not just like the lines on a road map but a topical map of the mountains and valleys of her life. Her knuckles were enlarged with arthritis which made her fingers look even thinner. I could tell it was hard for Murn to leave her; the difficulty and fear were in her voice when she would say, "Mom, we're going to have to get on the road. Debbie has school tomorrow, but I'll be back to check on you in a day or two."

Grandma would whisper a barely audible, "Okay." No requests, no pleading not to leave, just a little whimper of a cry and a tear in her eye.

Murn would lean down and kiss Grandma on her cheek and say, "I love you, Mom," and Grandma would mouth, "I love you, too," and nod her head.

Murn always talked to the nurses and the sister supervising the nursing home wing before she would leave, letting them know when she would be back. I didn't think of it then, but it must have been so very hard for Murn to leave her mother in that condition and to be so far away. It must have brought back memories of having to leave Aunt Kitten. As a teenager, I didn't realize the strain the past year had placed on Murn. At Grandma's age, I'm sure Murn knew that this was probably not going to end well. The loss of Daddy and EtEt both was so sudden and unexpected. The shock was difficult enough but the grief that followed was a day-to-day battle. It must have been difficult and heartbreaking for Murn to know that every time she left Grandma it might be the last time she would see her alive, hold her hand, feel Grandma's hand on her face or hear, regardless of how faint, her mother say, "I love you."

When we arrived home, Murn would wash our clothes and prepare everything for the next week when she would be traveling up and down the road to check on Grandma. She must have been exhausted. It was visible that the emotional weight of the past year had gradually affected her physical strength. She was tired. We had been here before. How much could Murn take? How much could *we* take?

Before Murn could return to Cairo, she received a call that one of the nursing home workers had left one of the bedrails down and during the night Grandma had tried to grab for the rail and had rolled out of bed and onto the hot radiator beside her bed. She was so weak; her little voice wasn't loud enough for anyone to hear her and she laid on that radiator until an aide found her. The radiator left deep burns on Grandma's chest and arms. Murn was furious! We never knew who left the bedrail down, but they were never left down again.

The next day, Murn left for Cairo. Starla and I stayed with Edna and Doc again while Murn left to be with Grandma. It wasn't but a couple of days before the call came that Grandma had passed away. How was it possible? It had only been seven months since we lost EtEt and the month before, Daddy. Murn was coming home to get us and return to Cairo for the visitation on Friday evening and the funeral on Saturday.

That upcoming weekend was the Illinois High School Association organizational contest. Our band was to play that Saturday and I was one of the first chair trumpet players. I never knew who initiated the discussion with Murn regarding my participation. She wanted me to be at the visitation, but told me, "There's nothing you can do for Grandma now, but performing with the band is important for the band and you. Grandma wouldn't want you to miss the contest." Somehow between Murn, my band director, and the English teacher who had stood with me as Daddy's flag was raised at the high school that fall, the decision was made that the English teacher was going to drive to Cairo Friday evening, pick me up at the visitation, take me back to her house, let me stay overnight, and then get me to the band bus on Saturday.

The evening of the visitation it was cold and dark and it had been snowing since that morning. The sidewalks were constantly being cleared for the visitors, but the snow kept falling. I helped Murn into the building the way EtEt had always done with Murn on his side holding on to his forearm. I had become accustomed to how to help her walk by letting her hold on to me. Once again, there we were: Murn, Starla, and me at the same funeral home where Aunt Kitten, Daddy, and EtEt rested. Their shadows stood around us.

Grandma looked so peaceful, so at rest. This time the casket spray had beautiful roses and a ribbon that said "Mother," one that said "Grandmother," and one that said "Great-Grandmother."

Grandma looked so petite and delicate lying there. She was wearing a pale lavender shroud and her hair was beautiful, as it always was. Aunt Ilene was a beautician and had always styled her hair each week. She had styled it this last time; how hard that must have been for Aunt Ilene. Uncle Wayne and Murn stood at the casket with his arm around Murn as they cried. I don't remember my Uncle Joe being there. He was the baby of her eight children and had not always been around when the family needed him. They were the only three left of her eight children. I don't remember crying; I guess I didn't have any tears left. I loved my grandmother dearly, but the previous eight months had robbed me of shedding a tear for her that evening. The snow continued to pound as the evening progressed. That didn't stop the mourners from attending; even the older members of our church came. The ladies in her Sunday school class always called Grandma simply "Troutman." I always thought that was funny. Her first name was Edith, but all the older ladies in her age group called each other by their last names. So did Murn's group of friends. It was as if they had all been on a basketball team or something.

The evening slowly moved along and my English teacher arrived. I looked up and there she was with that grin to one side that she always had when she was being genuine and compassionate. She offered her condolences to Murn and introductions were made to our family, small as it was. Murn thanked her for her willingness to make the trip and allow me to stay with her in order for me to attend the contest. They spoke for a few minutes and then Murn said we needed to get on the road because the snow wasn't letting up. She cautioned us to be careful and told me to play well at the contest. She said she would probably be back home by the time I got back to the school from the contest and if for some reason she wasn't, Edna would pick me up. It was hard leaving Murn that night – leaving her in her sorrow, with Starla to take care of, a snowstorm, and knowing how tired and exhausted she must have been. She assured me that Uncle Wayne would help her get to the car and follow her to the motel.

My teacher and I made our way to her Volkswagen Beetle and began our journey home. The snow was unforgiving and the roads had barely been plowed. I'm sure the roads were covered again as soon as the plows had made their pass. It was like a whiteout. We could see nothing and we were moving at a snail's pace, just creeping along. The closer we moved toward home, the snow began to let up a bit. What should have been an easy hour drive took a little over two.

It was strange being at my teacher's mobile home, but she made it very easy for me. She was always up on the newest songs, television shows, and pop culture in general. Earlier that day she had just received the new Simon and Garfunkel album, *Bridge Over Troubled Water*. She placed the record on the stereo and we listened while we had a soda. She had to make a phone call and went back to her bedroom. I sat on the couch in her living room and played the song over and over.

I loved all of Simon and Garfunkel's songs, but this song resonated so strongly with me. The music was certainly stirring and moving but there was something more. Many of the words that were used in the lyrics were as if they were chosen just for me and what I was feeling. I was so *weary* after losing Daddy, EtEt, and Grandma; we all were weary. It seemed as if there were always *tears* in my eyes. It was one of the *roughest* times in my life and while I had *friends*, I couldn't find friends that understood my feelings. I felt as if *darkness* swallowed me and *pain* surrounded me every waking moment. I had several *bridges* that covered my turbulent waters daily. Murn was certainly my bridge, but there were also a few of my teachers, the school librarian, and the school secretary. They *comforted* me and *eased my mind* day after day allowing me to keep moving forward to the end of the school year. Music has always touched my heart and was a way for me to express my feelings. "Bridge Over Troubled Water" was much more than any other song; it was a recording of my teenage life.

That song became my voice; it resounded in my heart daily for months and the next few years. That evening, it saved me. I fell asleep on the couch listening to it. The next morning came and my teacher dropped me off at the band room to catch the bus for the contest. She had gone so far out of her way to help us in my time of need. She was the perfect person to comfort me at that point. She just had a way that resonated with me as a teenager. I was always grateful to her for her understanding and kindness throughout my sophomore year and the friendship that continued throughout my high school years.

Being with the band the day of the funeral helped take my mind off of the sadness. We performed well at the contest and received a first. But even with the distractions, I continued to worry about Murn. The snow had stopped earlier in the wee hours of the morning, but it had piled up several inches, more so in Cairo. That weekend was one of the record snowstorms for Cairo, Illinois. The plows had had more success in clearing the roads, so I wasn't as worried about Murn and Starla driving home. The band bus didn't arrive home until early evening, and Murn and Starla were there waiting for me. As it turned out, there was no graveside service for Grandma. The ground was too frozen and when they did reach the correct depth, the grave kept filling with water. Grandma wasn't buried next to Grandpa Burris until later that spring. As I look back, that must have been hard for Murn and Uncle Wayne, waiting to have their mother placed in her final resting place.

Grandma's rent had been paid for the month which gave Murn, Uncle Wayne, and Aunt Ilene the time needed to separate and organize Grandma's belongings. Murn would send me off to school as she had all my life, then she and Starla would drive to Cairo and spend the day completing the hard task of going through Grandma's personal belongings, household items, and furniture deciding what to keep, who should be given what, or what to do with various items. Then she would return home, emotionally and physically exhausted, before I got out of school.

My days at school always began in the auditorium before the bell rang for classes to start. The auditorium was always empty and dark. I just didn't want to be in a large group of my peers. I was now more than ever introverted with my sadness. I had purchased the sheet music to "Bridge Over Troubled Water" and sat at the grand piano in front of the stage and played it over and over until the bell rang. Often I would see my English teacher standing inside one of the doors which led from the second-floor hallway to the balcony watching and listening, but she never said a word. Just like when she stood next to me as Daddy's flag was raised, she was just there, "...like a bridge over troubled water." The waters that had swallowed me that school year had left me depleted with no air to sigh, no tears to weep, and no words to cry. I was simply floating. It was as if I were sitting at the bottom of deep water.

One day I came home from school and there where our light blue Ford Comet station wagon had always sat was a brand-new 1969 white Ford Maverick. Murn had purchased a new car. We had never had a new car; they were always used. Then, of course, EtEt and Daddy were alive and they knew how to fix something or EtEt would just take it to the garage to be fixed. Murn was happy, I could tell. She said that we needed a dependable car since it was just us girls, so she bought a new one. It was strange how that car marked our year of grief, 1969–70. I'll always remember how Murn looked in that car. She was so short; you could just see her head above the steering wheel. Here was this brand new car sitting next to Daddy's old Ford Fairlane. In some way, it represented what now was and what used to be. The three of us, Murn, Starla, and I, were truly on our own, alone.

That spring we continued to drive to Cairo to go to church. I could tell Murn loved driving the Maverick. She was a good driver with a bit of a lead foot. The route we would take to Cairo was very hilly and had some large curves. I was often afraid, going down one of the huge curving hills, that we were going to go flying into space. Murn would just laugh and say, "We're fine, I'm in control." I'm sure the carpet was a little thinner from my foot "braking" on the passenger side of the car every time she took one of those hills! She was always in control regardless of the situation, literally or figuratively.

Summer came and the anniversary of Daddy's death came with my birthday that June. But that was my 16th birthday and I was getting my license. His car was not suitable for me to drive. It had not been driven for a year. Murn agreed to let me trade it in for a red Volkswagen Beetle. It was hard saying goodbye to Daddy's car. I could still smell his cologne mixed with cigarette smoke, see him sitting behind the wheel, and see his arm waving out the window when he would drive away.

I was on wheels and slowly smiles, laughter, and happiness began to replace the sadness that had consumed me during the past year. Most summer days were spent sleeping late; 9:00 was about as late as late could be at our house. For the first time, I was beginning to feel like a teenager. I played in the Murphysboro Municipal and Union Band that summer on Monday and Thursday evenings and got a paycheck for playing. My VW had bouts of not starting or simply stopping as I was driving! Sometimes I think I pushed it as much as I drove it. We never did figure out what was wrong with it. When it wouldn't start that summer, my band director, who owned a VW Karmann

Ghia, would come by the house and get it running. He was so important to me in my teen years and how grateful Murn was for him. I loved that red bug, not so much because of its lack of dependability, but because in many ways it helped to free me from the shadows of the previous summer and the darkness of the recent winter. It allowed me to see just a glimmer of sunlight again.

CHAPTER 13

Leaves of the Branches

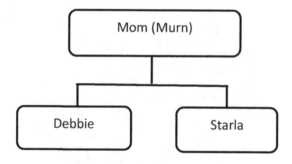

CHAPTER 13

Life Goes On
Summer 1970 - Spring 1972

I had a group of friends, all who were in the band, that I spent free Saturday nights with the summer before my junior year. Three of us were going to be juniors and three were to be seniors, two girls and four boys. We were good kids, responsible, and no trouble to anyone. Our exciting evening was spent getting something to eat, usually pizza, and then bowling. We were always home by curfew and were in the mature, responsible hands of one of the seniors who always drove his parents' tank of a car. We often ate boxes of raisins in the car as our senior chauffeur picked us up and delivered each of us safely home. There was only one time during our Saturday night routine when we worried our parents.

One summer Saturday night our driver, Chris, was delivering the first drop-off when he turned left off of a two-lane highway onto a blacktop country road. His turn was a little wide and the wheels caught the mud shoulder and the tank slid into the ditch! Raisins and balled-up socks from bowling flew throughout the car like a hailstorm of sock balls. When the motion stopped, there we sat, three in the front, three in the back, crushing the passengers on the passenger sides of the car. Shoulder to shoulder, cheek to cheek, stacked like the three monkeys in the front and the back – hear no evil, see no evil, speak no evil. Silence. From the outside in the pitch black, we must have looked like a family of raccoons inside the car with only the whites of our big eyes visible.

After what seemed like an eternity, the silence was broken by our chauffeur in a low, quiet, nasal, matter-of-fact voice saying, "Well, I don't think we're going to make it home by curfew." A loud burst of laughter ensued with shouts of "Get off of me! You're crushing me! I can't move!" filling the car as we all began climbing up and out of the driver-side doors like clowns exiting a clown car at the circus. There we stood in darkness while two of the guys walked up the hill to a house – the only house with a small light shining in the window. No one got in trouble that night except the car, which had to be towed the next day. Those guys never knew, but they were my freedom from worry, from responsibility, and from music, even if it was just for one night a week. It was those Saturday nights with them when I felt my age, finding laughter and peace of mind.

Starla started kindergarten for a full day this year. Murn would take her and pick her up each day. Starla and I didn't interact very much; 10 years is a big difference in age when it's between a teenager and a youngster. Murn and Starla spent most of their time together. Murn would hold her on her lap and read to her. They would put puzzles together, play board games and practice all the things she was learning in kindergarten. Considering everything, Starla appeared to be a typical five-year-old. Through the years Murn had always stopped her housework during the day to watch her favorite soap operas, *Search for Tomorrow* and *As the World Turns*. It seemed to be the only thing that Murn truly did for herself.

As a 16-year-old beginning my junior year in high school I was a dichotomy walking, an antonym between my emotional and physical age. While I experienced some healing during the summer and Murn did her best to create a home full of love and happiness, encouraging me to be a typical teenager, it couldn't change the darkness that hung inside me. What for my age should have been a glass full and running over, the losses in our life had instead left my teenage glass half empty. At the same time, the losses had forced me into adulthood resulting in a glass half full. I was caught between young and old, a rock and a hard place, and night and day. I wore a solemn, serious exterior that protected me from the world and further hurt. My biggest fear was that I would lose Murn, too. I felt the weight of fear and responsibility, not because Murn had placed it there, but because I knew the weight she was carrying and I didn't want her to do it alone.

My mind was focused on only two things: Murn and music. This was the year that I learned what it meant to worry. I worried daily that something would happen to Murn. I worried when she took Starla back and forth to school that she would have car trouble. I worried when she said she was going to the grocery store that she might have a wreck. I worried when she would wash the clothes and hang them on the clothesline; there was a decline in the yard that sharply dropped off to the gravel alley and I was worried that she might lose her balance and fall. I worried that she would have another heart attack. And most of all, I worried that she might die.

It was 1970 and the Vietnam war was still taking young lives; protests were escalating on college campuses by rioters in hip-huggers, sandals, love beads and hair, lots of hair! The air was filled with the smoke from joints and smoke bombs, a mixture that divided the youth and the police. While drinking, drugs or toking was common among college students, they had also found their way into high schools. Some of my classmates partook of one or the other or both.

The love and obsession I previously had for music was minimal compared to what it was about to become; it had been my drug of choice, but shortly it was going to become my full-blown, mind-altering, raging addiction. If I wasn't in class, I was absorbed in music – before school, lunch, after school, evenings, at home, and always on my mind. The hours I spent in chemistry, trigonometry, upper track English, and American history were boring to me. I had no interest. The one hour of band each day wasn't enough. The fall semester gave me weekends with parades and halftime shows at the football games but I needed more.

I began practicing my trumpet more than ever. I had always participated in solo and ensemble contests, auditioned and earned a chair in camp bands, district bands, and festivals, and played in the Murphysboro Municipal and Union Band during the summers. This year I increased my practice time to make sure I earned a seat in the All-State band or orchestra. I spent hours after school practicing with my band director to prepare for many opportunities. I earned the first chair first in the All-State band that year, the top trumpet player. I earned a first on my solo and duet at the contest and played for the basketball games almost every weekend. That still wasn't enough. With the blessing of the administration, I started what became known as Funny Company. I organized a show, selected music for a pit band, rehearsed all the music, recruited classmates to perform, directed the show, and conducted the pit band. We performed the show for the entire student body and it was a hit! I was a Judy Garland and Mickey Rooney all rolled into one!

I guess I was getting a little too big for my britches that year. Murn and I always got along and I don't ever remember but a couple of occasions where we had disagreements. I do remember one specific time when she was in the utility room folding clothes from the dryer when I walked in to ask her a question. Murn was a stickler for cleanliness and between cleaning the house, cooking meals, and washing clothes, she was always busy. I would come home from school, change clothes, go back to a rehearsal, and when I came home later that evening, the clothes I had taken off after school had been washed and were hanging in my closet. As I started to leave the utility room she reminded me that she had told me I needed to clean my room and I'd better have it done that day. Well, she kept talking about it and as I was walking away, I mumbled under my breath, "Oh just shut up!"

Before I knew what had happened, her hand came from behind me and popped me in the mouth! "Don't you ever talk back to me again!" she said. That was the first time Murn had ever done that. I had never been disrespectful and she had never slapped me. I started crying immediately and went to my room and shut the door.

Murn had a way of being done with something once she had her say. Before I could sit down, she came to my bedroom door and said, "Open this door." Then in this sweet, kind voice, she said, "What do you want for dinner tonight, Debbie girl?"

My junior year passed and soon another summer rolled around and again it was all about practicing and playing in the municipal and union bands. While many of my friends had jobs during the summer and often during the school year, Murn had always told me that my job was to make good grades in school and her job was to provide everything I needed.

I had an interest in photography and owned a Mamiya Sekor SLR camera with lenses. I often went to a photography shop to ask questions and buy film. For the summer the owner asked if I wanted to make some money by placing corrective fluid on black and white photos. I used a tiny brush and had to black out all of the white filaments that showed up on the prints. I made 50 cents an hour. That job didn't last very long and I'm sure it contributed to my having to eventually wear glasses!

On occasion, my band director would take me with him to a music store about 30 miles away to search for contest solos and ensembles for the year. Some weekends I was allowed to go with my band director or the assistant band director to play a dance gig with their combos. These were such good men and Murn trusted them or I never would have been allowed to go. I learned so much musically from those experiences and, without knowing it, they helped to fill that void of my dad and EtEt.

We had stopped driving to Cairo for church on Sundays. I think the trip was getting harder for Murn. Grandma and Daddy weren't there to visit and I was so involved in activities I think Murn realized I didn't want to be gone over the weekend. There was a little country church about 18 miles away from where we lived and Murn had some connection with the minister there, so we began attending that church. Our church in Cairo had been Bible-based and that's what Murn wanted. While Sunday mornings we were in church, I think she was worried that Starla wasn't having the rich religious upbringing and church activities that I had growing up. That was a major concern for Murn. So every opportunity she found for Starla to attend Vacation Bible School or a youth activity with one of her little friends, Murn encouraged it and made sure she attended.

One would have thought my activities during my junior year would have been enough but they weren't. During my senior year I was president of the Band Council and not only did I have parades and football games, but my director let me design and teach a football show. I was first chair first in our band and was often allowed to conduct the band. I developed a new Funny Company show and produced it during the fall semester. This time I included faculty in the skits. I was still practicing for auditions in the district and All-State band/orchestra along with preparing a solo and ensemble for the contest. I sat first chair first trumpet in the All-State orchestra that year, the best in the state.

During the basketball season, my band director would often have to leave early because he had a gig most weekends. When he had to leave he would hand me the keys to lock up the band room afterward and I would conduct the band for the remainder of the game then lock up once the instruments

194

were all put away and everyone cleared out; I made sure everything was locked tight. Still, it all wasn't enough.

My reputation as a fine young musician was relatively well known throughout the area. I was asked to rehearse the band and choir at a high school 20 miles away. The teacher was going to be absent one day and it was very close to an organizational contest for bands and choirs. I asked Murn if I could skip school to do it and she agreed; she knew how important it was for me. That morning in my red Volkswagen I made my way to that high school and conducted the rehearsals.

I decided I wanted to direct a musical during the spring semester. I went through all of the channels and the school approved it and paid for the royalties and costs involved. *Bubble Trouble*, an off, off, off-Broadway musical was my first musical theater production; I directed, conducted, designed the set, organized the costuming, and handled the publicity. I recruited crews and gave directions as to their jobs. I had a set of keys to the school and held rehearsals after school, and in the evenings and built the set on weekends. As I said, Judy and Mickey had nothing on me.

I would also ask to go to the auditorium to work on the set during classes I just wasn't interested in. One particular class was physics. The teacher was kind and a good teacher, but I just didn't care about the subject. I would never have wanted to take physics but the guidance counselor said I was a high-track student and I should take it. I probably pushed to leave his class more than the others because he was so nice about it. I would turn in my assignment if there was any and ask if I could go to the auditorium. He always said yes. One day I was in the auditorium and the principal came over the loudspeaker and asked, "Debbie, are you in the auditorium?" I quickly responded and then he asked that I come to the principal's office.

195

I was used to getting called to the office to sign for lumber, printing, or general deliveries for the musical so I thought nothing of it. When I got to the principal's office the secretaries who knew me so well gave me the raised eyebrow with their eyes rolling with a tilt of their head over to his office and pointed for me to go in. When I came around the counter I saw my physics teacher sitting there with his grade book in hand. I was told to have a seat and my teacher began to read off to the principal all the days I had not been in class. I was furious! I challenged him by saying, "I asked you if I could go and you said yes!"

The principal looked at me and in no uncertain terms made it clear: "Debbie, you will attend this class every day from now until school is out. Do you understand?"

In as cold a response as I could muster from behind my gritted teeth I uttered, "Yes." I had NEVER been in trouble at school. I was so angry when I left the principal's office that I pushed the door so hard it flew open and hit the lockers just outside the main office, making an explosion of a sound. Then as I never had done before, I dropped the F-bomb. "Fuck you!" I bellowed.

After hearing my commentary echo through the halls, I have to admit I was a little scared that administrators and teachers would be pouring into the hallway to give me a detention. But nothing ever came of it and I went to physics every day from that day forward and had nothing to say to my teacher for the rest of the year. This was probably my first act of intentional passive-aggressiveness! Despite being required to attend classes daily, the musical was a hit at school and in the community. At the end of the performance for the school, the principal came up on the stage and called me up from the pit. He presented me with a dozen long-stemmed red roses. Little did I know until years later that the roses were from my physics teacher.

As my senior year was coming to an end, I was still haunted by Simon and Garfunkel's "Bridge Over Troubled Water." I wanted to arrange the song for the band and conduct it at our spring concert. For one whole week, I spent the wee hours of the mornings arranging the song, writing the score by hand and preparing the manuscript part for each instrument. I conducted that piece at our senior band concert. It summarized my years in high school and expressed what I couldn't express with words. It was the culmination of what music had been to me. Music had been not just a raging addiction, but the bridge over *my* troubled waters along with Murn.

I had always planned on going to college and Murn had always encouraged me. She said she wasn't sure how we would handle it financially, but I *would* go to college. I'm sure she had prayed about it for most of my high school years. Of the eight children my grandma Troutman bore, only Murn went to college. She attended Brown's Business College in Cape Girardeau, Missouri. As a young woman, she worked as a bookkeeper at Sullivan Electric Company in Cairo. I guess that was where she was working when she met Harry before they were married. She worked for several years until she began having nightmares where she was trying to put large font numbers into tiny little squares. That was the point that she decided it was time to quit.

Murn valued education. There was never any question when purchasing items for school, regardless of what it was. Although money was often tight, I remember the day a salesman came to the door selling encyclopedias when I was in elementary school. Murn reviewed the samples carefully and decided that it would be good for me to have my own set at home. I'm not sure where the money came from, but I'm pretty sure it was a monthly payment. I used that set of *Compton's Encyclopedia* throughout my education.

While Julliard School of Music in New York had always been on my mind as to where I wanted to go to college, my dad begged Murn not to allow me to go before he died. He said that I was too timid and wouldn't be safe in a big city. When it came time to apply to colleges, it was never an issue. There was no possible way I would have left Murn alone to raise Starla or even to leave Murn.

I was named an Illinois State Scholar for excellence in music and the arts that year. It guaranteed my college tuition for four years. I also had knee issues, which eventually was identified as Osgood-Schlatters disease. The condition was identified during my senior year by a state rehabilitation agency which had been alerted by my high school guidance office, based on a request for a physical education waiver from my physician. I wanted to be a band director and according to them, I wouldn't be able to march by the time I was 30. Because of this, they would have paid my tuition to college. But since I was an Illinois State Scholar and my tuition was covered, instead they paid for my mileage to and from school, my books, and a stipend for my lunches. Because I was going to college, my Veteran's and Social Security benefits from my dad would continue until I was 22. The prayers of Murn resulted in more bridges over our "troubled waters" than we ever imagined!

My high school graduation was finally here. It was really "our" graduation. Murn deserved it as much as I did. She had completed and exceeded all the requirements of a parent in raising a child, taught me everything a soon-to-be 18-year-old should know about life and living, grounded me in a Christian education, and maintained an A+ average in all she did throughout everything we had been through. In fact, *she* was a valedictorian!

Murn was determined that she was going to see me walk across the stage and receive my diploma. I was worried because the ceremony was to be held at the football field. Parking and maneuvering the bleachers were going to be difficult for Murn. She said for me not to worry, she was going. We went early, very early, and parked right in front of the gates and I helped Murn up the ramp and found a place on the bottom row of the bleachers. Starla and she sat there throughout the ceremony and waited until I came to help her back to the car.

I'm sure she cried during the ceremony – tears of joy, pride, relief, and tears of sadness, loss, and loneliness. There were just the three of us. She must have worried whether she would ever see Starla graduate and who would sit at Starla's graduation. Murn was approaching 65 and Starla was going to turn eight that year. Ten more years before Starla would walk across the stage. Murn must have wondered if she would live to see it and if she had the strength to help her grow and guide her into her teen years as she had me. We had been through so much and she had worked so hard to see that I was successful. I'm sure she was happy with who I had become and I'm sure EtEt and my dad would have been too.

Mother didn't come for my graduation. Since she never had one and didn't really value education, I don't think she realized the milestone and I know she didn't understand the magnitude of my achievements. By this time in my life, Mother didn't know anything about me or my interests or accomplishments. But she loved me as much as she knew how and I loved her for who she was. It was okay that she wasn't there because the person who had always been there for me was Murn.

My best friend and neighbor who had graduated the year before came on her brother's motorcycle and we were going out for pizza afterward. Once Murn was safely in the car and on her way home, I left with my friend. I'll never forget us riding off of the football field with me on the back of that motorcycle with cap in hand and robe flowing in the breeze as she took me home to change. Murn was so proud and I know relieved that despite everything we had been through, we made it. Regardless of what life had thrown at us in the past, I learned that life goes on. We never got over what we had been through; we just learned to build bridges over the hard times. Murn, Starla, and me.

CHAPTER 14

Leaves of the Branches

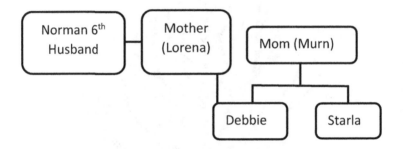

CHAPTER 14

A Coming of Age
Summer 1972 – Summer 1973

The summer after my graduation began with a senior band trip to Gatlinburg, Tennessee, chaperoned by my band director and his wife along with their three young boys. What a great time we had. I turned 18 while we were there and purchased my first beer at Lum's restaurant. Eighteen was the legal drinking age in Tennessee at the time and I must say we abided by the law. Before we left on the trip, I shared with Murn that the drinking age would be 18 and I would be there on my birthday. She knew where I was going with this discussion but I was hesitant to ask the question I was hedging. Then Murn, in her all-knowing way, said, "You know I believe the beer I liked the best when I tried a few was Miller High Life." And that recommendation was the one I followed when purchasing my first beer and toasting Murn.

I had decided to attend the summer session at Southern Illinois University in Carbondale, Illinois. No sense putting it off until fall. The campus was large and there were so many students from so many different countries. I entered as a music education major and trumpet was my primary instrument. That summer I also took over as conductor of the Murphysboro Municipal and Union Band. What an honor to conduct a band filled with professional musicians and area music teachers along with community musicians and peers. Monday nights were rehearsals at the band shell in the park and Thursday evenings we played two concerts, one always at the park and one usually at one of the nursing homes.

My little red Volkswagen wasn't dependable enough to drive the eight miles to college every day so it was traded in for a 1968 Ford Mustang. It was metallic green with a dark green material-covered roof. Oddly enough, my best friend who lived next door was given an identical Ford Mustang but a 1967. Mine was an automatic and hers was a standard; they sat side by side in our parking lot. Murn had cashed out the $1,000 insurance policy that she had cashed out many times and then paid back for so many things: partial payments on funerals, my trumpets, down payments on my cars, and eventually things for Starla.

Taking classes in the summer allowed me to take a few general studies classes to make way for more practice time in my schedule during the fall and spring. Science was never my strong area so one of the classes I decided to take was Geology 105. It was my first experience with a class where the teaching associate was an international student. I couldn't understand a word he said! The professor had turned the class over to him and I was not only subject bored but language bored! Our class was held in a small lecture hall that held about 75 students.

One day as I sat trying to find something of interest to focus on during the hour, I noticed that other students were drinking sodas, eating snacks, and smoking – SMOKING! After class, I made my way over to the cafeteria and purchased my first pack of Marlboro cigarettes. I carried that tiny red and white package with what I thought would be boredom breakers the rest of the day until I could get home to my best friend to teach me how to inhale! That evening I almost made myself sick as I struggled to become a truly skilled smoker. My geology class became more bearable as I puffed away the remaining class meetings along with my soda and snacks to keep me entertained. I had become a true college student.

When July came Murn asked me to sit down at the table with her. When I sat down Murn slid my Veteran's and Social Security checks across the table to me. They had my name where it had always before said Murn's name "for Deborah Burris." I wasn't sure why the change or why Murn was giving them to me. Softly Murn said, "Debbie, I'm no longer your custodian. You're an adult and now your money comes directly to you. You'll need to get a checking account and manage your own money."

My heart dropped to my stomach! "What do you mean? Do you want me to leave? Do I have to move out?" Tears started rolling down my cheeks, my nose started running, and I began heaving uncontrollably. I didn't want to leave. I wanted to stay with Murn and commute to college.

Murn smiled and almost laughed at me! "No, honey, you don't have to move out. I'm just doing what I'm supposed to do. This is your money now; I can't be in control of it any longer. We'll get you a checking account set up and if you need me to help you, I will."

I wiped my tears and began to breathe normally. "Don't you need this money for the house?"

"No, I can handle the house expenses. But if you'd like to contribute to the living expenses, that would be nice," she said.

While my friends were excited to go away to college, living in a dorm or apartment, I was terrified that I might have to. Just like when I was seven years old, I knew where I wanted to be – with Murn. I knew at 18 where I wanted to be. I loved our home, I loved Murn, I knew she needed me but she would never have held me back. She couldn't have pushed this bird from the nest with a bulldozer. Along the way she would often ask, "Debbie, wouldn't you like to get your own place?"

That would send me into a panic attack. "Why do you say that? Do you want me to leave?"

"No, but I want you to know it's alright if you want to. You don't have to stay here because of me. I'll be okay," she'd say. I loved her for loving me enough to let me go but loving me more to have me stay.

My general studies classes were pretty low on my priority list but I survived and my professors survived me. In addition to summer classes and conducting the municipal band, I was also directing and conducting a musical for the local festival held each September. *Anything Goes* was the first Broadway show I selected. We were all teenagers but we did it ourselves. Even though I had graduated, I still had keys to the school with their permission and signed for all purchases. The musical was scheduled for two nights and we sold out both; we thought we were stars! The municipal band and the musical kept all of us busy. There was no time for us to get into teenage trouble, at least not as much as those who weren't involved perhaps did.

Fall came and I was deep into my music classes and ensembles. By now I had become a Marlboro woman! I was foolish to think Murn didn't know I was smoking just like she knew I wanted to try beer, but I was 18; I was smarter than she was. It wasn't odd for me to run over to my friend's house in the evenings or maybe go to the Dairy Queen for a soda during warm weather to grab a smoke, but it was getting colder and not comfortable to sit outside. The Marlboro man began calling me before bedtime and I would tell Murn I was going out to get a soda. But now I was having to sit in the car to smoke and to stay warm. And that was my downfall.

It never entered my mind that Murn would smell it on my clothes. Lots of people smoked then. It was very common, except in our house. One night when I casually told her I was going to get a soda, she called me into her bedroom and asked me to sit down on the bed. Murn placed her hand on mine and said, "Honey, that cigarette isn't going to keep you very warm in the winter, so if you're going to smoke, smoke at home."

Oh my gosh! How did she know? "What? What do you mean?" I retorted.

"I know you're smoking, I can smell it on your clothes. I wish you wouldn't, but if you're going to, I'd rather you not run out at night driving around in the car."

After recovering from the shock that Murn knew I was smoking, I was perplexed that I didn't receive a stern lecture. As I thought about it, I remembered a moment when I was about 12 or 13 when we lived in Cairo. One early morning after EtEt had left for work I came downstairs and found Murn struggling to set a tea cup on one of the top shelves in the cabinet over the sink. She could barely reach the top. Her arm was extended as her other hand held tightly to the sink, and her crippled leg was off the ground as she stretched with all her body to place the cup on that top shelf. I surprised her when I asked what she was doing because that wasn't where the cups were stored.

She was startled and brought the cup down and the look on her face let me know she had been caught, but for what, I wondered. As I moved closer, I saw it: a partially smoked cigarette and a new one. I knew EtEt smoked but why were those in a cup that she was trying to place on the top shelf that she could barely reach? Murn knew she had to explain it. She confessed. She told me she sometimes got nervous and just took a couple of puffs then put it out; that she didn't do it all the time and she never smoked a whole cigarette.

I never saw Murn smoke ever after getting caught. I can't help but wonder if she ever took a couple of puffs again or she simply hid the tea cup where she could reach it. Murn wasn't a hypocrite so I guess she probably never smoked again. I guess she figured there were many more things I could be doing other than smoking. It was a long time before I ever smoked in front of Murn. For months, I only smoked after she went to bed. It sure was better having a smoke at home after 10:00 than sitting in my car in 30-degree weather, and I didn't have to hide mine in a tea cup!

Mother and her husband had moved to Montana that summer. I never understood what the draw was, but he wanted to live there and Mother went along. They would come for a visit and then be on their way to visit her brother James and my half-brother and sister south of us later in the day. They never stayed with us, which was fine with me. I didn't care for my stepfather. He was a know-it-all and I don't think he treated my mother well at times. I had seen less of Mother since Daddy and EtEt died. There was one time when I think Mother came alone and stayed with us but that was before they had moved to Montana. But now I think they had less money so their visits were few and far between. When they did make the trip from Montana, most of the time was spent in Kansas City with his family. She wrote more letters and we talked on the telephone, but I was coming into my own and making my assessment of things. It was spring that year when they came for a visit and the world turned upside down while Mother and I were standing by their truck.

Mother was expressing how proud she was of me and how Murn and EtEt had done so much for me. Then Mother made a fatal comment, "You know, honey, your daddy never did anything for you."

It was the wrong thing for her to say. I felt my jaw lock, my lower lip protrude and I could feel my eyes turning a cold, steely grey locking under my brow just like my dad. I'm sure she recognized that Gilbert in the flesh was standing before her. She could have delivered the statement with "honey, sweetie, sugar," or any other descriptor she often used, and it still would have been received with a bitter, stingingly cold taste that prompted the words that spewed from my mouth. "Daddy was always around. Daddy served in a war and provided me with a monthly pension. I'm going to college because Daddy died and I have his benefits. What did *you* ever do for me?"

There it was. It was my coming of age. The timid, respectful child had slammed full force into adulthood, brave and willing to challenge jealousy, selfishness, and hurtfulness over that one sentence. I'm sure my mother was not only taken aback but hurt in some way. The truth can be hard and painful, but it had to be told. She never should have tried to diminish my dad. She had no right. He wasn't there to defend himself. He had never, ever said anything negative about her to me.

That exchange standing by the truck with my mother that afternoon defined the people in my life and their behaviors justified me in adjusting their titles. Mother was my mother. She gave birth to me and in her own way, as much as she was capable of, loved me. Murn was my mom. I had known this deep within me for many years. She raised me, good times and bad, gave me everything I needed and more, loved me, taught me to love my mother and dad, worried about me, encouraged me, healed my wounds, celebrated my successes, was always proud of me, and corrected me when I needed correction. She followed me every step of the way throughout my life, shining a light for me to see and helping me to choose the best path. *She* was my mom and *she* deserved and had earned the title.

After Mother and her husband had left, I went inside and told Murn what had happened. I also told her that from that moment on, I was calling her what she was: *my mom.* I never called her Murn again when I spoke to her; she was Mom. Starla had always called her Mom. Murn was the only mother she knew.

It's odd how labels or titles are simply assumed or given to people without them earning it. Perhaps titles should be re-evaluated or not applied to people until they prove that they fulfill the requirements or live up to the expectations. Murn had been an aunt only by a label; by actions and requirements, she had always been my mom since I came into the world. I understood that day what

Murn had always said, "I love your mother, I just don't love the things she does." I, too, loved my mother, just not the thing she did that day.

CHAPTER 15

Leaves of the Branches

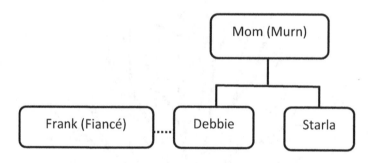

CHAPTER 15

Defense and Offense
Fall 1973

My first year of college was completed and another summer had arrived. I continued to take a few classes, conduct the municipal and union band, direct and conduct *Hello, Dolly!* for the annual city festival, and began teaching guitar on Saturdays at the local music store. At 19 I was still consumed by the addiction that had grabbed me in high school. It was as if I were running from past heartache and music was the only thing that fueled my forward motion.

Rehearsals for the musical were still held in the high school auditorium. After a couple of years, my association was no longer as a student and I wasn't a district employee. I was told that for liability and insurance purposes I needed to have an employee of the school district in the building while we were rehearsing. Having had many favorite teachers and staff members who were also wonderful supporters when I was a student, recruitment was not a problem. Each weekend I would line up a "babysitter" for each rehearsal during the upcoming week. We ended up with the same few people who were willing to sit with us for the three to four hours I would hold a rehearsal and yes, I still had the keys.

Believe it or not, one of our regular sitters was the physics teacher who secretly purchased the roses I had been given my senior year following the musical *Bubble Trouble.* Following the summer festival production of *Anything Goes,* he asked me on a date. I had dated several guys up until then, but he was

much older – 10 years. I was always busy but I thought, "What would a date hurt?" Besides, that guy without a tie and his gradebook looked a lot different with his summer tan, white tennis shorts and shirt, and blue eyes and blonde hair – thinning, but blonde. Well, one date led to another and the next thing I knew, Frank and I were dating. Our dating was a little different from most dates. In order to see me, he ended up helping build sets, babysitting rehearsals, going to performances, and on occasion, going out to dinner on weekends and having dinner during the week with me at our house.

It was getting to the point that I spent very little time at home. Mom and Starla were on their own. I was in just enough to change clothes, sleep a few hours, then out the door to classes, rehearsing, building sets, teaching guitar, or spending time practicing. Looking back, I realize this was when the distance between Starla and me became as wide as the Grand Canyon and as silent as deep space. Mom and I would find time to talk in between my entrances and exits but I had little daily interaction with Starla. The daily personal interaction was abandoned to Mom and Starla.

What had been just the three of us became the two of them. I think loneliness crept into our home. Many of Mom's friends in Cairo had passed away and there were only our two neighbors whose friendship consisted of daily short exchanges, along with her close friend in town, Edna, with whom she talked daily on the telephone. Little Ruth was our neighbor and she and Mom would talk through the kitchen window with each other.

Starla was at school, but I think it was hard for her to associate with her friends. Most of them had younger parents, a mother and a dad, and they hadn't experienced the losses Starla had nor did they carry the fear of potentially losing their moms that she carried. Even though Mom changed with the times, encouraged Starla to spend time with her friends, and did her best to see that she had the same opportunities and activities that her friends had, it wasn't the same for Starla. She saw her world as very different from that of her friends. At nine years old, feeling like you're different isn't a good thing, it's isolating.

We knew what music had done for me so Mom and I both encouraged Starla to learn an instrument and be in the band. She would have the same band director that had been so dear to me in high school. He also taught all the beginning woodwinds, assisted with the junior high band, and was a saxophonist. Starla decided she wanted to play the saxophone. So Mom signed the contract and made monthly payments on the horn. Mom was so supportive of activities that provided us with opportunities and skill development. Starla was talented as a beginner. Mom and I were so happy she was part of a group and participating in an activity that would encourage her and build her confidence. She marched in parades, played in concerts, and even took a solo to contest and received a superior. Starla was also a very good artist for her age. Hopefully, she would find comfort and a deep interest in these activities.

While I was gone so much with all of my activities, Mom and Starla spent many hours together entertaining each other. They both loved jigsaw puzzles. They would sit together for hours at the kitchen table putting them together. I hated those puzzles! On occasion, I would sit down and try to work a puzzle with them. I would search and search for a piece and they would find one after another while I never found even one! They would just howl at my frustration. I finally realized that it was something special between the two of them, similar to the marble shooting Mom did with me in our empty guest room. Playing cards was another activity that belonged completely to them. Rummy was the game they loved to play.

When I was home they would invite me to play and I too enjoyed playing Rummy. I would sit down to play with them and I often noticed that Mom would start singing non-songs on simple syllables; do-da-doo. Then Starla would start smiling and laughing. Mom would just keep staring at her cards and singing those made-up songs. Starla or Mom would win, game after game! What on earth was happening? The more we played the more frustrated I became and the more smug and snickering the two of them became. How was it possible that I couldn't win a hand? Then I caught them! They were CHEATING! They were passing cards under the table. When I caught them they would laugh and laugh, thrilled that they had fooled me. I was sure Mom had instigated it! She was a feisty gal and often liked to tease.

Mom did have a sense of humor, more mischievous in her younger years, and by today's descriptors, she probably was what we'd call a "hot mess." She told of walking on the sidewalk along the main highway through Cairo wearing a half-slip that was a little too big for her. She said she knew it was slipping down but she just kept on walking. Soon it was almost to her knees. The traffic was passing by heavily and she simply stopped, shook it all the way down, stepped out of it, rolled it up, put it under her arm, and walked on as if nothing had happened. Her silliness didn't stop as a young woman. She and a few of her church girlfriends would go down to the major intersection of town and stand on the corner staring up at the sky pointing until other people walking down the street would stop and start looking up to see what they were looking at. Then she and her friends would move away from them and just start laughing! When she was much older I always loved to watch her and her lady friends when they got together. There was always laughter as soon as a conversation started. Mom was definitely sweet and spicy – perhaps a little spicier than sweet.

Anything Goes and *Hello, Dolly!* opened the floodgate to Broadway for me. I barely had time for classes during my sophomore year in college. Several of us developed an organization named Southern Musical Productions. We saw

Mom's faith had always been supernatural. It was as if she had a superhuman connection with God. She seemed to know outcomes before they happened, what to say before it was said, and what to do before it was done. Murn and EtEt had always attended church; it was just who they were. But not so with Mom's first husband.

A dear Christian friend of Mom's asked her advice as to how to get her husband to attend church. Mom told her the story of Harry during the early years of their marriage. Harry wasn't a religious man. Sundays would come and Mom would dress for church while Harry was having his coffee. "Harry, don't you want to come with me to church?"

Harry would respond with, "No, honey, not this Sunday."

Mom would say, "Alright, honey, I'll see you after church."

Mom told her friend that this went on every Sunday for several years, and every Sunday she would ask him the same question and every Sunday he would respond with the same answer. One Sunday as she was dressing for church she repeated her Sunday question, "Honey, don't you want to come with me to church?"

Harry responded, "You know, honey, I believe I will."

From that Sunday on, Mom and Harry attended church together. Mom told her friend, "If he doesn't go with you when you ask the question, he won't go with you with begging, pleading, lecturing, or nagging. Keep showing him your behavior and inviting him to go with you; one day he might surprise you." I remember the Sunday that friend and her husband walked down the aisle of our church. I watched as she and Mom made eye contact and shared an all-knowing smile. That was the beginning of his remaining years accompanying his wife to church each Sunday.

Mom never gave up on anything or anyone. I believe she prayed every minute of every hour of every day. Sometimes I think God must have answered her prayers just to shut her up. Her persistence and perseverance were as superhuman as her faith. Mom never preached to us as we were growing up. She simply led us by her example and, of course, her expectations. When I brought a problem to her she often assured me that it would be alright; that it would work out. I knew right then and there that she had started praying about it. I often wondered how many promises she must have made God throughout the years or maybe he simply rewarded her as his good and faithful servant. Either way, she and God were tight.

I was busy rehearsing and staging *Mame* after that heartbreaking interview and my fears had somehow faded. My major professor on my committee was on sabbatical during the fall semester and I was going to have to have the show videotaped for her to see when she returned. I simply threw myself into the production and not to sound sacrilegious, I let go and let Mom and God handle the job situation. Within a week after I had interviewed for the first job, I came home after working on the set all day and there was a phone message Mom had taken. It was from the superintendent at one of the largest high schools in the area asking if I would be willing to interview for a position. Mom simply smiled and said, "I told you things would work out."

The next morning before I could call to arrange for an interview, the other superintendent called offering me the job at the small district. I begged for a little more time without telling him I had another interview. He gave me another few days. I returned the message I had received from the large high school district and arranged for an interview the next day. It was my dream job: band, orchestra, choirs, jazz band, swing choir, and an all high school district. No elementary general music. In essence, I was replacing three and a half men. Upon approval by the board of education, I was recommended for hire as the new director of music and was confirmed by the board the following evening. Before it was announced, I notified the smaller district I had accepted another position. I was starting a huge new job and directing a musical at the same time. Mom and God – what a team!

CHAPTER 16

Leaves of the Branches

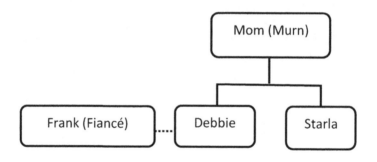

CHAPTER 16

Dissonance in an Unfinished Melody
Fall 1977 – Summer 1980

I was consumed with my new teaching position. My day started by arriving at the school at 7:30 in the morning and most days not leaving for home until around 9:30 in the evening. There wasn't a time I arrived home that Mom wasn't sitting up watching television or lying in bed waiting to hear me come through the door. "Debbie honey, is that you?" she would always ask. I would always go back to her room and sit beside her on the bed to see how she was and perhaps tell her about my day.

Starla was usually still awake or just getting ready for bed. At times we would acknowledge each other but Starla was becoming more and more non-communicative. She was approaching 13, which is a tough time for any teenager, but it seemed to be more difficult for Starla. Her violent outbursts had been replaced with blatant, punitive silence and suspicious indifference and compliance. She appeared to have no interest in participating or engaging in anything as part of our family. She complied with requests but offered no discussion, no comment, no interaction other than a smug facial expression with no eye contact. Mom tried to be caring and kind, and Frank always tried to communicate with her about school, while the relationship between Starla and me became totally disjunct. Starla was creating tension in our home by her presence that was increasingly concerning. My position required weekend performances and travel which left Mom alone with Starla. Frank often spent time at the house when I was gone to be with Mom not just for company, but

I think to protect her, too. We knew something was about to boil over in Starla, we just didn't know what or when.

Mom always hung clothes on the clothesline when the weather was warm. We had a dryer but I think she loved to be outside and thought the clothes smelled so fresh. I came home one afternoon early and saw a T-shirt hanging on the clothesline that I knew was Starla's and I was sure Mom had no idea what was on it. I went inside and asked Mom, "Do you know what's on that T-shirt of Starla's hanging out there? It's a marijuana plant! Where did she get that?" I exclaimed.

I could see Mom's embarrassment and anger in her eyes as she headed out the door to take it off the line. She came right back in, T-shirt in hand, took a pair of scissors from the kitchen drawer, and began cutting it up. Starla came into the kitchen from her bedroom and the anger in the room began to rise. This time, however, Starla's anger was no match for Mom's and she knew she couldn't intimidate Mom with me standing there, not to mention I think she might have been a little afraid of the consequences she might face as a result of Mom's anger. The house was very quiet that evening. I think they both were contemplating their next steps.

When I arrived home the next evening Frank was still there and Mom was visibly upset. Starla had not come home from school. Mom called all of Starla's friends that we knew of and Frank had checked with the junior high. Starla had not gone to school that day. I could see in Mom's eyes that she was blaming herself for Starla's actions and was fearful of where Starla might be or if something had happened to her. Filing a police report required that she be missing for over 24 hours but Frank and I knew the officers and one in particular that we were comfortable contacting that evening. He assured us he would do some checking and keep an eye out for her. The police knew some places and individual homes where kids her age who were smoking marijuana, drinking, or defiant at home often frequented. There was nothing else for us to do that evening so Frank went home. I went to bed but I'm sure Mom barely shut her eyes that night. She was too busy praying.

Frank and I had to go to work the next day and Mom was home alone hoping she would hear from Starla. Late that afternoon, the officer we had spoken to arrived at our house with Starla in tow. Starla made a beeline to her bedroom. The officer shared with Mom the information that he had found Starla at a house where the adults living there allowed teenagers to hang out and skip school.

It wasn't long, maybe a few months, before Starla ran away again. This time she was hanging out in a van at the park with a guy who shouldn't have been with a minor, but both separately assured the police that she was there voluntarily and all they did was drink beer. Once again she was escorted home by the police. Going to work every day for me was a relief from the situation but I worried about Mom's health and safety when I was away.

Summer was upon us and I was home more. Mom was showing signs of wear. We were always waiting for the next shoe to drop. Starla had made it to the eighth grade and we had hopes that she had calmed down and perhaps had passed through a difficult phase. Every day she left for school, appeared to be a part of our family in the evenings again, and was somewhat enjoyable to be around. Starla was so very bright and very pretty as a young teen. She was probably much smarter than I. She seldom brought home a book, which concerned Mom regarding her grades. She was making Bs and Cs but was capable of making all As. At the end of the school year, we were alarmed to see she had missed 44 days of school! We never had been notified. Mom, Frank, and I were furious! We weren't upset with Starla but livid with the school. She was running with a bad group and skipping school to go behind the Dairy Queen to smoke cigarettes and probably pot and then off to do who knows what.

We decided that we had to get her away from the crowd she was running with. I contacted a state senator from our district whose wife I was on faculty with and asked his help in moving Starla to my school district without having to pay non-resident tuition. We were so grateful when he intervened and she was able to start high school at my school that fall.

Every morning she and I would go together and if I had a late day, Mom would drive over to pick her up. It didn't last very long. While it did get her away from her old crowd, it put her in a situation where she didn't have any new friends to interact with after school hours. Once again we began struggling.

Soon she ran away again. Frank and I spent so many hours driving around trying to find her. This time it was much longer than overnight. A few days had passed and the officer who had always helped us let us know she was staying at the house of a woman who was essentially harboring young people who weren't happy at home and he was pretty sure they were drinking and smoking there, but the police had difficulty proving it. The police went to the house and once again brought Starla home.

We found a teenage counseling service in town and suggested that Starla might like to talk to someone to help her with whatever she was feeling. She agreed that she would be amenable to that. Her counselor was a young, new counselor and Starla seemed to enjoy having someone to talk with. She would meet with her counselor after school weekly and then would walk home. We never heard from the counselor but trusted it was important that Starla felt her conversations with her were private. Little did we know that Starla had developed into a skillful, manipulative liar. Suddenly we received a visit from Division of Children and Family Services (DCFS). Starla had made accusations against Mom and me and falsehoods about our home. After the visit, the caseworker informed us he was calling the report unfounded. He knew my reputation and certainly knew Frank as a school district principal.

Little did we know, the youth counselor had put into motion the paperwork requesting that Starla be legally identified as an emancipated minor and that she receive her own Social Security and Veteran's checks, allowing her to live on her own. Mom was brokenhearted. It was a situation where you just couldn't believe what was happening. How could this be? We reached out to an organization to help us and our family ended up being destroyed. Starla was placed in her own apartment, receiving her own checks, and as far as we knew, not attending school. And this was the counselor's solution for Starla. We were sick, angry, frustrated, and disappointed with the system. There was nothing for us to do; what was done, was done. Mom was visibly devastated. I, on the other hand, was relieved and so was Frank.

We didn't hear from Starla nor did we even know where she was living. I was seldom home due to my teaching position but Frank spent much time with Mom in the evenings. One evening when I was on the football field in a marching band rehearsal, Frank came walking into the stadium to tell me Mom had been admitted to the hospital with chest pains and probably a heart attack. She was stable but I needed to go to the hospital. Frank was certified and knew the administrators in my district so he said he would stay there with the band and let them continue to practice while I went to check on Mom. When I arrived at the hospital she was stable and assured me she was alright. It was a mild heart attack and they were going to keep her to monitor. She would see me tomorrow; she just needed to rest. I stayed at Frank's that night; I just didn't want to be home alone.

Mom had had so many heart attacks that her doctor called her his cat with nine lives. She was already well past nine and I worried as to how many more lives she had. I knew this time it had been building over Starla's behavior and the emancipation decision. I'm not sure how it happened, but the young counselor was fired. It might have been the DCFS caseworker or maybe even Frank. We never knew.

The dissonance that Starla had created in all our lives, especially in her own, was more unsettling to Mom than any of us. The melody that Mom had begun composing with Starla as a 19-month-old was unfinished. Mom could not resolve the dissonance in Starla's melody and, sadly, that uncompleted song would haunt Mom for the days that followed. The dissonance that was yet to come would be earth-shattering.

CHAPTER 17

Leaves of the Branches

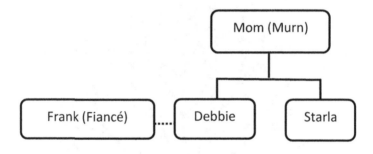

CHAPTER 17

The Volcano Erupts
End of Summer 1980

The ring of a telephone seldom raises anxiety and fears in most households, but our family had been conditioned to expect the worst with that startling ringing. Except for Starla, there were few family members left for us to worry about. I had resigned myself to believe that she was a lost cause. My patience with her behavior had been tried beyond my limits. During the past years, she had grown more and more difficult, disrespectful, and in some ways dangerous. I was a high school teacher and worked daily with kids her age and none were as disrespectful as she was. Much of my resignation was based on how angry I was with her because she had hurt Mom so deeply and insisted on living a life completely opposite from how she was raised. Mom's golden years should have been filled with peace and joy. Instead, her life was filled with worry, disappointment, and the guilt that a mother feels when she interprets a child's poor choices as her parental failure to the child. Mom didn't fail Starla, Starla failed Mom. That's what fueled my anger. How could Starla be so ungrateful, so unloving, and uncaring? Each day Mom woke up worrying about Starla and each night went to bed fearing what had happened to her during the day and what might happen to her throughout the night. I watched Mom's eyes fill with tears daily and I could see her heartache as it carved the lines in her face each day that Starla was gone.

One day that fright-filled ring of the telephone came with a city police officer on the other end. The police had been called by the landlord to the apartment where Starla was living. There had been an incident where the apartment had been wrecked and there was no sign of Starla. The officer asked that Frank and I meet him at the apartment before he speculated as to what had occurred. We knew many of the city police officers personally, mostly from the many times Starla had left home and they had tracked her down and brought her home.

Walking into the apartment we were met with a scene I had only viewed in a crime drama on television or in movies - ashtrays were heaped with ashes and numerous brands of cigarette butts and remaining joints, beer cans and liquor bottles covering the tables and floor, furniture scattered and tipped over, and a bed with sheets in terrible disarray. The stench in the air was a sickening combination of cigarette smoke, pot, stale beer, filthy clothes, and body odor. There was no sign of Starla. Her purse including her billfold and the contents were strewn across the floor. The officer questioned us as to whether we had seen or heard from her within the past few days. We had not. She had cut all communication with us since she moved out of our home and into that apartment. The officer told us that they would notify us as soon as they had any more information or if they found her.

Frank and I dreaded returning home to tell Mom what we had found. As we drove home my thoughts turned from Starla to my fear that this information would challenge the failing strength of Mom's broken heart. When we arrived the three of us sat down at the kitchen table and I began to share the disgusting details of what we had seen. Watching the tears roll down her cheeks and the wringing of her aged hands as we described the scene made my anger grow even greater toward Starla. For the past couple of years, Starla had been a constant heartbreak for Mom. Throughout the years with all our family losses and trials, I had watched Mom persevere, strong and steady. Starla had broken her. She had crushed Mom's joy and usurped her strength.

At this point, we didn't know whether Starla had been kidnapped or killed. All we could do was wait and, of course, I knew Mom was praying.

Later that day came another phone call. The police had found Starla and were transporting her to the local hospital emergency room. They asked that we meet them there. Frank and I left immediately and as we pulled in toward the emergency entrance we saw two city police cars, a sheriff's car, and a state police car. As we approached the cars on foot, we began to hear screaming resembling that of an attacking wild animal or the devil incarnate. The officers were removing Starla from the back of the sheriff's car. There were three city police officers, a deputy sheriff, and a state police officer all trying to hold on to a 110-pound, not yet 16-year-old girl. An officer was holding on to each appendage and one was holding around her waist. She was like a wild beast: kicking, biting and spewing profanity which shook the very ground we were standing on. This continued as they carried her into the emergency room where she was placed in restraints on a gurney. As she continued screaming and threatening everyone around her, one officer was recovering from a kick to the groin, another was treated for a bite, and the others stood outside the room catching their breath and sharing with us what they had pieced together.

As I look back, this was probably the day that I truly understood that we each define actions and events based on our own personal perspective, life choices, and experiences. The police told us that, based on what they could gather, Starla had had a party in her apartment the night before with many young males who had gotten out of hand and she had been gang-raped. As soon as the phrase "gang-raped" left his lips, Starla began screaming, "I wasn't raped! They're my friends! They're my friends! I wasn't raped!"

According to her, she was not gang-raped, she had "pulled a train" for her friends. Frank and I were mortified beyond embarrassment. The police continued to probe her as to who was involved. They had pieced together who one of the individuals was, but she refused to give up the names of her friends. Every time Frank or I tried to talk to her or even get close to her she would break into a blood-chilling eruption of projectile profanity in what could only be described as a satanic, possessed voice – the same voice I had heard when she had Mom backed into a corner.

Our family doctor admitted her to the hospital and ordered a psychological examination. He said he was going to sedate her for the evening and suggested that we go home and that he would contact us tomorrow after the psych exam. He knew Starla had been a major behavioral problem for the past few years and I'm sure he was concerned about Mom and the emotional strain this would physically have on her heart. I was so glad to leave the hospital. I was exploding with a variety of emotions: embarrassed at the situation, angry at her behavior, painfully sad over the whole event, glad that she was safe in the hospital, and sick knowing that once again, I had to tell Mom these tragic details.

Over the next few days, we were provided with the results of the psychological examination. While we all had survived the losses in our family, the losses and their impact affected each of us differently. During the first 10 years of Starla's life, she had lost all of the generations above her other than Mom. She had lost her mother, daddy, EtEt, Grandma Troutman, her Grandpa Treese, and aunts and uncles. She didn't know her half-brothers but had some interaction with her half-sister. It was explained to us that in her mind everyone she loved died. Therefore, she had decided not to love us. She didn't want to be like us. She didn't want our values, our beliefs, or our love. In short, she didn't want us and certainly didn't want to live with us. There was nothing left to be said or done other than what the future held for Starla. She was still a minor and could not return to the living situation arranged by the youth services organization that had placed her in that apartment. We contacted an attorney, a man who had been very good to me when I had been hit in a car accident, and a school board member supportive of the music program. We needed his help to guide us in a situation that was foreign to us. More importantly, we needed him to help us save Starla from herself.

The day we appeared in court was gut-wrenching. Just getting Mom to the courtroom was difficult. Although we had a wheelchair, getting her to the courtroom required maneuvering three levels while the emotional intensity increased at each floor, with Mom becoming more subdued with each passing level. When we arrived in the courtroom our attorney met us with a kindness that I have never forgotten. He helped position Mom at the table and then sat down next to her. He took her hands, covered them with his, looked into her eyes, and in a gentle, soft voice assured her that this was the best thing for Starla and then explained to her how the proceedings would be conducted. As we sat waiting, Mom was silent. She looked tired, beaten, defeated; yet it was evident that she wasn't sure if we were doing the right thing. Suddenly there was a loud, echoing sound of the courtroom doors opening then closing. We looked to the back of the courtroom and watched Starla along with her representative as they walked down the aisle, then sat at the table across the aisle from us. Mom smiled, wanting so badly for Starla to see the love she had for her. Starla was hard; she wouldn't look at us. I'm sure she was angry but knowing Starla I'm sure that was her way of punishing Mom. I'm sure she knew that not acknowledging Mom would hurt her. I knew by looking at her that she had no idea what was coming. She had a defiant look on her face that translated to an attitude that she had somehow won and she was in control.

The judge hearing the case knew me and Frank as well. He knew we were a good family. Our attorney began to present the case that Starla was out of control. He submitted to the court the psychological report that had been completed during her stay at the hospital, shared the actions that landed her in the hospital, recounted the numerous activities Starla had engaged in that we had dealt with, and asked the court to identify her as incorrigible. I watched Mom as he shared this with the judge. I had never seen her in such despair. It was as if all life had left her. Suddenly the judge's voice rang throughout the courtroom. "Mrs. Lipe, I'm sorry you are having to endure this. It is apparent to me that you have given this young lady a loving home from the time she was 19 months old. You have clothed and fed her, cared for her when she was sick, seen to her education, given her a religious upbringing, and raised her with the values and expectations that should be expected in raising a child to be a productive member of society. Unfortunately, Starla has chosen not to follow the path nor take advantage of the opportunities that have been provided her. It is evident that she does not appreciate the love and the home she has had all her young life. Mrs. Lipe, you have done your part. You deserve peace in your older years. Therefore, I am relieving you of this burden and I am taking control of Starla from this point forward. Starla, please stand up. It is the decision of this court that you be transferred immediately following this proceeding to the Huddleston Baptist Children's Home by a sheriff's deputy. You will remain there until you are 18 years of age and have completed your GED. I wish you the best and hope that you will reflect on what you had and what you have forfeited. Mrs. Lipe, I hope you and Debbie find peace. It is the order of this court."

The drop of the gavel echoed like a grenade exploding throughout the room. Starla and her representative left the room without a word nor a glance, hard as a rock. She gave us nothing.

I think a part of Mom died that day. She had always solved problems, fixed things that needed fixing, cared for everyone who needed comfort or support, and made sure everyone had what they needed. In her mind, I think she felt that she had failed Starla, that somehow *she* was responsible for Starla's choices; that *she* had done something wrong. Again, Mom didn't fail Starla, Starla failed Mom. In the big picture perhaps life failed Starla as a child. But without question, Starla had failed Mom.

The days and weeks that followed were empty for Mom. She wrote Starla letters and sent her cards without any reciprocal response from Starla. I hated that for Mom, but I was so glad the drama and the ugliness were over. It was months before we ever heard from Starla. When we finally did, I couldn't help but wonder when the ground would shift and the fiery, molten lava would burn our lives again.

CHAPTER 18

Leaves of the Branches

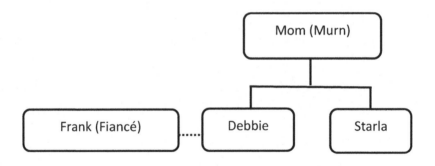

CHAPTER 18

Quiet Isn't Always Peaceful
Fall 1980

I've always heard that it gets very quiet before a tornado, but it's also eerily quiet afterward. Once the tornado has roared through there's no sound, no movement. Then when the people begin to come out from their safe and secure places, the silence begins to diminish and the faint whispers of astonishment and muffled sounds of crying fill the air. So much lost, so much to repair, so much work to rebuild, and some things can never be replaced or rebuilt. It is quiet but it is not peaceful. Starla had been our tornado. For Frank and me the quiet was finally peaceful. He and I were relieved. We didn't have to worry about where Starla was, what she was doing, having to track her down, and more than anything, how much worry, hurt, and anxiety she was inflicting on Mom. We returned fully focused on our jobs and daily activities. Starla had been an inconvenience and an irritant for Frank and me. However, for Mom, the quiet was not peaceful. It was crushing. The devastating damage Starla had imposed on Mom destroyed Mom's spirit for life.

The days and weeks after Starla was sent to the children's home, Mom spent her days continuing to write letters and cards, enclosing stamps and spending money for Starla, which resulted in no response. I was so involved with my position at the high school I was seldom home until late at night on weekdays and only on Sundays on weekends. Frank was so good to Mom. Often he spent time with her in the evenings while working on his administrative paperwork or writing computer programming projects. For the first time, Mom had no one to lean on or share her feelings with. EtEt was gone, Mom's mother, sisters, and two brothers, along with many of her friends had passed away, and I was all she had left yet I was seldom home. She would never have leaned on Frank or me with her hurt or pain; she wouldn't have wanted us to worry, even though we did. Mom had always taken care of family members, juggled a household, and raised children. Now her hours were spent cleaning a clean house daily, washing fewer clothes, cooking meals for us when Frank and I were home for dinner, reading her Bible and praying, always praying. But for the most part, Mom was alone with her devastation; her life's purpose had been demolished. For the first time in her mind only, she must have felt the pain of the two miscarriages she had had, the loss of Freida many years ago, and now she had lost Starla. There was no peace in her quiet.

It was no surprise when Mom had another serious heart attack. What she had endured was more than she could bear. Teaching and running to the hospital every day was difficult emotionally and physically for me. How many more heart attacks could she withstand? I didn't want to stay at home alone so I stayed at Frank's. Mom rebounded relatively quickly but there had been a complication. Her crippled leg had always been cold due to poor circulation, but suddenly they couldn't find a pulse in the foot and a sore had developed. After a week the sore slowly began to heal and the pulse had returned. But her ability to walk had been compromised. While she could still walk, she couldn't walk for very long periods so I purchased a wheelchair for her. She was such a small woman I was able to purchase a lightweight child-size wheelchair.

Since I was on campus in classes it was difficult for her to contact me if she needed me. While cell phones were not common at that time, I secured a voice pager. All she had to do was call the number and talk as if she were calling me on the phone. The pager would sound five rapid beeps and then I would hear her talking. One day it was very stormy and I was in one of the required doctoral classes with only five other students and a professor who reminded me of the Kentucky Colonel of fried chicken acclaim. Although he didn't have a beard, he did have a white mustache, white hair, glasses, a thick Southern accent, and was tough! My pager was in my backpack on the floor when suddenly it started beeping and before I could get to it I heard Mom, along with the whole class. "Debbie honey, there are tornado warnings posted. You need to be careful and be ready to take cover. I love you." I was mortified!

The professor, in his most sarcastic Southern drawl asked, "Miss Burris, do you need to take cover or should we proceed with our class?"

The longer it took to get home, the angrier I got. When I got home I scolded Mom harshly, telling her that the pager was not for weather updates. She said she would never do something like that again. There are only two times in my life that I'm ashamed of how I spoke to Mom and I would give anything to take back my words. The first was when I was a teenager and said for her to shut up under my breath and now this time. It's awful when caring what other people think is more important than hurting a person who does something because they truly love you.

Thanksgiving and Christmas were calm and Mom had recovered enough that she fixed a modified special dinner like she always had and Mom, Frank, and I spent the holidays together watching television and just spending time together. It didn't matter what we did or said, Mom's face told us her heart was aching over Starla not being with us. She didn't talk much about Starla, but it was obvious that she was consumed with Starla's absence. Starla may have been living in a restrictive space but so was Mom. Mom was alone in the house day in and day out with her memories of Starla growing up and EtEt sitting in his favorite chair. I know she wished EtEt was still here for her to talk to and to comfort her.

The 1980/81 academic year was my fourth year at the high school and I had had most of the students from their freshman year and they now were in their senior year. The program had expanded in many ways and so had my load. I was teaching a marching/concert band, guard (flags and rifles), orchestra, sophomore choir, junior/senior choir, jazz band, show choir, a musical, and state music contest with solos and ensembles, along with a men's chorus, women's chorus, and madrigal choir for the organizational contest. I was gone on weekends for competitions, conferences, concerts, and a week-long tour in the spring. In addition, there were two freshman choirs taught by my colleagues. I was blessed to have had amazing and outstanding students each of my four years, but this year they were exceptional and the activities were unbelievably exciting and exhausting! It all paid off during the spring when it was announced that we had won the state championship music sweepstakes for our Class A-AA school size. This was the first time since the year I was born that the music department had achieved such an honor. Mom was so proud of me as she always was.

People always asked where my musical ability came from. I didn't know; maybe it just came from my heart. Since I came into the world singing you would think it was genetic. Mother didn't play an instrument but she had pretty good pitch when she sang along with country songs. Her brother, my Uncle James, played guitar and sang in the old country style of Hank Williams with the characteristic nasal twang. I was told my grandfather Luther was musical but I never heard him play or sing anything. The Burris side was even less musical. Daddy had a beautiful voice but didn't play an instrument. Mom carried a tune well as evidenced when she was doing her housework. EtEt never sang, not even when he was "working on the railroad." Growing up there wasn't a lot of music in our home. Like many young children, I had a suitcase record player and a stack of old 45s that my mother had given me; not the popular songs that children listened to, but the music of adult listeners. I think the early variety of music I was exposed to established my taste for wide and varied genres of music.

The music that was most consistent in my life was the music found at church. There were hymns where we all sang, organ and piano preludes and postludes, vocal solos or ensembles, the choir, and often trumpet and trombone solos and duets. When I was in college I bought Mom a cabinet stereo for the living room. She played music all day long: Tennessee Ernie Ford, Jim Nabors, the Blackwood Brothers – all performing Christian music.

But I don't think the music was what drew me to music; it was the people. Whether it was learning piano or music theory, it was the teachers I adored before I began to take lessons. When I began playing trumpet, my interest started when I listened to the handsome pastor's son perform in church. It was my beginning band director I was fond of, my private trumpet teacher that I loved, and the band directors I worshiped. But the most important factor was that Mom and EtEt supported my interest, encouraged my participation, and had confidence in my ability.

I guess the question as to where my musical ability came from was much like the question "Which came first, the chicken or the egg?" I had to work hard at being a good musician. I believe it was the people that inspired me. They led me to the hard work to develop my love of music and it was music that permitted me to feel. Perhaps this is why I was drawn to conducting and teaching music rather than becoming a professional performing musician. Maybe I wanted to be the person who inspired young people to discover the power of music and how it could permit them to feel. Perhaps I wanted to give them something that allowed them to express what words can never express when life breaks you down as it did me during high school.

The school year ended with the opportunity for me to serve as an assistant director for the state youth chorale in a European tour. Eight of my students were singing in the chorale and it was a wonderful opportunity for all of us. I was hesitant based on my fear of leaving Mom alone. I would be gone two weeks touring five countries. The emotional state Mom was in and the stress that the "tornado" and the months spent without Starla had created on her physical well-being weighed heavily on me concerning her heart and the potential for another heart attack. What if she fell or had another heart attack and I couldn't get back home? What if I got home too late? As always, Mom assured me and insisted that she would be just fine and I should go. Frank promised that he would look after her and would see her every day. Between the two of them, I agreed to go on the tour.

Between the final escalation event of Starla being sent to the children's home and the demands of my job, I was worn out and simply drained. More and more I was feeling the pull to return to college to seek a doctorate. I didn't want to quit my job, and the loss of a paycheck I had grown used to were barriers that I didn't know how to break through. I just knew that I needed time and space to renew my commitment and energy to what I loved: teaching music. Most importantly I needed time to spend with Mom. We both had had a difficult year.

The time I spent on the plane and the bus as we traveled throughout Europe allowed me to consider how I might be able to go back to school. The tour was wonderful and there were no emergencies at home. When I returned home following the tour I had a long talk with Mom. As always, Mom was supportive of what I wanted to do and was always confident that the financial issues would not be a problem. She assured me that she could handle the home expenses. In other words, she had already started praying that God would provide.

I asked for a leave of absence from my position at the high school, which would protect my tenure and assure the administration that I would return the following year. The school board granted my request. I think they knew I had earned it. The next steps were jumping through the hoops for graduate school and applying to the program from which I was seeking a doctorate. Since the university didn't offer a doctorate in music, I was seeking a Ph.D. in curriculum and instruction in education with supplemental courses in music. While it didn't match my paycheck, once again, Mom and God worked it out that I was offered a full-time graduate assistantship for the year, complete with a tuition waiver for both semesters and with just enough money monthly to pay my expenses.

While it was difficult watching from afar as someone else directed my ensembles at the high school and took over the administrative and office duties of the position, I was enjoying my time back at the university as a student. Several of those amazing high school students I had, who had just graduated high school or earlier, were also attending the university and my graduate assistantship was in the School of Music where my assignment was working with ensembles in which they were members. My studies were stimulating, my graduate assistant assignments were engaging, and I was loving having more time to spend with Mom. Most evenings and weekends were spent at home. Mom, Frank, and I were the family now, along with a couple of special friends that Mom loved.

My friends were always welcome in our home. Often friends would come to visit when I wasn't home and they all called her Murn. I came home from my college classes one day to find one of the kids who was in all the Apple Festival musicals I directed sitting at our patio table with Mom. He was such a handsome young teenager with a twinkle in his eye, relatively long black, curly hair, and a smile that made you smile. He was between his freshman and sophomore years at the time. When Cliff was nine his dad died from a congenital heart issue. As fate would have it, Cliff was diagnosed with the same issue. It was not something that could be reversed or contained and each day Cliff knew his impending fate, as did his friends and the people he was close to. All the kids who were in the musicals knew I had lost my dad and EtEt and that Mom had survived many heart attacks. I guess that's why Cliff came to talk to Mom.

The three of us had sat around the table for a few minutes exchanging pleasantries when Mom said, "I need to get in there and start supper." Cliff stood up and hugged Mom. I thought Cliff was waiting to talk with me but immediately following Mom's departure, Cliff said, "I need to get home."

I went into the house and said to Mom, "Why did Cliff come to talk with you? I thought he wanted to talk to me but he didn't say anything."

Mom turned from the sink and in a broken voice and a tear in her eye she said, "He wanted to talk to me about dying." I guess he felt safe talking to her about his fears, leaving his mom behind, and what it might be like for him at the end. I never really knew. Mom never shared their conversation with me. It was private, between Cliff and her. Cliff met his fate his senior year in high school and Mom took their conversation with her to her grave. It was puzzling how so many young people were drawn to Mom, seeking her advice and comfort while Starla pushed her away.

Mom always surprised me with her forward thinking and adjusting to the cultural changes. Nadine was one of my dear friends from college that Mom had met several times. I think Mom really liked Nadine, perhaps because she saw some of herself in her. Both were small in stature, feisty, and quick-witted. After we graduated with our master's degrees, Nadine left to return to teach at her alma mater university in New Orleans. It wasn't long after that Nadine announced she had married. Although I had never met him, I knew he must be special because Nadine would not have married anyone less.

One day I got a call saying they would be passing through, wanted to see us, and wondered if they could stay all night with us. I told Nadine I was sure it would be fine with Mom and that I knew she would love to see her. Nadine's call couldn't have come at a better time. Murn needed some enjoyment and a distraction from the rubble Starla had left. Suddenly in our conversation, Nadine raised the important question, "Are you sure Murn will be okay with Rick and me staying all night?"

I knew Mom would be fine with that young, sparky little black woman visiting our house throughout the years, but how would she feel about an interracial couple staying all night? I have to say, I was a little surprised when it seemed to be fine with Mom; she just wasn't sure what the neighbors would think. I think Mom needed the visit.

Nadine and Rick arrived and here was this small, young black woman with a young man she introduced as her husband. Mom's happiness to see Nadine overshadowed the unexpected vision of her husband. Since they arrived close to suppertime, Mom had decided to fix tacos. Of course, we had no idea that Rick didn't eat meat! No problem. Rick ran to the grocery store and bought tofu to make his tacos. Mom finished frying the meat for our tacos and then Rick began fixing his tofu crumbles. The looks between Nadine and me, Mom and me, and Mom watching Rick were minutes of my life I will never forget. Here stood this tall, thin, red-headed, ultra-white man, married to this little black gal, and Mom was disgusted by this thing called tofu! I think she was now more concerned with what the neighbors would think about tofu in the house as opposed to an interracial couple!!!!

Dinner ended and Nadine helped Mom with the dishes while I entertained Rick. I could hear them laughing and chattering on. When they were done we all settled in the living room and watched television. Mom was quiet, which could be worrisome. You never knew what she was thinking or what she was going to say. Thank goodness Rick was a friendly guy and was good at making conversation, not to mention that Nadine and I were Chatty Cathys trying to keep Mom from having an opening to say whatever or ask whatever she was thinking. It got close to Mom's bedtime and she said, "I'm going to leave it to you young people and I'm going to bed!" We all told her good night and Nadine and Rick thanked her for supper and told her not to do anything for breakfast. They were going to leave early and eat somewhere along the way. Nadine and I just collapsed with relief while Rick, I believe, was oblivious as to our freedom from tension.

The next morning, we all were up bright and early and Mom was in the kitchen asking if they were sure they didn't want anything for breakfast. Hugs were shared by all, even Rick and Mom. The visit had deflected Mom's daily routine of mourning Starla and it was good to see her laugh and communicate with Nadine like she used to. We never really talked about the interracial aspect of our lodging guests. It was just another way that Mom was capable of adapting and accepting people for who they were as human beings, not based on cultural or racial biases. The only bias I remember Mom having other than that of alcohol was cleanliness. She used to always tell me, "Debbie, there's no excuse for not being clean. A bar of soap costs only 25 cents." Nadine and Rick's visit was also the jump-start that Mom needed to get back to living life finally for herself rather than for other people.

The year flew by quickly and Mom began to hum again as she did her housework. She even started going to the local Walmart, spending time looking and shopping for things for herself. Mom had always bought things for everyone else and seldom anything just for her. She started buying what I called her Garanimals, like the mix-and-match tops and bottoms brand for little kids. They were colorful, flowered polyester, shirt collar blouses. The blouses were interchangeable with the pairs of elastic waist polyester pants she bought in several different colors that she could mix and match. She was so proud to have so many new outfits. I couldn't even remember the last time she had bought herself new clothes. She even bought herself cologne. She loved Tabu and bought the combination set complete with the cologne and body powder. I was so happy to see her returning to her old self, laughing, smiling, and beginning to enjoy life.

At the end of the spring semester, I realized I wasn't ready to return to my teaching position at the high school and formally requested a second year leave of absence to complete my course work. The school board once again being gracious, granted me a second year's leave. During the summer I continued to take a class and Frank and I played golf when we had a chance. Life was calm and we had adjusted to a family of Mom, Frank, and me.

Wine coolers had become popular and Frank asked Mom if he could bring some for us to try. After allowing me to smoke in the house, I wasn't sure if she had expanded her thoughts enough to allow alcohol in the house. I know she knew that Frank and I drank alcohol when we went out. She was the one who told me what kind of beer to get when I turned 18! But bringing it in the house? I wasn't sure that was going to happen and I wasn't going to be the one to ask. Mom was always full of surprises. She said yes, she thought it would be okay. To this day, I'm sure it was only because Frank asked.

It wasn't long before one evening Frank walked in with a four-pack of California Cooler wine coolers. Of course, Frank, the gentleman that he was, asked Mom if she would like to try one. And of course, her answer was no. As the summer went on, there were more four-packs coming in the door, not daily, but not unusual on the weekends. Frank had stopped asking Mom if she'd like to try one. Suddenly the earth shook one evening when Mom said,

"Frank, give me just a little taste in a glass," as she motioned showing him about three-quarters of an inch between her thumb and forefinger. I knew the shaking of the earth was that of my dad spinning in his grave and EtEt chuckling with a belly laugh in his.

"Why sure, Murn," Frank said with a slight grin. I was in shock! Frank and I watched as she took her first sip. Mom tilted her head and said, "That's pretty good." Frank offered her more but she declined. "No that's fine. I just wondered what it tastes like."

Frank would bring a four-pack of coolers for us to have in the afternoon or evening watching television on Sundays. Each time Mom was offered one and she always replied, "Just a sip." It wasn't too long before, as always, Frank asked and Mom said, "I believe I'll have one."

Frank and I almost broke our necks as we turned to look at each other. We were stunned watching her tip the bottle. She pursed her lips in a smug little smile, raised her eyebrows, and tipped her head from side to side as she sat in her favorite chair, California Cooler in hand, and watched television. Yes, it was a new day and a refreshed Murn! Finally, there was a little peace.

CHAPTER 19

Leaves of the Branches

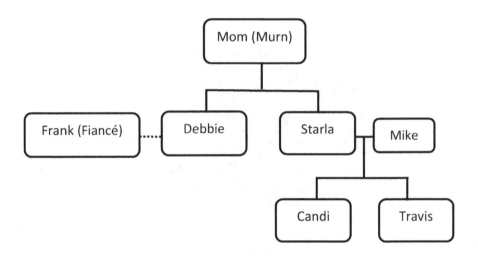

Chapter 19

The Prodigal Child Returns
Spring 1982

F all came with a new graduate assistantship assignment in the College of Education. I was assigned to public relations and accreditation prep for the dean's office one semester and teaching a teaching strategies course the next. Most of my course work was done and I was taking my prelims to advance to my dissertation work. As the calendar year was coming to an end it was bringing Starla's 18th birthday. The court had ordered that she would remain at the children's home until she was 18 and had completed her GED. Starla was extremely smart and I knew she would complete it with flying colors and probably already had. The question was, when would she show up on our doorstep and what weather would she bring?

Spring in Southern Illinois can be very unsettled regarding the weather. Quite often it brings lots of rain, storms, and damaging winds along with the possibility of tornados. But it also can be a beautiful time in nature with blooms and the crispness in the air. It's often said that spring is a time of new beginnings and fresh starts in nature. I guess this same theory can apply to people too. All I knew was that we couldn't survive another "tornado."

One spring day Starla appeared on the doorstep with a young man who she introduced as her husband. Mike was a handsome guy and Starla appeared to have settled down. They made an attractive couple. Starla seemed happy and Mike was kind and respectful to Mom, Frank, and me. They were young and had secured an apartment in town that they could afford. Mike was working manual labor and Starla was pregnant before long. Mom was so happy to have Starla back and on good terms. She seemed to be excited at the thought of having a little one in the family and comforted that Starla had married a young man who seemed to be good for her. I, however, was waiting for the downpour and high winds.

I was still angry with Starla. Our interaction was strained and it was easier for me to interact with Mike than it was with her. I didn't trust her and I was afraid she was going to reignite the anxiety and hurt she had kindled in Mom before. But Mom was happy and they were renewing their relationship through phone calls and her visits to our house. Frank and I both worried as to what the future held with Starla back in our lives, but we acquiesced to Mom's happiness.

The months passed, Starla grew larger, and Murn and she had renewed their relationship to what it had been to some degree when Starla was young. I have to admit it was heartwarming seeing them together. They laughed and talked like a mother and daughter who loved each other should. Starla would share the doctor's report after each of her visits and talk about Mike, their plans, and everyday events.

I was relieved. I didn't worry so much about Mom. She seemed much happier, Starla was behaving and I was beginning my dissertation work. The holidays were approaching and life just seemed to be more enjoyable than it had for the past few years. Starla could easily have played Santa with her huge baby bump! We were hoping the baby would come on Starla's birthday but the baby had a different date in mind.

The first week of January brought in a new year along with a new little one into the world. Mike called to tell Mom that he was a new daddy and Starla and little Candice were doing well. Mom was just beaming and couldn't wait until she could meet Candice. I couldn't help but think that between Mike and Candice maybe Starla's life was finally going to be settled and stable. When she brought Candice to meet her great-aunt Marian, the joy that was on the faces of Starla and Mom was accented by a tear or two that Mom wiped from her eyes as she held Candice in her arms.

As spring came in like a lamb I waited for it to leave like a lion. I was busy working on my dissertation but kept a watchful eye on Mom and Starla. They continued a warm relationship and Starla and Mike appeared to be doing well. I still was very skeptical but I must admit perhaps I was wrong. I couldn't help it; I was predisposed by Starla's old behaviors. The only lion that roared that spring were the actual storms that blew us into summer.

My second leave of absence was ending and I needed to prepare for my return to the high school. I spent my summer selecting music and designing the field show for the marching band, going into my office to select music for all the other ensembles, filing entry forms for competitions, submitting purchase orders, and organizing instruments, uniforms, and equipment. The first time I walked back into my office I wanted to cry. Dust covered everything, music that had been played during the past two years was stacked in piles on anything flat, the couch and chair set one of my groups had purchased for the office had been poorly treated, the carpet they had also purchased was filthy, and the meticulous files were a disaster. I wanted to scream. I was not prepared to have to physically rebuild a department I had left in excellent condition. I guess this was the roar of the lion that brought in my summer.

With Mom's encouragement, Frank's help, and the help of a few students who were freshmen and sophomores when I left and were now to be juniors and seniors who came to my rescue, we put things back the way they knew I had expected them to be on my return. My students always knew that my expectations were high not only regarding their musical performance but also for their behavior, how they presented themselves and how we maintained our physical surroundings. I came by it primarily from Mom, but my mother and dad were both particular regarding physical appearances. My problem now was incoming freshmen who were brand new, sophomores who came in under my substitute, and juniors and seniors who once knew my expectations but for two years did not have those expectations reinforced.

Following one of the many days of cleaning and putting things back where they belonged at school, I came into the house one day and was met with the news that Starla was pregnant again and due in December. "What!?" I exclaimed. "She just had a baby! Two kids born in the same year? Do they not know about birth control?" Mom just chuckled and all I could do was roll my eyes.

There was already a rumbling of the waning honeymoon between Starla and Mike and all I could think of was more worry for Mom and disappointment if they split up. Starla was so very smart but only had her GED. What kind of job could she secure and how could she go to college with two babies 11 months apart? I hoped Mom had started praying because this news just about sent me into a high-speed come-apart!

Fall is always hard on marching band directors. Parades, field competitions, and football games consume a high school music teacher yet there are all the other ensembles they must give their attention to as well. It was hard coming back. It wasn't long before I was exhausted, concerned, disappointed, frustrated, and just plain discouraged. The good thing that encouraged me was that I was a much better teacher because of the time I had spent in doctoral courses. While I was a musician, I was now teaching as a teacher rather than as a musician alone. I was designing instruction in a much more focused and educational delivery rather than just the common "Pete and repeat" approach, even though it contributes greatly. My dissertation had to be placed on the back burner. I had completed all but one chapter. It was a big chapter, and I knew what I was going to write but now was not the time. My focus now had to be on hands-on application rather than research and theory.

December brought a Christmas break at school for Frank and me and a lot more work for Starla. Now she was managing a newborn and a soon-to-be one-year-old. Mom was in her splendor. A baby boy to hold and a little girl to sit on her lap, just as she had with Starla 19 years earlier and me 10 years before Starla. The joy that was on her face now I'm sure was the same all those years ago with us. This was the first Christmas where the absence of all our family members who had passed didn't overshadow the holiday. The house was full: Frank, Starla, Mike, the two little ones, and me and Mom. There was new life in the air over Christmas. In all honesty, we had to thank Starla for that.

I guess in a way, Starla and I were both prodigal children, not in the sense of wealth or the true definition of the word, but we both left what we had that was rich in goodness. Starla had left a home where she was loved, protected, and supported but found her way back to a mom who had loved her with all her heart since she was 19 months old. I returned to the high school music program I had loved so much and had worked so hard for the students and the program to be successful. And yet, we both were struggling: Starla keeping a marriage and family together and me trying to rebuild a program I had already built once before.

CHAPTER 20

Leaves of the Branches

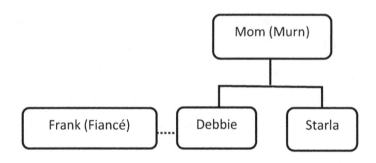

CHAPTER 20

Saying Goodbye
Summer 1984

Only one year back after my leave of absence and I was already exhausted. This time it was more than tired from the demands of teaching such a diverse load; it was hard building the program back. I guess I was just frustrated. I was so happy school was out for the summer and I could spend time focusing on myself. I hadn't worked on my dissertation at all. I just didn't want to have to think about anything academic. I did have to do some physical work at school, check instruments that might need repair, tag new instruments that had been ordered, hang new plaques from competitions, and do general housecleaning in the music department rooms.

I had ordered new storage boxes for band and orchestra files. Currently, music was stored in manila envelopes. Each new box needed the title, composer, and file number written on it. It was a perfect job for Mom to help me with. She had very good printing and it was something which allowed her to spend time with me in the office. With her wheelchair loaded up in the car, she and I left early one morning to work together at the high school. Various students would stop by and Mom loved to talk with them while she worked. It's as if young people were always drawn to who they all called Murn. It's amazing how simple moments in time can become such a lasting memory. I can still see my students interacting with her.

One day I was talking with a friend and she shared that there was a little house next door to her that would be perfect for Mom and me. I hadn't thought about buying a house, but it was in the town where I taught and would mean not driving seven miles each way from home to work at all hours. I talked to Mom about it and she said it didn't hurt anything to check with the realtor and see what it was like on the inside and if we could manage the purchase. I made the call that day.

The house had two bedrooms, one-and-a-half baths, an eat-in kitchen, living room, and dining room or could be used as a family room. The half bath was off one of the bedrooms that would be perfect for Mom. The dining/family room had a glass sliding door that looked out onto a covered patio and a large backyard. It also had an attached garage which would be nice for me to drive into late at night and keep me from having to scrape snow and ice in the winter. It was a perfect little house in a very nice residential section just on the outer edge of town. The asking price was $48,000 and the realtor thought I would have no problem qualifying and the monthly payment would be within my financial limits. The call finally came and the papers were ready for my signature. I was so very excited. I was going to be a homeowner! We had lived in the housing in Cairo and then Murphysboro since 1964. Now Mom and I were going to be in our own house and a cute one too!

The middle of July was spent packing and preparing for the move. We rented a truck and between Frank, me, and a few friends we loaded and unloaded our belongings to the new house. I left my car at the new house and Frank drove me back to our old house. We returned to the house so I could get Mom and take her to our new home in her car.

When we drove up Mom was standing by the back screen door with a broom in her hand wiping tears from her eyes. I came inside and asked, "Mom, what's wrong? Don't you want to move?"

262

Through her tears and her choked-up voice she said, "Yes, I'm just thinking of Everett dying here and the years I raised you and Starla. There are just a lot of memories here."

I had been so wrapped up in my excitement that I had never entertained the thought that this move might be difficult for Mom. In typical Murn fashion, she dried her eyes, handed me the broom, picked up her purse and handed me the keys to her car, grabbed my arm as she had since EtEt died, and said, "Let's go to our new home, Debbie girl." With that statement, she walked out the door, got in the car, and never looked back as I closed the door on the love that had filled our home in good times and bad during the 15 years since 1969.

Our new house had a one-car garage and Mom wanted me to use it for my car. Mom's car sat off the driveway close to the garage. Mom hadn't driven the little Maverick for quite a while. The most recent heart attack had taken away her ability to walk very far and she was basically in the wheelchair other than standing for short periods when she could hold on to things. Frank and I had taken her out for lunch one Sunday in his car on a famously hot southern Illinois day. When we drove into the driveway, Mom said, "I think I want to drive my car around the block."

Frank and I looked at each other with total fear. Not that she wasn't a good driver, but since her last heart episode she hadn't been driving. But Mom was determined to drive her car. I started to get in the passenger side but she said, "No, I'll be fine. I've driven longer than the two of you put together!" She had the keys in her purse and before we knew it, she was backing out of the driveway. Our house was on the edge of a suburban area where there were many internal roads. On the edge, however, was a busy two-lane highway. We were relieved when she backed out heading toward the neighborhood roads.

Off she went, the brake light flashing on and off. She had always driven with her good leg resting on the brake and her crippled leg on the accelerator.

Frank and I stood in the yard, sweating literally and figuratively, waiting for her to come back up the road from the way she left. After what felt like an hour, it seemed she should have already returned by then. The car hadn't been driven recently. Maybe she had car trouble, maybe a flat. Our tension was building and Frank was about ready to go looking for her. I just happened to look over toward the highway and there she sat in the far lane waiting to make a left turn on to our street as cars were whizzing by her. We were so relieved! I could barely see her little head above the side of the car. I'm not sure how she saw over the steering wheel! As we took a deep breath and relaxed, "Crash! Bang!" There sat Mom, the driver-side front fender pushed straight up in the air! We ran across the property next to ours to reach her. Mom yelled out her window to us very calmly, "I'm okay." Then she turned on to our street and parked in front of our house.

It happened that a young woman with her baby in a carseat in the back seat had reached around to check on the baby and crossed the dividing line and had driven directly into Mom's front fender. Mom was as calm as the proverbial cucumber. She sat in the car as we waited for the police to come.

When the officer came he first spoke to Frank and me as witnesses and then went to talk with the young woman. I could tell the heat was taking its toll on Mom so we asked the officer if we could get her in the house and he agreed. Mom pulled the car into the driveway and we helped her into the house. The officer came in and was so kind to her. She told him her side of the events and he assured her that the young woman said it was her fault and the officer agreed, particularly since Mom was stopped. To complete the report, he of course needed to see Mom's driver's license. Mom handed it over with such confidence. The officer knelt in front of her and very kindly said, "Mrs. Lipe, are you aware your license has expired?"

Mom's confidence quickly turned to shock and embarrassment as she exclaimed, "What?!" She had been in the hospital during the spring with a heart attack and had just come home after her birthday in June. Needless to say, her driver's license had not been a priority at the time. The police officer said, "Mrs. Lipe, I'm not going to give you a ticket. The accident wasn't your fault but I'm going to have to give you a warning regarding your expired license." The young woman didn't have insurance and Mom had dropped hers to liability only. So Frank pushed the fender down so it wasn't acting as a lightning rod and we parked it back in its parking space.

Little did I realize that Mom finding her driver's license had expired and the little Maverick too damaged to drive was such a hard goodbye for Mom. As long as she knew she could get in her car and go, she still had her independence and her control. Now she was dependent on me or Frank. She was confined not just to a wheelchair, but to our home. So the little Maverick sat damaged in the driveway while little Murn sat damaged in her wheelchair.

Fall was like most fall semesters for me: football games and parades for the marching band, concert preparations for the choirs and orchestra while the jazz band and show choir prepared not only for concerts but for community groups asking for entertainment. It was so nice having a very short drive from our new home to and from work every day and weekends and evenings. I was able to run home between the end of school and an evening performance or rehearsal, which I had never been able to before. Frank came over most evenings as he always had and Mom was spending more time in her wheelchair. It seemed like she was losing weight and the upper-body muscle that she had always had. She was, for the first time in my eyes, showing that she was aging. She still stood at the sink and washed dishes, rolled in her wheelchair to furniture surfaces she could reach to dust, cooked, and carried folded clothes and linens on her lap as she delivered them to the room where they belonged.

Starla and Mike's relationship was not surviving. Two children in one year, one crawling and one toddling was now becoming Starla's sole responsibility. She secured an apartment in a tiny little town north of Carbondale. I have no idea how she paid the bills. Maybe Mom was helping her. Mom started to show signs of worry, not because Starla was behaving badly but because she was just turning 20 years old with two babies alone. There were fewer visits from Starla but she and Mom spoke often on the telephone.

Mom was becoming quieter and quieter. I'm sure she was lonely. She would sit in her wheelchair in front of the storm door and watch for any sign of life. This was an area where there were no sidewalks and most of the neighbors worked, so there were very few people for her to interact with. Directly across the street lived an elderly couple. Bill was retired and often sat on his porch during the day. They became "waving friends" and sometimes he would walk across the street and talk with Mom on our porch. His wife seldom came outside but when she did she became part of the friendship. As the weather grew cooler and the doors were closed more often, there was very little interaction with Bill and his wife. Mom was more isolated.

Christmas was once again upon us but not as light-hearted as the Christmas before. It was hard for Starla to manage the two children and drive over to visit. Truthfully, I don't remember if we saw her and the kids at Christmas. She might have gone to Mike's family so he could be with the children. Mom was so very, very quiet as Frank and I handed out the presents. In the previous weeks, there were times when Mom would be holding her chest and I'd say, "Mom, are you okay?" She would say, "Just let me be still for a bit." I was so scared every time I would see her do this.

Mom's heart issues were not due to a diseased heart but a damaged one. The stress she had been under before her first heart attack had caused severe damage. Mom's blood pressure had always run high with a top number around 240. She was never able to wear a watch because the electricity in her body moved the minute hand like a second hand, so it would never keep time. She suffered from tachycardia, a heart rhythm issue where the beats were greater than 100 beats per minute and then would create an irregular heartbeat. Basically, it was an electrical problem in addition to all the damage from each heart attack. Finally, she would say, "I'm okay." Frank and I continued handing out the gifts and Mom sat in her wheelchair, leaning forward, elbows on the chair arms and each hand holding the other. It was a quiet Christmas.

Christmas break was over and Frank and I were back at work and Mom was alone each day. There was something about this Christmas that left me empty. I wasn't sure why; maybe it was just having to return to work or just the end of another year. Perhaps it was just not having Starla and the kids with us. Mom had said goodbye to our family members, her church friends, our church, our home filled with memories, her car and the freedom she felt it gave her, and Mike was now gone from our family. Were we going to have to say goodbye to Starla again? Or maybe it was something more.

CHAPTER 21

Leaves of the Branches

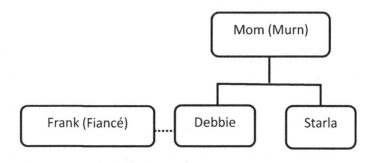

CHAPTER 21

The Last "I love you"
Winter 1985

How many times in our lives do we utter the words, "I love you"? Do we just automatically allow those words to fall out of our mouths day in and day out? Is it a phrase that flows like water out of a faucet: transparent, empty, and available? Do we ever really even look into a person's eyes as we say the phrase when it's not in the heat of passion? "I love you" – three words meant to express our deepest feelings for a person we love with all of our heart.

As a teacher with late bird classes, I was fortunate not to have to report at 8:15 to start the school day and was assigned a late start of 10:30. I had ensembles that had to meet for credit after the regular school day. These classes lasted until 5:00 and then, of course, there were evening rehearsals just about every night. I was grateful to sleep a little later in the mornings before having to start what commonly were very long days.

Little did I realize this morning how very much longer the next few days would be. I was getting ready to walk out the door when Mom asked me to pick up a half-gallon of milk on my way home. "I can get it now if you need it," I responded.

"No, that's okay, I've got enough to get me through the day," she said.

"Bye Mom, love ya."

The supermarket was two blocks from our house and on my way to school. Since my night rehearsals often go late, I decided to go to the store right then rather than wait. I came back into the house and placed the milk in the refrigerator. Mom rolled around the corner in her wheelchair "Honey, you didn't have to get that now. I told you it could wait."

I stopped and just looked for a moment at this sweet little woman, then walked over, leaned down, and placed a kiss on her soft, smooth, cheek and said "I love you, Mom," and patted her what then seemed like a thin, frail arm.

"I love you too, honey," she replied with a smile on her face.

I didn't know why, but that moment seemed so special, so heartwarming, a phrase we said to each other for almost 31 years, morning, night, any time either of us left the house and sometimes just in the middle of the day. I guess we often sounded like the television show *The Waltons*. I know we did at bedtime when I was young and Starla was at home.

"Goodnight Mom, goodnight Starla."

"Goodnight Mom, goodnight Debbie."

"Goodnight Starla, goodnight Debbie. Sleep tight girls, I love you."

"Love you too, Mom."

"Me too," Starla would chime in.

But today it was different…special, "I love you too, honey." There was something different in her voice.

The fourth period of the day was a class called Independent Instrumental Instruction. Students who wanted to study an instrument could take this class and receive instruction and have daily practice time with me there to assist them. There were only about six or seven students in the class that semester so it didn't take long to get everyone started on their plans for the period. My office was attached to the music room and I kept the door open during classes. It was common to have phone calls often throughout the day and today was no exception. The phone rang and it was my sister, Starla. She now lived in a neighboring town about 15 miles from our house and had two little children at home. It was odd that she would be calling me, especially at work. She and I did not have the best relationship at the time and I have to admit I was short with her and somewhat annoyed.

"Debbie, is Mom taking a shower this morning?"

Since she had become weaker and primarily used a wheelchair, Mom would tell me when she was going to take a shower. That way if she didn't answer the phone I wouldn't panic. I think it also might have been her fear of what had happened to her sister Jean years before.

"No, she didn't say anything about taking one. Oh Starla, you probably dialed the wrong number. Try it again."

Within a few minutes, the phone rang again.

"She's not answering, Debbie!"

I'm not sure if my irritation at that point was with Starla or whether it was the fear that something might be wrong. "I'll call and then I'll let you know."

Mom always carried the cordless phone beside her in the wheelchair. Had it fallen out and she couldn't find it? Was it dead because it had not been recharged last night? All these thoughts were running through my head as I dialed the phone. It rang and rang, no answer. At that point, my heart began to pound and I knew something was horribly wrong.

I gathered all of the students together and told them to follow me. They must have sensed the seriousness in my voice because no one said a word. I led them to my department chair's classroom and told him I had to leave immediately, something was wrong at home. I ran straight to the parking lot and sped through the back roads to our house. What usually would have taken six to seven minutes seemed like hours, yet probably took less than five at the speed I was driving. What could be wrong? Maybe she fell and couldn't get to the phone. Maybe she was taking a nap and left the phone in the kitchen. Why wasn't she answering the phone? It seemed like the garage door took longer than ever to go up. I drove into the garage. Why? Why didn't I just park in the driveway and go in? Was I just not thinking?

How many times do we put a key in a doorknob and turn it with no anticipation or consideration of what might be on the other side? My heart was beating so hard and fast I couldn't hear anything but what sounded like the beating of a bass drum. What would I find? Why couldn't I get the door open? C'mon! I busted through the door and there she was.

"Oh, God! No! Please God, no!" There she was, in front of the kitchen sink. "No, no, no, no, no! Momma! Momma! No, no, no!"

She had collapsed like a book that had been closed. She was folded at the waist. Her head was between her legs and her arms straight out as if she had held on to the sink and tried to lower herself to the chair. The wheelchair must have been pushed back as she fell to the floor. I threw the wheelchair out of the way and grabbed her around the chest to lay her flat. She was a bluish-purple I have never seen in the many years since. Her jaw was set with drops of saliva running over her lips. How long had she been here? Conscious and in pain? Alone. I reached for the kitchen wall phone and started compressions. I dialed 911 through a flood of tears. I could barely see the numbers. I screamed for an ambulance. "Oh God, please don't take her! Please, Lord!"

It seemed like it was taking the ambulance forever! People talk about being in the moment. This moment was a horrible place –a total eclipse – no sun, no moon, all dark. How could this happen again? Uncle Everett and now Mom? My arms were getting so tired; the compressions weren't working! I couldn't get her to take a breath. I just kept up the compressions, crying. What was taking the ambulance so long? I failed before with Uncle Everett, I can't fail now with Mom!

Finally, the EMTs arrived. There was a pulse but faint. I couldn't stop crying. The ride to the hospital was with a full siren and fast. I struggled to answer their questions. "What medications does she take? Were there any symptoms preceding the event? How long was she down? Has this ever happened before?"

Some I could answer, but others I had no idea. I didn't know what exactly had happened other than surmising that she had had a heart attack.

I was physically and emotionally exhausted. I was sick at my stomach, my head was pounding from my sobbing, and I kept hearing the hammering of my heart. The emergency room doctor said it was a massive heart attack and she was in critical condition. They were transferring her to the cardiac care unit. I was dazed.

I sat in the cardiac ICU waiting room for almost three days. I don't remember ever leaving. The waiting room had this bluish-green aura, cold and quiet, like sitting at the bottom of the ocean. This can't be happening. I can't lose her. I don't know life without my Mom in it. At 31 years old, I knew I would never love anyone as much as I loved her. She had had a total of 19 heart attacks before now: four major ones and 15 small ones. She had made it before; I knew she could make it again! She had to. What would I do without her?

My thoughts drifted to when I was three years old and my mother wanted to dress me in frilly little dresses for various activities. Mom would come to the house and convince me to put the dress on. She had magic that my mother could never conjure up. Where's that magic, Mom? Use that magic to pull out of this! My thoughts were interrupted by the doctor.

"She's stable right now but her condition is critical. Do you know how long she had been non-responsive?"

I told him I wasn't sure and that we had been trying to call for at least 10 minutes and then it was five to 10 minutes before I found her and started compressions.

"She is still unconscious and we have no idea as to the amount of brain damage that she has sustained based on the lack of oxygen she suffered. You may see her now if you like."

The rules of the cardiac ICU were very rigid, allowing only one visitor at a time, 10 minutes every hour. I wanted so badly to be in the room with her all the time, but they assured me this was best for her and would allow her to rest.

When I entered her room the sounds of the machines filled the room with a rhythm characteristic of the ticking of a metronome or in this case, it could have been a bomb. The lights of the machines were green and blue with splashes of red, flashing the vitals that represent life and death. I stood alongside her bed and placed my hand on her arm, that same thin, frail arm that I had laid my hand on hours earlier. Now it was cold and lifeless. Her arms had always been so muscular. Having polio, her upper body strength and arms had been firm and defined. Age and time in a wheelchair had diminished those muscles. When I was little I would crawl up on her lap, she would hold me in her arms as she rocked me and sang "You Are My Sunshine" and sometimes "Babes in the Woods." The latter always made me cry. I could hear her voice as I stood there. I felt like that little girl again. I wanted to crawl into her arms and have her rock me as she sang. My time with her was up for another hour. Oh, how I hated leaving her. I wanted to be there when she opened her eyes. I wanted her to know that I was there, she wasn't alone, I came home and found her.

As I returned to the waiting room a nurse gave me some crackers and peanut butter because I hadn't eaten all day. As I began nibbling on one it took my mind back to a special time with Mom. In the summer when I stayed with them at times as a little girl, EtEt would go to work, Mom would do her wash or housework, and then she would make peanut butter and cracker sandwiches, place them in a brown paper bag, fill a thermos with milk and off we would go to the park for a picnic lunch. I didn't care for peanut butter but with Mom everything was good. We would sit and talk. I can't imagine what the conversation was like with me at four or five, but she would sit at the picnic table and listen to every word. The smell and shade of the magnolia trees along with the summer breeze made for a perfect picnic – just Mom and me.

I was startled from my memories when Frank and Starla finally arrived. They both had so many questions and were so distraught, I really couldn't tell them anything to calm them. Starla was in tears and her small, thin frame was shaking. She had two little ones and no car. She had gotten a neighbor to babysit with the children and Frank had picked her up. I never thanked Starla for calling me that day. I wish I had. They stayed for most of the late afternoon and early evening. Each of them took their turn to go in and see her.

I had never seen Frank so somber and sad. I think she had been like a mom to him, having lost his mother years ago and his dad many years before that. Mom thought the world of Frank. He was the son she never had and Mom filled a space similar to that of a mother for him. Frank had been with us through several cardiac events with Mom throughout the years, but I think he knew this was not going to end like the others. That night I saw how much he loved her. He could barely talk.

They both left for the evening and again I was swallowed by the blue-green aura in that waiting room, cold and alone.

Nighttime in a hospital is a very aural experience. The sounds of machines in the rooms are faint, voices of the doctors and nurses are whispers, and the sound of wheels on the medicine carts rolling in the hallways or being moved from room to room are like a grinding and then a stop, grinding then a stop from place to place. The sound of the wheels on the cart took me back to when I was seven years old.

We had an empty bedroom in our house with aged, solid wood-planked floors. Each board seemed to have a ridge between it and the next. There was nothing in the room but an ottoman in one corner. I would place marbles at different spots around the room on those grooves. Mom would sit on that ottoman for hours and we would shoot marbles, trying to hit the ones I had strategically placed at different spots on the floor. "Grrrrrrr smack! Grrrrrr smack, smack!" We laughed and laughed as we would hit each other's marbles. Oh, what I would give for an hour in that room with her. Instead, the only hour I had was waiting for 10 of each 60 minutes to spend with her in that mechanized room. No change. Just time spent watching the heart monitor, watching her respiration, and holding her hand. The minute hand moved slowly and the hour hand crept, but every hour brought with it another hour she was alive and another 10 minutes I could spend with her. The night was long. I didn't dare go to sleep. I didn't want to miss that precious 10 minutes each hour watching her breathe, holding her hand, watching the machines monitor her heartbeat, and hoping and praying that she would wake up and everything would be okay.

The second day began with a changing of the shift of nurses, doctors on the floor, and lab techs scurrying quietly from room to room. A new patient had been brought on the floor. The family was filling the waiting room. There must have been four or five people there. Having spent the last 20 hours in that secluded room alone, I felt like I had been imposed on. They were talking and the noise from their pacing, sitting, and standing irritated me. Didn't they know there was sadness here? It was hanging on every wall and sitting on every chair. Maybe I was just jealous. I was alone. They had so many family members; I had none. Why was all of our family gone? There should be more than just me. Thank God my 10 minutes finally came.

Before I could get to the room, the nurses came running past me. Was this it? What was happening? Where was the doctor? I stood outside the room, confused and scared. What had happened? A doctor finally came to the room and within minutes came out. Mom had had a grand mal seizure. The doctor said it was over and I could go in and see her. Still no change. The day crawled on, hour after hour. Around noon the other people left the waiting room; their family member had been moved from the cardiac ICU to another room. Once again, I was alone with my anguish and fear.

In mid-afternoon, I looked up and two of my colleagues from the high school were standing in the doorway. Jenny was the women's physical education teacher and Shirley a guidance counselor. They didn't know my mom, but I guess they knew how close we were. Shirley brought me a little stuffed mouse. It was dressed in a pale lime dress with a matching bonnet. I was surprised at such a token, but that little mouse brought me comfort as the hours passed. There was very little said but their presence said a great deal to me. Frank and Starla arrived around dinner time. Once again we shared the visits. The nurse finally let us share the 10 minutes, but still only one at a time. There was little conversation among us. We were empty, suspended in time, waiting for some type of change. The evening passed and Frank and Starla had to leave.

Around midnight a "code blue" was called. If you've never been in a hospital when a code blue is called, it's similar to a fire alarm in school, not the bell, but an electrical buzzer of sorts. Then you hear an announcement "code blue, code blue." People started running down the hallway, directives were being shouted, and machines were being pushed through the halls. My heart jumped into my throat; I was paralyzed. Everyone ran to Mom's room.

I couldn't breathe. The tears began to flow. I stood in the doorway of the waiting room watching. Within a few minutes, people started to leave her room. A doctor came to me and said she responded and was still with us.

About an hour later, the head nurse came to the waiting room and told me she was conscious and that I could see her. It wasn't time for my 10 minutes but I think the nurse knew that we were close to the end. As I walked into the room it was no different from the many times I had been in the room over the past two days, but seeing her, well, this time *I* was different. This small, weak, tired, once fierce little woman lying in the bed, hooked up to all the machines and tubes, who had been my strength, my protector, my greatest supporter, and my savior, finally opened her eyes and looked up at me. She had been a David against so many Goliaths for so many people throughout her life. But now her eyes were a watery, pale blue and the lids were so very heavy. I took her hand in mine and kissed it as she turned her head toward me. She was tired, life tired. Not the tired we all feel after a hard day's work, but a tiredness that comes with 76 years of fighting battles, caring for others, defending those who can't defend themselves, and raising other people's children.

I read somewhere that there are two types of tired: one that requires rest, and one that requires peace. Mom deserved both. As much as I wanted her to stay in this world, I knew it was time. She had earned her rest and her peace. I knew I had to give her permission. I started crying uncontrollably, patted her cheek and said "I love you, Mom. You've been the best Mom I could have had. Thank you for being my Mom. I know you're tired. It's okay; you can go. I'll be okay."

She nodded as much as the respirator tube would allow. I leaned over the bedrail and kissed her forehead and stroked her hair. She squeezed my hand, closed her eyes, and exhaled slowly as if an incredible force had been lifted.

Giving someone, one you love with all your heart and soul, permission to leave this earth is the hardest thing I have ever had to do in my life. I knew when I left her room it was only a matter of when.

As I left the room I was sobbing so hard I could barely breathe. It was the kind of sobbing that felt like you have the hiccups while crying. What had I done? How could I have told her it was okay to die? What was wrong with me? Perhaps for the first time, I realized the magnitude of my love for her.

I think that night I learned what it meant to love someone enough to put their needs above your own. I now understand how very much she had loved me to fight heaven and earth to be there for me all my life. I now understood what *agape* love meant in reality.

It wasn't long before another code blue was called. This time they were in her room much longer. Slowly, one by one, each person quietly and slowly left. You could see it in their faces as they walked out. It was done. Frank had just gotten home in bed when I called him. I called Starla but of course, she couldn't leave the children. I was so consumed by my grief I never thought about how she felt, home alone with her two little children – no one to hold her as she cried, no one to tell her it will be okay. Mom always did that for us. Starla was only 21 years old and had just recently repaired her relationship with Mom. One more loss in her young life.

When they had removed the tubes and turned off all of the machines, the nurse came to tell me I could go in. There she was, her face calm. She was at peace. The white hospital sheets seemed to glow around her like she had already been given her wings and was now heaven's angel. It looked like she was smiling. I believe she was with Uncle Everett, Harry, her mom and dad, and most of her brothers and sisters: Margaret, Jean, Kitten, Charles, and Gilbert. She was finally home and at rest.

The days that followed were a blur. Frank had come to the hospital and taken me home. I was exhausted. I must have lain down on the bed and slept for almost a day. When I woke up my best friend Cynthia had arrived from Iowa and was greeting people as they stopped by.

Planning a funeral is not only strenuous but a heart- and gut-wrenching act. However, Mom had already taken care of most things. She always told me to go to her lockbox if anything happened to her. And there it was: a manila envelope with writing that had been scratched out and rewritten many times over the years. It was filled with instructions, insurance policies, burial plot ownership papers, who to contact, and a Helen Steiner Rice card addressed to Starla and me. Mom's organization and training from Brown's Business College were in her DNA.

Frank went with me to the funeral home. I've often thought the death of a loved one is the hardest pain. But that moment of loss is only the first of the pains to follow. Planning a funeral brings a distraction until it's time to select the casket. I had watched Mom prepare for so many family members' funerals. Selecting the casket brought on another wave of heart-wrenching sobs. Part of me wanted to scream, "I don't want to be here!" but she deserved the best and I would make sure she had it. I selected a beautiful mahogany casket. The expense was more than I was prepared for or her life insurance would cover but Frank assured me he would help me with it. He did. She never had a lot in life, but she would have the best for eternity.

Cynthia helped me select the music for the funeral. I couldn't pick hymns. I couldn't bear it — I don't think I could have made it through the funeral. When Mom washed dishes, she always sang "What a Friend We Have in Jesus," "In the Sweet By and By," "Rock of Ages," or one of the many hymns we sang in church. I'm sure she was singing just before she collapsed. Instead, I selected classical music. It had played a large part in my life and there were beautiful pieces that were comforting and soothing. Cynthia and I recorded those selections on a cassette tape to be played at the funeral.

Our past minister from our church in Cairo, who was then pastoring a church in Fort Scott, Kansas, came to preach her funeral. Mom should have had her funeral in our church in Cairo but she left instructions for me not to. Most of our family and her friends were gone and she said it would be too hard on me. She had written in her instructions to have her funeral at the funeral home she selected in Murphysboro.

The funeral home was filled with people. Her old friends that remained came from Cairo, her friends from Murphysboro, my friends and colleagues, and Starla and Frank's friends.

My mother didn't come; neither did my older half-brother and sister. I knew my mother probably didn't have the money, but I'm sure the pain was too much. Murn was more than a sister-in-law to Mother, she was like a mother, accepting her unconditionally, always providing her a shoulder to lean on, cry on and always depend on. Many thought Mother should have been there for me. It was okay, it didn't upset me. She had never been there for me. I don't say that in a judgmental way, but factually.

Starla's half-sister on her mother's side was there with her two adopted parents, Mom's dear friends who were left from Cairo. Most of our family was gone, but numerous "chosen" families were there. The pallbearers were her nephew Wayne's oldest son, Darryl Wayne, and young men who had been around our house and had grown to love her.

There wasn't a dry eye in the place. Everyone who knew her loved her. All of my friends who came around our house loved "Murn" and were there. Brother Travis preached a traditional Baptist funeral – reverent and Bible-based. He praised Mom's life – raising children, her dedication to God, our church, and the Christian life she had led. He read the scripture from Second

Timothy, verses 7 and 8: "I have fought a good fight, I have finished my course, I have kept the faith; Henceforth there is laid up for me a crown of righteousness, which the Lord, the righteous judge, shall give me at that day: and not to me only, but unto all them also that love his appearing."

"Marian will have a crown full of jewels," he said. The one thing he said that I have held in my heart since that day is, "They say when two people live together long enough, they begin to look and sound alike. Debbie looks and sounds like Marian and Starla shares her love for children."

As the guests said their last goodbyes and processed by the casket, I had chosen the song "The Promise of Living" from *The Tender Land* by Aaron Copeland to be played. Another death…saying I love you and goodbye to her physical form for the last time…the last look upon her face…the last touch of her face and pat on her hand. Closing the casket is conclusive, another pain. It is finished. Starla, Frank, and I stood as we held each other and sobbed.

The ride to the cemetery was quiet. We had nothing left in us. The cemetery was about 55 miles away. I remember how slowly we moved as we passed the cars that had stopped as the funeral procession passed. I'm always taken back to this day when I stop for a procession. My heart aches for the family and friends, knowing there is one more heartache, one more pain before it's done. Soon we were on the highway and the car's speed had accelerated. Following the hearse was a constant reminder of our loss. As we turned into the cemetery and followed along the winding road to the top of the hill, we could see the line of cars behind us.

Mom's best friend Alice had purchased a plot with six graves, using three for her and her parents. She gave Mom and EtEt the other three. Alice's mother and father had been buried there and Alice was to be buried beside them. EtEt was already buried there and their headstone was mounted after his death. The plot was on a hillside with them facing toward the top of the hill and the sky. We sat in the car while the pallbearers moved the casket from the hearse to the gravesite. Brother Travis followed the casket and stood beside it as we exited the car and moved to the seats under the tent. This was the final I love you and goodbye.

It was February and it was cold. There had been remnants of snow that had frozen hard and it proved difficult to maneuver, especially for Mom's elderly girlfriends from our church. I remember that one of them slipped – not bad, but enough to cause the men who were there to start assisting everyone as they came to the tent. I loved those dear old friends of Mom's. They were going to be there for her regardless of the weather, the distance, or come hell or high water.

I was cold and began to shake. It was the kind of cold that goes beyond temperature. It's the cold I acquaint with death. My jaw was locked yet my teeth were chattering. I couldn't stop shaking. Tears were like crystals on my cheek and then they stopped as if my tear ducts had frozen.

Brother Travis was such a quiet, kind man. I never realized how hard it must have been for him to preach the funeral for so many old friends. As he read the 23rd Psalm, I knew we had come to the end of the graveside service. All that was left was a prayer.

Another death, Mom's death. How could I walk away and leave her there? It was cold and dreary. My only consolation was that she was there with EtEt. The tear ducts unfroze and the tears began to flow again as we walked back to the car. Final condolences, hugs, and words of comfort from her dear friends came to Starla and me as we moved to the car. I was numb. There's no recession from a funeral. The cars all pull out of the cemetery and everyone goes on their way and the loved ones are left alone.

I returned to the same house, the same belongings, the same passing hours, but the wheelchair sat empty. I stood by the wheelchair as that little lost six-year-old many years ago: scared, afraid, and lost. Nothing will ever be the same.

Through the years I've come to believe that life promises us only one thing – those we love we *will* lose. That *is* the "Promise of Living." Every moment counts. Always get the milk right away. It might be the last "I love you."

CHAPTER 22

Leaves of the Branches

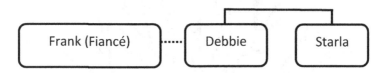

CHAPTER 22

Houses Are Made of Bricks and Stones
End of Winter 1985

T he week following Mom's death wasn't difficult for me because I felt nothing. I slept often, barely ate, had no tears left to cry, and spent my waking hours reviewing the documents and instructions Mom had left for me in her lockbox, getting death certificates to send to various agencies, notifying GM&O regarding her pension, changing the utilities to my name and so many more end-of-life necessities. Somehow I managed to resolve all of the paperwork that needed to be filed or submitted finalizing Mom's life. I was fortunate that I had a week's leave of bereavement from my teaching duties at the high school. I was glad; the joy that I had always had as a teacher seemed to have vanished. My joy in life was gone; I was simply going through the motions of living, taking one breath at a time. This was the first time in my life I had lived alone; that kind of silence I found was deafening. The decibels of grief are louder than any sound known to mankind. I was back to being that little six-year-old who was lost many years ago.

I missed hearing Mom's gentle voice every morning making sure I was awake. I missed our conversation as to what my schedule for the day was and what I wanted for dinner. I missed hearing her humming a hymn as she rolled her wheelchair through the house or as she stood at the sink washing dishes. But most of all, I missed hearing her voice from her bedroom, regardless of how late I came home, asking, "Is that you, Debbie girl?" She never went to sleep until I was safely home. Frank was in and out of the house and Starla called, but I had nothing to say. All of my emotions had been snatched by that "thief in the night." The plaque that had always hung in our kitchen was no longer true for me. "Houses are made of brick and stone. Homes are made of love alone." My home was now just a house; Mom had always made it a home.

Every activity in my life was altered. Frank and I were sitting in a restaurant on Sunday before I had to return to work. There were no cell phones as there are now, so we always told Mom where we were going and how she could reach us. I remember sitting next to Frank when the phone at the restaurant rang. Frank and I both gasped and jumped as if we had been shot. Suddenly we both realized that Mom wasn't calling and we never had to worry about that ever again. The tears rolled down both of our cheeks and we sat quietly for the rest of our lunch.

My time off had run its course and I had to return to work. First period I had concert band. The students were very respectful and seemed to be on their best behavior that morning. I'll never forget that moment back on the podium. I quietly asked them to pull up the piece we were going to work on. I placed my arms in the "ready" position and suddenly I couldn't move. My arms were in the air, the kids had their horns up ready for the downbeat, but I couldn't move. My throat began tightening; breathing became harder. It was as if I was holding my breath; something was bubbling up from the very bottom of my soul. My throat became closed; I couldn't talk. My heart was pounding and I could feel the pressure in my ears. My head was down and suddenly an explosion of tears gushed out of my eyes. The tears were falling one after another on my score and I still couldn't move. My arms were suspended in the air and I was terrified as to what my closed throat was holding back. I couldn't compose myself. I was paralyzed. I just stood there for what seemed like hours with my tears continuing to flow without slowing. I wanted to let out a bloodcurdling cry from the depth of my gut. I wanted to scream like an animal caught in an iron trap, but I couldn't utter a sound.

I finally was able to release the air that had been contained in my throat and chest. I swallowed hard and managed to look under my brow at my kids. I could see my pain in their faces and my tears roll down their cheeks as they sat quietly and reverently as I began to wake up emotionally and feel again. Nothing was ever discussed with me about that morning with my students. I often wondered why that emotional breakdown happened in front of my kids. I guess it was because we were like a family; we spent hours together traveling, rehearsing, and performing. Other than Starla and Frank, I had no one to grieve with. My students grieved with me that morning.

My transition to living without Mom was life-changing, challenging at the least. I had to find my life. She had always been right behind me, shining the light for me to find my way. Now alone, with no immediate family other than Starla and Frank, I had to find my way through complete darkness. Mom had raised me and now it was time for me to be strong and all that I could be without standing on her shoulders. I had to walk forward with her memory. So began my journey in the dark, walking alone with all my angels. Death is hard; living is harder. The house was now simply bricks and stones and I was left with love alone.

EPILOGUE

Love, Loss, and Perseverance

The word "love" conjures many definitions in the minds of individuals. To some, how they define love is determined by the use of the phrase "I love you" and/or the various words of affection that are spoken. To others, love is synonymous with actions of affection or sex. And to still others, love is defined by general, daily behaviors or deeds. To many, defining love is more difficult than defining what love is not. Life has taught me to believe that love is a five-dimensional concept and each dimension is contingent upon the other. How is it that each of us comes to an understanding of the meaning of the word love and the concept itself?

I believe we each reach our definition of love based on our measurement of each of the five concepts: quantity, quality, longevity, how love has been experienced by the giver, and the receiver's expectations of love. Love is often further complicated by the type of relationship two individuals have. For instance, love between a parent and a child brings a very different type of love compared to the love perceived to be in a romantic, a friendship, or a family relationship. Relationships themselves, regardless of the type, are at times difficult to maneuver without the complication of the emotion of love.

If we consider quantity as a measurement of one's definition of love, a simple question that is difficult to answer is how much love is needed for a person to feel loved? How much is too much or how much isn't enough? How can we quantify an emotion? Does how much we love a person depend upon the day, the situation, or an event? Do we each come into this world needing the same amount of love and life changes our requirements? Or are we each born with the love we are given and we seek more or less love depending on what we received?

To determine the quality, we must examine what it is we value as love – in other words, the scale by which we measure the quality of love. Do we measure the quality of love based on what we perceive to be valuable? Is it the amount of money spent on us or things given to us? Is it the time spent with us by someone? Or perhaps the display of affection we receive from an individual? Or maybe it's just simply being with someone. It's often very common for someone to say "I love you" to someone and then that person responds with "I love you more." How is *more* determined and by what measurement? Why does one person believe they love the other more than the other loves them and how do they know?

We must consider how love over time changes. Does it grow deeper, richer, or shallow and unrecognizable? Does it change based on our behavior or that of another's? I often pondered the phrase, "I love you more today than yesterday." How is it *more*? How is it different today than it was yesterday? What changed? I believe deep in our hearts we may truly believe that our love for someone deepens each day. But how do we identify it? Is it just a phrase we say because we are limited in how we show or express our love?

Since love does not exist in isolation, measurement is also affected by what each individual gives, based on their own experiences and perceptions of love and what each person expects from someone who loves them. Therefore, an individual measures the love that is being given based on their own expectations of what love should be and gives love in a manner based on what they believe love is.

But the one love that meets all requirements that love can entail is that of *agape* love – a love that is unconditional and rises above and beyond events, situations, or occurrences. A love that is consistent, devoted, and steadfast. It comes from a heart that is selfless and pure. It is the very essence of the word love – a love so rare it is seldom experienced.

Agape love sustains an individual through loss – those who give that love and those who receive it. Certainly, the loss of someone we loved leaves us with sadness and grief. It often makes us re-evaluate who we are and what we will do without them. What emptiness will we be left with and will we ever be able to fill the hole that their absence leaves? While the loss may be hard for those who remain, it may be the best for the individual who left. The loss of the love that the departed gave us is often painful, but our love for the person we have lost is our true loss. We suffer in loss whether it's through death or simply the end of a relationship. What was no longer exists, but the love that was may linger with us for a lifetime.

Life is filled with loss, obstacles, and difficulties. Not one person can escape such interruptions or inconveniences. There are so many instances in life which require our undivided attention. But some of those events are the most shattering to our lives. Those which stop us in our tracks often leave us with grief or fear or anger or simply lacking the will to live. To continue to live requires courage and courage is necessary for us to persevere, to move forward when we see no tomorrow at the time. Courage is without value unless we have perseverance. Perseverance requires us to put one foot in front of the other, to look forward rather than back, to complete our purpose in life believing that tomorrow brings a new day with the faith that we can and must complete our earthly task, to live our life. Perseverance leads us through what we see as impossible to that which is possible.

Love, loss, and perseverance were the essence of the life of *A Woman Called Murn.*

Photographs of our past become a

Homecoming of people, places, and memories that

Occupy places in our hearts and minds with

Timeless recordings of our lives, of

Others, and ourselves; we are

Grateful for those we have loved and those who have loved us.

Reclaiming the feelings of days gone by and the

Assurance of our place in their lives, their affection, and the

Precious effect they had on our lives; we can relinquish things we may

Harbor deep within our soul and reflect as we view the
   photos which revive

Sentimental acceptance of the past which serves as the significance of
   where we are today and our choices for the future.

-dlburris

Mother

Dad

EtEt and Murn

Grandpa & Grandma
Burris

Grandma Burris Troutman

Mum & Grandma
Troutman

Starla & Murn

Starla & Mother

Starla, Mike, & Candice

Starla & Debbie

Starla, Murn, & Candice

Debbie's
Beginning

Debbie and Mother
St. Louis Zoo

At the TB
Sanitarium

Debbie & Mother
Kansas City Visit

Mother, Tom,
Debbie & Pam

Debbie, Mother, Dad, Pam & Tom

Debbie,
Murn, & EtEt
Happy & Loved

Ann & Dad
Starla's Mother

Murn, Grandma,
EtEt., & Debbie

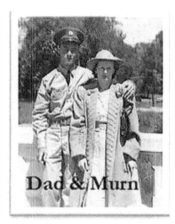
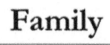

Dad & Murn

Family

Mother & Murn

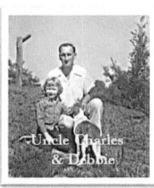

Uncle Charles
& Debbie

Aunt Kitten

Harry & Murn

My Uncles – Joe, Dad,
Charles, & Wayne

Aunt Jean

Grandpa Luther

Maudie Mother's Step-Mother

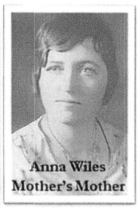

Anna Wiles Mother's Mother

More Family

Nonita, Grandpa Luther, Grandma Maudie, Mother, Tom & Pam

Mother & 2nd Husband Howard

Mother's Brother Uncle James & wife Aunt Fay

Bob, Mother & Pam

Mother, Me, & Murn

Debbie

Debbie & Starla

306

 A Woman Called
Murn